NOW
T

Nearly a m____ ____ ____ ____ ____ __-One
*Calorie Counter* can attest to the advantages of
having such a valuable source at their fingertips.
Now, well-known nutrition expert, Jean Carper
has completely revised and updated this book with
the latest information available from food manufacturers and the U. S. Department of Agriculture.
This convenient and important handbook con-
tains over 5,500 entries on just about every kind
of food imaginable—including the top fast-food
chain foods.

AN INVALUABLE BOOK
IF YOU ARE CONCERNED
ABOUT YOUR WEIGHT.

# The All-In-One Calorie Counter

### Revised Edition
### By Jean Carper

**BANTAM BOOKS**
TORONTO · NEW YORK · LONDON · SYDNEY

THE ALL-IN-ONE CALORIE COUNTER

*A Bantam Book | published by arrangement with
Workman Publishing Co., Inc.*

### PRINTING HISTORY

*Bantam edition | January 1974*

| | |
|---|---|
| 2nd printing ............. May 1974 | 8th printing ...... August 1977 |
| 3rd printing ........ August 1974 | 9th printing ...... October 1977 |
| 4th printing ........... April 1975 | 10th printing .... January 1978 |
| 5th printing .. December 1975 | 11th printing ...... January 1979 |
| 6th printing ............. July 1976 | 12th printing ........... May 1979 |
| 7th printing .. November 1976 | 13th printing . November 1979 |

*Revised Bantam edition | July 1980*
15th printing ...... September 1980
16th printing ................ June 1981

ISBN 0-553-20339-8

*Published simultaneously in the United States and Canada*

---

*Bantam Books are published by Bantam Books, Inc. Its trademark, consisting of the words "Bantam Books" and the portrayal of a bantam, is Registered in U.S. Patent and Trademark Office, and in other countries. Marca Registrada. Bantam Books, Inc., 666 Fifth Avenue, New York, New York 10103.*

---

PRINTED IN THE UNITED STATES OF AMERICA

25 24 23 22 21 20 19

# Contents

# Introduction

"Counting calories is not just the best way to long-term weight maintenance—it's the only way," says Harvard nutritionist Dr. Jean Mayer. It is that unit of energy—the calorie—which determines how much weight you put on and take off, he says. And certainly there are hundreds of thousands of successful calorie-counting dieters who would agree. Take in fewer calories than you burn up each day, and you're bound to shed pounds.

But how to do it? Unfortunately, there aren't any mysterious secrets for making dieting actually fun. But in this book you'll find loads of information that I hope will take some of the monotony out of dieting, enable you to eat some foods on your diet you never dreamed possible, and clear up some misconceptions you may have about which foods are high in calorie content and which aren't. For example, many calorie-conscious persons avoid potatoes and spaghetti like the plague (which by themselves are fairly low in calories) and load up on "protein" foods like beef (which is comparatively much higher in calories).

With potatoes and pasta, it is not the basic food itself but the way they are prepared or the embellishments that make the calorie difference. A medium-sized boiled potato weighs in with only 104 calories, whereas only 10 French fries have 137 calories. Of course, if you want to splurge occasionally and eat French fries or load up your baked potato with butter and sour cream cheese sauce, why shouldn't you as long as you consider the calorie difference?

And why shouldn't you eat a Mars bar if you want one? Or a slice of Sara Lee's rich cake? Or Jeno's pizza? If you don't exceed your daily limit. Dieting—even if you are counting calories—doesn't have to be a Monklike experience —ascetic and uninteresting. Of course, overindulging in these goodies at the expense of well-balanced nutrition is not in your best interest.

The only stumbling block may be that you don't know how many calories are present in these products. For unlike pure, fresh foods, when the ingredients get into a company chef's kitchen, they are all mixed any which way according to the company's special recipe. Only the company can tell you how many calories are in their foods. And that's the kind of information you will find in this book: a comprehensive listing of not only all common "generic-type" foods, but commercially prepared foods—from Durkee's appetizer frozen puff pastries to Mrs. Paul's frozen zucchini sticks.

You'll see that the number of calories in similar grocery products can vary greatly, and you'll find that simple knowledge can trim calories off a product quickly. For example, it is almost startling to realize that if you use a 7 ounce can of Chicken of the Sea white tuna complete with oil, you accumulate 507 calories—but if you drain off the oil before use, you're left with only 328 calories—a saving of 179 calories!

If you've bought or are thinking of buying this book, you're probably already committed to losing weight, so there's no use wasting time telling you why you should reduce, or all the terrible medical problems that may confront you if you don't. But there are some facts about calories that you may find valuable. A calorie is a unit of energy in foods. Technically, it is the amount of heat needed to raise the temperature of one liter (about a quart) of water by one degree. The body constantly takes in calories through food and expends them through activity.

Theoretically, if you took in precisely as many calories in a day as you used up in energy, you wouldn't lose or gain a smidgen of an ounce that day. But when you take in more calories than your body can use, you store them as fat. The rule of thumb is that a moderately active person needs about 15 calories per day per pound of body weight to "stay as you are." That is, if you weigh 120 pounds and want to stay that way, you should consume about 1800 calories a day. If you're happy at 150 pounds, you take in 2250 calories a day. Now if you want to get rid of some of that stored fat by counting calories, the calorie intake should dip below that. How much you want to lose and how fast is up to you.

According to the American Medical Association there are about 3500 calories in each stored pound of fat. So if you want to take off a pound, you have to get rid of that 3500 calories somehow. One way you can do it is to shave 500 calories a day for seven days off your caloric intake. Thus, if you're 120 pounds and want to take off a pound a week, you would cut your regular 1800 calorie daily count to 1300; and if you weigh 150, you'd go down from 2250 calories daily to 1750. It's an easy formula and you can work it out for yourself according to your own weight and diet aims.

As far as giving you the basic facts necessary to follow your diet, you'll find in this book the calorie counts on all kinds of foods—both fresh and processed (by brand name, of course)—from A to Z. Included are not only the usual brands you see everyday on grocery shelves and on TV commercials, but also the "house brands" of the A & P and Safeway supermarkets—such as Ann Page from A & P and Lucerne from Safeway. (If you wonder why we didn't include other major supermarkets, it's because, though we asked, they did not make such information available.) And there's a whole special section on fastfoods— everything from Big Mac's to Dairy Queen sundaes— valuable information, not found in any other popular book to my knowledge.

A word about the figures in the book: This book was first published in 1974 and has been an enormous success. Dozens of people have written to say how much it helped them lose weight, and it is used in organized weight-loss clinics. It has sold over 7 hundred thousand copies. Since the original publication, some of the calorie counts have changed due to new analyses or reformulation of products, and new products have been introduced. Thus, new figures were gathered in 1979 for this complete revision. Of course, some of the calorie counts are the same or similar, since the calories in many basic foods, such as milk, cheese, bread, as well as alcoholic drinks, don't change much. And a few companies did not have any new information. But I would estimate that fully two-thirds to three-fourths of the figures are brand new. For example, the baby food companies have eliminated most or all of the sugar in their fruits and vegetables, in some cases reducing the calories in a jar of baby food by 100 per cent. Many companies now have their products analyzed in a laboratory instead of "calculating" the calories from the food's recipe as they did in the past. That means in some cases slightly altered figures.

All of the figures bearing brand names in this book were provided by food companies and are the latest the company had available. If some of your favorite products are missing, it is because the company does not have the information or did not provide it.

In some cases the information from the company has been translated from 100 gram units or other serving sizes (for example to one slice of bacon or one slice of bread) to make it easier for you. This translation may account for some minor variations in figures.

Within the last few years more companies have started putting nutritional information on their products, although they are not required by the federal government to do so, unless they make specific nutritional claims for the food. However, if they do label, they must provide the information in a standardized form. Still, it is difficult to make comparisons among various brand name foods without running all around the supermarket. Thus, another benefit of this book:

you can pick out the lower calorie items *before* you go shopping.

Most calorie counts, now that companies have done more analyses, should remain exceedingly stable over the years. However, occasionally a food maker will change the composition of a product, severely changing the calorie count. For example, during the lifetime of this book, some soft drink companies came out with saccharin-sweetened drinks that slashed the sugar and thus the calorie count to virtually nothing. Diet Rite, for example, instead of having 48 calories per 8 fluid ounces, as listed in the book, had only one, and advertised that fact. Many readers wrote in to ask which was correct.

This happens only rarely, but in such cases of conflict, you can believe the calorie information on the label. The accuracy of a food company's labeling is regulated by the federal Food and Drug Administration, and a company would be subject to severe penalties for putting out a label that was grossly inaccurate.

Also, some manufacturers have asked me to point out that their figures are the best average calculations or analyses they have on specific products, but because of normal variations beyond their control, there may be ever-so-slight variations from batch to batch from the same manufacturer. Even such factors as seasonal conditions or soil composition may influence final food nutritional values.

All of the calorie counts without any brand name or company attribution are from the U.S. Department of Agriculture. And here, too, some calculations were done to make sure the figures were in the most convenient form.

To sum up, the new revised *All-In-One Calorie Counter* will provide you with the latest, most accurate data available about fresh foods, processed foods and fastfoods.

Jean Carper
January, 1980

# How To Use This Book

The most important organizational fact about the *All-In-One Calorie Counter*, as you will quickly see, is that it is alphabetized for easy use according to food categories. That is, you don't have to look in the front of the book under B for bean soup and then flip to the T's to find out if tomato soup is lower in calories. It runs through the alphabet, starting with appetizers and ending with yogurt. All the breads are listed together in the B section, all the fruits are grouped together under F, the vegetables under V, and so on. Simply by looking at the Table of Contents in the front of the book, you can quickly spot which category a food is in and turn directly to that section. You'll then find the foods alphabetized within the sections. Some foods, to be sure, just don't fit easily into categories, and rather than force them into some artificial grouping, we've listed them alphabetically too, even though there may be only one or two of a kind; for example, baking powder and cornstarch have listings of their own. And for the first time we've included a special Fast-Foods section at the end of the book.

In other words, the book is akin to a dictionary—with headings at the top of each page, too, to help you out. If you get stuck and can't decide where a food might be, just consult the index.

We have tried to standardize the language and food serving sizes as much as possible to make them useful, but here again we haven't strained the point.

We have tried to be realistic. For example, under cereals, you won't find all of them in either 1-cup or ½-cup portions. The reason: simply because they are not really comparable. A person may easily sit down to an 8-ounce cup of puffed rice, but rarely to a full 8-ounce cup of the heavier All-bran. A more realistic portion for bran is ⅓ of a cup. Therefore, we have followed the manufacturers' recommendations and provided single serving sizes they believe appropriate.

For some items, for example, frozen pies, we've given the calorie content for the entire pie. Often the producer provides the information in portions of 1/6 of a pie. But it seemed to us that a person who wanted to eat only ⅛ of a pie when we had given figures for only a 1/6 wedge would have to go through the laborious procedure of first figuring out the total calorie content of the whole pie and then dividing by eight. Consequently we've stated the calorie count of the entire pie. A person can then cut it anyway he wants and figure accordingly; he's not tied down to a single serving size arbitrarily decided by us.

Whenever you see the word "prepared" the figures are based on the assumption that the food has been prepared according to the manufacturer's directions. If you alter the preparation, for example, by adding meat drippings instead of water to a gravy mix or using milk when water is called for on the package or adding other embellishments of your own, you must figure these extras in. Whenever milk is called for in a preparation, we assume it is whole milk—not skim or nonfat or condensed milk. If you use any of the latter —either raising or lowering the calorie content in the finished product—you will have to make provision for it.

In most cases companies prefer to tell you how many calories are in the finished prepared product— for example, a cup of pudding from pudding mixes, because it's rare that the powder would be used in any other way. But in some instances you will find the calorie count for the dry mix only—*before* preparation. That way, if you want to add another ingredient to your mix, you're free to do so and add up the extra calories. Also on this note: whenever you merely add water to a mix, you're not adding calories—for example, when you make a Lipton's soup. If you use the dry soup mix in any other fashion, say as a dip mix, you have the same calorie count in the dry mix as in the cup of prepared soup.

In keeping with our determination to make this book easy to use, we've taken due note of the power of identity of brand names. Whenever possible, without interfering with the organization, we've used brand names for quick identification. Thus, when you look up a certain cookie, cracker or cereal, you don't have to peruse the whole list searching for a description of your cookie. We don't have Cheez-Its listed under "crackers, cheese;" we have it simply alphabetized under Cheez-Its. And we have Oreo cookies under O and not under "chocolate creme sandwich." The same goes for Franken Berry cereal (under F in the cereal section). Of course, it was not always possible to do this without creating a chaotic organization, and in many cases the only identifying factor is a description of the product (chocolate chip cookies, for example) and the name of the manufacturer.

Within the listings, we repeat the measurements frequently, even though they are the same, rather than place the portion size at the head of a section which may be a page or two back. However, on items like cookies and crackers and frozen "TV" dinners, where the portion size is not confusing—one cookie or cracker or a complete dinner—we've simply noted the portion at the head of the section. This has also been done on fairly short listings.

To avoid confusion, whenever possible, we have stated the measurement in the most easily used terms: cups and tablespoons and fluid ounces for liquids and items such as canned fruits and vegetables; and weight ounces for items like cheese and frozen fish fillets.

Despite our best efforts, there's no way we can save you from doing some figuring on your own, simply because no one, including yourself, wants to eat the same amount of a certain food at every sitting. And, of course, when you use your own recipes, there's no way possible that we could give figures on the finished product, because home recipes vary greatly just as do recipes for commercially prepared foods. If you're whipping up your own tapioca pudding, we can tell you how many calories are in the dry tapioca, in the eggs, milk and sugar, and you'll have to take it from there. Only you know how much of an ingredient you really use.

For doing your own conversions, here's an equivalency table that may be of help:

> 1 tablespoon = 3 teaspoons
> 2 tablespoons = 1 fluid ounce
> 4 tablespoons = ¼ cup
> 5⅓ tablespoons = ⅓ cup
> 16 tablespoons = 1 cup
> 1 cup = 8 fluid ounces
>       = ½ pint
> 2 cups = 1 pint
> 2 pints = 1 quart
> 1 pound = 16 ounces

Happy calorie counting!

# Abbreviations

| | |
|---|---|
| art | artificial |
| diam | diameter |
| fl | fluid |
| in | inch |
| lb | pound |
| med | medium |
| oz | ounce |
| pkg | package |
| swt | sweetened |
| tbsp | tablespoon |
| tsp | teaspoon |
| unswt | unsweetened |
| w | with |
| wo | without |

# Appetizers

| | CALORIES |
|---|---|
| **Frozen** | |
| Cheese straws: 1 piece / **Durkee** | 29 |
| Frankfurter: 1 piece / **Durkee** Franks-n-Blankets | 45 |
| Puff pastry: 1 piece | |
|     Beef puffs / **Durkee** | 47 |
|     Cheese puffs / **Durkee** | 59 |
|     Chicken puffs / **Durkee** | 49 |
|     Chicken liver puffs / **Durkee** | 48 |
|     Shrimp puffs / **Durkee** | 44 |

# Baby Food

## BAKED GOODS

| | |
|---|---:|
| Biscuits, teething: 1 piece / Gerber | 50 |
| Cookies, animal shaped: 1 cookie / Gerber | 30 |
| Cookies, arrowroot: 1 cookie / Gerber | 30 |
| Pretzel: 1 pretzel / Gerber | 23 |
| Toast, zwieback: 1 piece / Gerber | 30 |

## STRAINED BABY FOODS

**Cereal: 1 jar**

| | |
|---|---:|
| High protein w applesauce and bananas / Gerber | 120 |
| Mixed w apples and bananas / Heinz | 90 |
| Mixed w applesauce and bananas / Beech-Nut | 85 |
| Mixed w applesauce and bananas / Gerber | 110 |
| Mixed w fruit / Beech-Nut | 110 |
| Oatmeal w apples and bananas / Heinz | 100 |
| Oatmeal w applesauce and bananas / Gerber | 100 |
| Oatmeal w fruit / Beech-Nut | 73 |
| Rice w apples and bananas / Beech-Nut | 86 |
| Rice w apples and bananas / Heinz | 100 |
| Rice w applesauce and bananas / Gerber | 110 |

CALORIES

## Cereal, dry: ½ oz

| | |
|---|---|
| Barley / Gerber | 60 |
| Barley / Heinz | 50 |
| High protein / Gerber | 50 |
| High protein / Heinz | 50 |
| High protein w apple and orange / Gerber | 60 |
| Mixed / Gerber | 60 |
| Mixed / Heinz | 50 |
| Mixed w banana / Gerber | 60 |
| Oatmeal / Gerber | 60 |
| Oatmeal / Heinz | 50 |
| Oatmeal w banana / Gerber | 60 |
| Rice / Gerber | 60 |
| Rice / Heinz | 50 |
| Rice w banana / Gerber | 60 |

## Formula, meat base: 2 tbsp / Gerber

| | |
|---|---|
| Infant Formula | 40 |

## Fruits and Desserts: 1 jar

| | |
|---|---|
| Apple betty / Beech-Nut | 69 |
| Apple blueberry / Gerber | 90 |
| Apple raspberry / Gerber Strained Fruits | 90 |
| Apples and apricots / Beech-Nut | 58 |
| Apples and cranberries w tapioca / Heinz | 130 |
| Apples and pears / Heinz | 70 |
| Applesauce | |
|    Beech-Nut | 59 |
|    Gerber | 60 |
|    Heinz | 70 |
|    and apricots / Gerber | 110 |
|    and apricots / Heinz | 100 |
|    and cherries / Beech-Nut | 72 |
|    w pineapple / Gerber | 60 |
|    and raspberries / Beech-Nut | 59 |
| Apricots w tapioca / Beech-Nut | 64 |
| Apricots w tapioca / Gerber | 100 |

CALORIES

| | |
|---|---:|
| Apricots w tapioca / Heinz | 70 |
| Bananas | |
|     w pineapple / Beech-Nut | 70 |
|     w pineapple and tapioca / Gerber | 100 |
|     w pineapple and tapioca / Heinz | 80 |
|     w tapioca / Beech-Nut | 66 |
|     w tapioca / Gerber | 100 |
|     w tapioca / Heinz | 90 |
| Cottage cheese w pineapple / Gerber | 100 |
| Dutch apple dessert / Gerber | 100 |
| Fruit dessert / Gerber | 100 |
| Fruit dessert / Heinz | 90 |
| Fruit dessert w tapioca / Beech-Nut | 64 |
| Hawaiian delight / Gerber | 120 |
| Orange-pineapple dessert / Beech-Nut | 64 |
| Peach cobbler / Gerber | 100 |
| Peach cobbler / Heinz | 100 |
| Peach melba / Beech-Nut | 59 |
| Peaches / Beech-Nut | 58 |
| Peaches / Gerber | 110 |
| Peaches / Heinz | 120 |
| Pears | |
|     Beech-Nut | 64 |
|     Gerber | 70 |
|     Heinz | 70 |
|     and pineapple / Beech-Nut | 77 |
|     and pineapple / Gerber | 60 |
|     and pineapple / Heinz | 80 |
| Pineapple dessert / Beech-Nut | 66 |
| Pineapple-orange dessert / Heinz | 90 |
| Plums w tapioca / Beech-Nut | 74 |
| Plums w tapioca / Gerber | 120 |
| Plums w tapioca / Heinz | 70 |
| Prunes w tapioca / Beech-Nut | 109 |
| Prunes w tapioca / Gerber | 110 |
| Prunes w tapioca / Heinz | 110 |
| Pudding | |
|     Cherry vanilla / Gerber | 100 |

CALORIES

| | |
|---|---|
| Custard / Heinz | 110 |
| Custard, apple / Beech-Nut | 90 |
| Custard, chocolate / Gerber | 120 |
| Custard, vanilla / Gerber | 120 |
| Orange / Gerber | 120 |
| Tutti-frutti / Heinz | 90 |

**Juices: 1 can**

| | |
|---|---|
| Apple / Beech-Nut | 52 |
| Apple / Gerber | 60 |
| Apple / Heinz | 60 |
| Apple-cherry / Beech-Nut | 47 |
| Apple-cherry / Gerber | 70 |
| Apple-cherry / Heinz | 60 |
| Apple-grape / Beech-Nut | 53 |
| Apple-grape / Gerber | 60 |
| Apple-grape / Heinz | 70 |
| Apple-peach / Gerber | 60 |
| Apple-plum / Gerber | 60 |
| Apple-prune / Heinz | 70 |
| Mixed fruit / Beech-Nut | 55 |
| Mixed fruit / Gerber | 70 |
| Orange / Beech-Nut | 54 |
| Orange / Gerber | 70 |
| Orange / Heinz | 70 |
| Orange-apple / Beech-Nut | 52 |
| Orange-apple / Gerber | 80 |
| Orange-apple-banana / Gerber | 70 |
| Orange-apple-banana / Heinz | 70 |
| Orange-apricot / Gerber | 60 |
| Orange-banana / Beech-Nut | 56 |
| Orange-pineapple / Beech-Nut | 59 |
| Orange-pineapple / Gerber | 70 |
| Prune-orange / Beech-Nut | 64 |
| Prune-orange / Gerber | 90 |

CALORIES

**Main Dishes: 1 jar**

Beef
| | |
|---|---:|
| Beech-Nut | 120 |
| Beech-Nut High Meat Dinner | 125 |
| Gerber | 100 |
| w beef hearts / Gerber | 90 |
| and noodles / Beech-Nut | 68 |
| and noodles w vegetables / Gerber | 70 |
| w vegetables / Gerber High Meat Dinner | 100 |

| | |
|---|---:|
| Cereal and egg yolks / Gerber | 70 |
| Cereal, egg yolks and bacon / Beech-Nut | 107 |
| Cereal and egg / Heinz | 70 |

Chicken
| | |
|---|---:|
| Beech-Nut | 106 |
| Beech-Nut High Meat Dinner | 83 |
| Gerber | 130 |
| Noodle / Beech-Nut | 55 |
| Noodle / Gerber | 70 |
| w vegetables / Beech-Nut | 54 |
| w vegetables / Gerber High Meat Dinner | 100 |

| | |
|---|---:|
| Cottage cheese w bananas / Heinz | 90 |
| Cottage cheese w pineapple / Gerber High Meat Dinner | 160 |
| Egg yolks / Beech-Nut | 190 |
| Egg yolks / Gerber | 180 |
| Egg yolks / Heinz | 170 |
| Grits w egg yolks / Gerber | 70 |

Ham
| | |
|---|---:|
| Beech-Nut | 112 |
| Beech-Nut High Meat Dinner | 135 |
| Gerber | 110 |
| w vegetables / Gerber High Meat Dinner | 100 |

| | |
|---|---:|
| Lamb / Beech-Nut | 122 |
| Lamb / Gerber | 100 |
| Liver, beef / Gerber | 90 |

| | |
|---|---:|
| Macaroni and cheese / **Gerber** | 80 |
| Macaroni, tomato sauce, beef / **Beech-Nut** | 80 |
| Macaroni w tomatoes and beef / **Gerber** | 60 |
| Pork / **Gerber** | 120 |
| Soup, chicken, cream of / **Gerber** | 80 |
| Turkey | |
|     **Beech-Nut** | 105 |
|     **Beech-Nut** High Meat Dinner | 111 |
|     **Gerber** | 130 |
|     and rice / **Beech-Nut** | 65 |
|     and rice w vegetables / **Gerber** | 70 |
|     w vegetables / **Gerber** | |
|         High Meat Dinner | 120 |
| Veal | |
|     **Beech-Nut** | 112 |
|     **Beech-Nut** High Meat Dinner | 90 |
|     **Gerber** | 90 |
|     w vegetables / **Gerber** High Meat Dinner | 90 |
| Vegetables | |
|     and bacon / **Beech-Nut** | 80 |
|     and bacon / **Gerber** | 100 |
|     and beef / **Beech-Nut** | 75 |
|     and beef / **Gerber** | 70 |
|     and chicken / **Gerber** | 60 |
|     and ham / **Beech-Nut** | 72 |
|     and ham / **Gerber** | 60 |
|     and lamb / **Beech-Nut** | 70 |
|     and lamb / **Gerber** | 70 |
|     and liver / **Beech-Nut** | 55 |
|     and liver / **Gerber** | 60 |
|     and turkey / **Gerber** | 60 |

**Vegetables: 1 jar**

| | |
|---|---:|
| Beans, green / **Beech-Nut** | 35 |
| Beans, green / **Gerber** | 35 |
| Beans, green / **Heinz** | 35 |
| Beets / **Gerber** | 50 |
| Beets / **Heinz** | 40 |

CALORIES

| | |
|---|---|
| Carrots / Beech-Nut | 36 |
| Carrots / Gerber | 30 |
| Carrots / Heinz | 35 |
| Corn, creamed / Beech-Nut | 90 |
| Corn, creamed / Gerber | 80 |
| Corn, creamed / Heinz | 80 |
| Garden vegetables / Beech-Nut | 55 |
| Garden vegetables / Gerber | 50 |
| Mixed / Gerber | 60 |
| Mixed / Heinz | 60 |
| Peas / Beech-Nut | 67 |
| Peas / Gerber | 60 |
| Peas, creamed / Heinz | 70 |
| Spinach, creamed / Gerber | 60 |
| Squash / Beech-Nut | 28 |
| Squash / Gerber | 40 |
| Squash / Heinz | 50 |
| Sweet potatoes / Beech-Nut | 70 |
| Sweet potatoes / Gerber | 90 |
| Sweet potatoes / Heinz | 80 |

**Yogurt: 1 jar**

| | |
|---|---|
| w mixed fruit / Beech-Nut | 74 |
| w peach-apple / Beech-Nut | 68 |
| w pineapple / Beech-Nut | 79 |

## JUNIOR BABY FOODS

**Cereal: 1 jar**

| | |
|---|---|
| Mixed cereal w applesauce and bananas / Gerber | 180 |
| Oatmeal w applesauce and bananas / Gerber | 170 |
| Rice cereal w mixed fruit / Gerber | 180 |

**Fruits and Desserts: 1 jar**

| | |
|---|---|
| Apple betty / Beech-Nut | 115 |
| Apple blueberry / Gerber | 160 |

CALORIES

| | |
|---|---|
| Apple raspberry / Gerber | 150 |
| Apples and apricots / Beech-Nut | 96 |
| Apples and cranberries / Heinz | 130 |
| Apples and pears / Heinz | 120 |
| Applesauce | |
|    Beech-Nut | 98 |
|    Gerber | 90 |
|    Heinz | 110 |
|    and apricots / Gerber | 200 |
|    and apricots / Heinz | 170 |
|    and cherries / Beech-Nut | 120 |
|    w pineapple / Gerber | 100 |
|    and raspberries / Beech-Nut | 98 |
| Apricots w tapioca / Beech-Nut | 106 |
| Apricots w tapioca / Gerber | 160 |
| Apricots w tapioca / Heinz | 140 |
| Banana dessert / Beech-Nut | 136 |
| Bananas w pineapple and tapioca / | |
|    Beech-Nut | 117 |
| Bananas w pineapple and tapioca / Gerber | 170 |
| Bananas w tapioca / Gerber | 150 |
| Cottage cheese w pineapple / Gerber | 210 |
| Dutch apple dessert / Gerber | 180 |
| Fruit dessert / Gerber | 160 |
| Fruit dessert / Heinz | 140 |
| Fruit dessert w tapioca / Beech-Nut | 106 |
| Hawaiian delight / Gerber | 200 |
| Peach cobbler / Gerber | 170 |
| Peach melba / Beech-Nut | 98 |
| Peaches / Beech-Nut | 96 |
| Peaches / Gerber | 170 |
| Peaches / Heinz | 200 |
| Pears | |
|    Beech-Nut | 106 |
|    Gerber | 110 |
|    Heinz | 120 |
|    and pineapple / Beech-Nut | 128 |
|    and pineapple / Gerber | 110 |
|    and pineapple / Heinz | 130 |

CALORIES

| | |
|---|---:|
| Pineapple-orange dessert / Heinz | 150 |
| Plums w tapioca / Beech-Nut | 124 |
| Plums w tapioca / Gerber | 200 |
| Prunes w tapioca / Beech-Nut | 180 |
| Prunes w tapioca / Gerber | 180 |
| Pudding | |
|     Cherry vanilla / Gerber | 170 |
|     Custard / Heinz | 190 |
|     Custard, apple / Beech-Nut | 150 |
|     Custard, chocolate / Gerber | 210 |
|     Custard, vanilla / Gerber | 210 |
| Tropical fruit dessert / Beech-Nut | 106 |
| Tutti-frutti / Heinz | 150 |

**Main Dishes: 1 jar**

| | |
|---|---:|
| Beef | |
|     Beech-Nut | 120 |
|     Beech-Nut High Meat Dinner | 125 |
|     Gerber | 100 |
|     and noodles / Beech-Nut | 121 |
|     and noodles w vegetables / Gerber | 120 |
|     and rice w tomato sauce / Gerber | |
|         Toddler Meals | 150 |
|     Stew / Gerber Toddler Meals | 110 |
|     w vegetables / Gerber | |
|         High Meat Dinner | 100 |
| Cereal and egg yolk / Gerber | 110 |
| Cereal, egg yolks and bacon / Beech-Nut | 183 |
| Cereal and eggs / Heinz | 110 |
| Chicken | |
|     Beech-Nut | 106 |
|     Beech-Nut High Meat Dinner | 83 |
|     Gerber | 150 |
|     Noodle / Beech-Nut | 87 |
|     and noodles / Gerber | 110 |
|     Stew / Gerber Toddler Meals | 150 |
|     Sticks / Gerber | 130 |
|     w vegetables / Beech-Nut | 87 |
|     w vegetables / Gerber | 130 |

CALORIES

| | |
|---|---:|
| Cottage cheese w bananas / **Heinz** | 150 |
| Ham / **Beech-Nut** High Meat Dinner | 112 |
| Ham / **Gerber** | 120 |
| Ham casserole w green beans and potatoes / **Gerber** Toddler Meals | 140 |
| Ham w vegetables / **Gerber** High Meat Dinner | 100 |
| Lamb / **Beech-Nut** | 122 |
| Lamb / **Gerber** | 100 |
| Lasagna, beef / **Gerber** Toddler Meals | 140 |
| Macaroni and beef / **Beech-Nut** | 128 |
| Macaroni and cheese / **Gerber** | 130 |
| Macaroni, tomato, beef / **Gerber** | 110 |
| Meat sticks / **Gerber** | 130 |
| Peas, split w ham / **Gerber** | 150 |
| Peas, split w vegetables and ham / **Beech-Nut** | 145 |
| Spaghetti, tomato sauce / **Beech-Nut** | 128 |
| Spaghetti w tomato sauce and beef / **Gerber** | 140 |
| Spaghetti and meatballs / **Gerber** Toddler Meals | 130 |
| Turkey | |
|    **Beech-Nut** | 106 |
|    **Beech-Nut** High Meat Dinner | 111 |
|    **Gerber** | 120 |
|    and rice w vegetables / **Beech-Nut** | 85 |
|    and rice w vegetables / **Gerber** | 110 |
|    Sticks / **Gerber** | 130 |
|    w vegetables / **Gerber** | 120 |
| Veal | |
|    **Beech-Nut** | 112 |
|    **Beech-Nut** High Meat Dinner | 90 |
|    **Gerber** | 100 |
|    w vegetables / **Gerber** | 100 |
| Vegetables | |
|    and bacon / **Beech-Nut** | 134 |
|    and bacon / **Gerber** | 170 |
|    and beef / **Beech-Nut** | 115 |
|    and beef / **Gerber** | 120 |

CALORIES

| | |
|---|---:|
| and chicken / Gerber | 110 |
| and ham / Gerber | 120 |
| and lamb / Beech-Nut | 113 |
| and lamb / Gerber | 110 |
| and liver / Beech-Nut | 87 |
| and liver / Gerber | 90 |
| and turkey / Gerber | 110 |
| and turkey casserole / Gerber Toddler Meals | 150 |

## Vegetables: 1 jar

| | |
|---|---:|
| Beans, green / Beech-Nut | 60 |
| Beans, green, creamed / Gerber | 80 |
| Carrots / Beech-Nut | 60 |
| Carrots / Gerber | 60 |
| Carrots / Heinz | 60 |
| Corn, creamed / Gerber | 120 |
| Corn, creamed / Heinz | 140 |
| Mixed / Gerber | 90 |
| Peas, creamed / Heinz | 130 |
| Spinach, creamed / Gerber | 100 |
| Squash / Beech-Nut | 47 |
| Squash / Gerber | 60 |
| Sweet potatoes / Beech-Nut | 117 |
| Sweet potatoes / Gerber | 140 |
| Sweet potatoes / Heinz | 130 |

## Yogurt: 1 jar

| | |
|---|---:|
| w mixed fruit / Beech-Nut | 124 |
| w peach-apple / Beech-Nut | 112 |
| w pineapple / Beech-Nut | 132 |

# Baking Powder

|  | CALORIES |
|---|---|
| Canned, 1 tsp / Most brands | 5 |

# Beer, Ale, Malt Liquor

|  | CALORIES |
|---|---|
| **12 fluid ounces** | |
| Ale / Red Cap | 160 |
| Beer | |
|     Andeker | 160 |
|     Black Label | 148 |
|     Budweiser | 150 |
|     Busch | 146 |
|     Coors | 138 |
|     Goebel | 145 |
|     Grenzquell | 150 |
|     Hamms | 138 |
|     Heidelberg | 143 |
|     Michelob | 163 |
|     Michelob Light | 134 |
|     Miller's | 150 |
|     Miller's Lite | 96 |
|     Natural Light | 110 |
|     Old Milwaukee | 144 |
|     Olympia | 140 |
|     Olympia Gold Light | 70 |

CALORIES

|                                      |       |
|--------------------------------------|-------|
| Pabst Blue Ribbon                    | 150   |
| Pabst Extra Light                    | 70    |
| Pabst Light                          | 100   |
| Rheingold                            | 159   |
| Schlitz (Regular)                    | 148   |
| Schlitz (Repeal)                     | 121   |
| Schlitz Light                        | 96    |
| Stag                                 | 151   |
| Stroh Bock                           | 157   |
| Stroh Bohemian                       | 148   |
| Stroh Bohemian 3.2                   | 126   |
| Stroh Light                          | 115   |
| Stroh Light 3.2                      | 115   |
| Tuborg USA                           | 148   |
| Malt Liquor / Budweiser              | 160   |
| Malt Liquor / Schlitz                | 175   |

# Biscuits

CALORIES

**Refrigerator: 1 biscuit**

|                                          |     |
|------------------------------------------|-----|
| Ballard Oven Ready                       | 50  |
| Hungry Jack Butter Tastin                | 95  |
| Hungry Jack Flaky                        | 90  |
| Merico                                   | 55  |
| Merico Butter-Me-Not                     | 90  |
| Merico Texas Style                       | 85  |
| 1869 Brand                               | 105 |
| Pillsbury Country Style                  | 50  |
| Pillsbury Prize                          | 65  |
| Baking powder / 1869 Brand               | 105 |
| Baking powder, prebaked / 1869 Brand     | 100 |
| Baking powder / Tenderflake Dinner       | 60  |

CALORIES

Buttermilk
    Hungry Jack Extra Rich    65
    Hungry Jack Flaky    80
    Hungry Jack Fluffy    100
    1869 Brand    105
    Prebaked / 1869 Brand    100
    Pillsbury    50
    Pillsbury Big Country    90
    Pillsbury Extra Lights    55
    Tenderflake Dinner    55
Corn bread / Pillsbury    95

# Bread

CALORIES

**1 slice unless noted: an average slice
weighs about one ounce**

Bran / Brownberry    75
Brown, plain, canned: ½-in slice / B & M    78
Brown, raisin, canned: ½-in slice / B & M    78
Cinnamon raisin / Thomas'    60
Corn and molasses / Pepperidge Farm    70
English muffin style / Mrs. Wright's    55
French
    Earth Grains / 1 oz    70
    Mrs. Wright's    65
    Pepperidge Farm    75
    Wonder    75
    Sourdough: 1 oz / Earth Grains    75
Garlic, frozen / Stouffer's    80
Gluten / Thomas' Glutogen    30
Gluten, frozen / Thomas' Glutogen    30
Grecian style w sesame seeds / Mrs. Wright's    95
Hollywood Light    70

| | |
|---|---:|
| **Hollywood** Dark | 70 |
| Honey bran / **Pepperidge Farm** | 58 |
| Honey Wheatberry / **Arnold** | 90 |
| Honey Wheatberry / **Pepperidge Farm** | 60 |
| Italian: 1 oz / **Pepperidge Farm** | 75 |
| Italian / **Mrs. Wright's** | 95 |
| Meal | |
|     **Colonial Country** / 6 oz | 75 |
|     **Kilpatrick's** Country / 1 oz | 75 |
|     **Manor** Country / 1 oz | 75 |
|     **Rainbo** Country / 1 oz | 75 |
|     **Roman** Meal | 70 |
| Naturél / **Arnold** | 65 |
| Nut / **Brownberry** | 85 |
| Oatmeal / **Brownberry** | 80 |
| Oatmeal / **Pepperidge Farm** | 65 |
| **Profile** Dark | 75 |
| **Profile** Light | 75 |
| Protein / **Thomas'** Protogen | 45 |
| Protein, frozen / **Thomas'** Protogen | 55 |
| Pumpernickel | |
|     **Arnold** | 75 |
|     **Earth Grains** / 1 oz | 70 |
|     **Pepperidge Farm** Family | 75 |
|     **Pepperidge Farm** Party | 23 |
| Raisin / **Arnold** Tea | 75 |
| Raisin / **Pepperidge Farm** | 75 |
| Raisin cinnamon / **Brownberry** | 85 |
| Raisin nut / **Brownberry** | 95 |
| Rye | |
|     **Arnold** Melba Thin | 50 |
|     **Arnold** Soft | 75 |
|     **Brownberry** Extra Thin | 65 |
|     **Earth Grains** Light / 1 oz | 75 |
|     **Earth Grains** Party / 1 oz | 75 |
|     **Pepperidge Farm** Family | 80 |
|     **Pepperidge Farm** Party | 18 |
|     **Wonder** | 75 |

| | CALORIES |
|---|---|
| Jewish / Pepperidge Farm | 85 |
| Jewish, seeded / Arnold | 75 |
| Jewish, unseeded / Arnold | 75 |
| Seedless / Pepperidge Farm | 80 |
| Sourdough / DiCarlo | 70 |
| Vienna w poppy seeds / Mrs. Wright's | 55 |

Wheat

| | |
|---|---|
| Arnold American Granary | 70 |
| Arnold Bran'nola | 90 |
| Arnold Brick Oven Whole Wheat (small family) | 60 |
| Arnold Brick Oven Whole Wheat 16 oz size | 65 |
| Arnold Brick Oven Whole Wheat 32 oz size | 80 |
| Arnold Melba Thin Whole Wheat | 40 |
| Brownberry | 85 |
| Brownberry Great Grains | 70 |
| Brownberry Sandwich Dark | 75 |
| Buckwheat | 75 |
| Colonial / 1 oz | 75 |
| Colonial Honey Grain / 1 oz | 75 |
| Earth Grains Berry / 1 oz | 75 |
| Earth Grains Earth / 1 oz | 70 |
| Earth Grains 100% Whole Wheat / 1 oz | 70 |
| Earth Grains Very Thin / 1 oz | 80 |
| Fresh Horizons | 50 |
| Home Pride Butter Top Wheat | 75 |
| Home Pride Wheatberry | 70 |
| Kilpatrick's / 1 oz | 75 |
| Kilpatrick's Honey Grain / 1 oz | 75 |
| Light Wheat Fiber | 55 |
| Manor / 1 oz | 75 |
| Manor Honey Grain / 1 oz | 75 |
| Mrs. Wright's Grain Belt | 80 |
| Pepperidge Farm 1½ lb | 90 |
| Pepperidge Farm Very Thin Whole Wheat | 40 |
| Pepperidge Farm Whole Wheat 1 lb | 70 |
| Pritikin 100% Whole Wheat | 65 |
| Rainbo / 1 oz | 75 |

CALORIES

| | |
|---|---|
| **Rainbo** Honey Grain / 1 oz | 75 |
| **Thomas'** Whole Wheat | 50 |
| **Wonder** | 75 |
| **Wonder** Whole Wheat | 70 |
| Cracked wheat: 1 oz / **Earth Grains** | 75 |
| Cracked wheat / **Pepperidge Farm** | 70 |
| Cracked wheat / **Wonder** | 75 |
| Dark style / **Mrs. Wright's** Special Formula | 50 |
| Granola bran / **Mrs. Wright's** | 75 |
| Honey bran / **Mrs. Wright's** | 85 |
| Light style / **Mrs. Wright's** Special Formula | 50 |
| Sprouted wheat / **Pepperidge Farm** | 65 |
| Wheat germ / **Pepperidge Farm** | 60 |

White

| | |
|---|---|
| **Arnold** Brick Oven 16 oz size | 65 |
| **Arnold** Brick Oven 32 oz size | 85 |
| **Arnold** Brick Oven (small family) | 65 |
| **Arnold** Country | 95 |
| **Arnold** Hearthstone Country | 70 |
| **Arnold** Melba Thin | 40 |
| **Brownberry** Extra Thin | 70 |
| **Brownberry** Sandwich | 75 |
| **Butternut** | 75 |
| **Colonial** / 1 oz | 75 |
| **Colonial** Butter / 1 oz | 75 |
| **Colonial** Contour / 1 oz | 75 |
| **Earth Grains** Very Thin / 1 oz | 80 |
| **Fresh Horizons** | 50 |
| **Hart's** | 75 |
| **Hearthstone** | 85 |
| **Hillbilly** | 70 |
| **Home Pride** Butter Top White | 75 |
| **Homestyle** | 75 |
| **Kilpatrick's** / 1 oz | 75 |
| **Kilpatrick's** Butter / 1 oz | 75 |
| **Kilpatrick's** Contour / 1 oz | 75 |
| **Light White Fiber** | 55 |
| **Manor** / 1 oz | 75 |
| **Manor** Butter / 1 oz | 75 |

CALORIES

| | |
|---|---|
| Manor Contour / 1 oz | 75 |
| Millbrook | 75 |
| Mrs. Karl's | 75 |
| Mrs. Wright's | 80 |
| Mrs. Wright's Butter and Egg | 75 |
| Mrs. Wright's Low Sodium | 50 |
| Mrs. Wright's Sandwich Bread Country Style (thin sliced) | 65 |
| Ovenjoy 16 oz | 65 |
| Ovenjoy 22 oz | 75 |
| Ovenjoy 24 oz | 80 |
| Ovenjoy Sandwich Bread 22 oz size | 60 |
| Ovenjoy Sandwich Bread 24 oz size | 65 |
| Pepperidge Farm Family | 75 |
| Pepperidge Farm Sandwich | 65 |
| Pepperidge Farm Thin Sliced | 75 |
| Pepperidge Farm Toasting | 85 |
| Pepperidge Farm Unsliced / 1 oz | 85 |
| Pepperidge Farm Very Thin | 40 |
| Rainbo / 1 oz | 75 |
| Rainbo Butter / 1 oz | 75 |
| Rainbo Contour / 1 oz | 75 |
| Safeway 16 oz size | 70 |
| Safeway (thin sliced) 16 oz size | 65 |
| Safeway (thin sliced) 24 oz size | 70 |
| Sweetheart | 75 |
| Weber's | 75 |
| Weight Watchers | 35 |
| Wonder | 75 |
| Wonder Low Sodium | 70 |
| w buttermilk / Mrs. Wright's | 80 |
| w buttermilk / Mrs. Wright's Sandwich Bread (thin sliced) | 65 |
| w buttermilk / Wonder | 75 |
| Refrigerator, to bake / Pillsbury Hotloaf | 90 |

## BREAD CRUMBS

| | |
|---|---|
| Bread crumbs: 1 cup / Contadina | 411 |

## BREAD MIXES

CALORIES

**Prepared: 1 loaf unless noted**

| | |
|---|---:|
| Applesauce spice / **Pillsbury** | 1920 |
| Apricot nut / **Pillsbury** | 1760 |
| Banana / **Pillsbury** | 1920 |
| Blueberry nut / **Pillsbury** | 1760 |
| Cherry nut / **Pillsbury** | 1920 |
| Corn: 1 pkg / **Aunt Jemima** Easy Mix | 1320 |
| Corn: 1 pkg / **Pillsbury** | 1280 |
| Cranberry / **Pillsbury** | 1920 |
| Date / **Pillsbury** | 2080 |
| Nut / **Pillsbury** | 1920 |
| Oatmeal raisin / **Pillsbury** | 1920 |

## BREADSTICKS

**1 stick**

| | |
|---|---:|
| Stella D'Oro | 40 |
| Stella D'Oro Dietetic | 43 |
| Onion / **Stella D'Oro** | 42 |
| Sesame / **Stella D'Oro** | 56 |
| Sesame / **Stella D'Oro** Dietetic | 57 |

## STUFFING MIXES

| | |
|---|---:|
| Chicken & Herb: 1 oz / **Pepperidge Farm** Pan Style | 110 |
| Chicken-flavored, prepared w butter: ½ cup / **Stove Top** | 170 |
| Chicken-flavored, prepared: ½ cup cooked w butter / **Uncle Ben's** Stuff'n Such | 198 |
| Chicken-flavored, prepared: ½ cup cooked wo butter / **Uncle Ben's** Stuff'n Such | 123 |
| Corn bread: 1 oz / **Pepperidge Farm** | 110 |
| Corn bread, prepared w butter: ½ cup / **Stove Top** | 170 |

CALORIES

| | |
|---|---|
| Corn bread, prepared: ½ cup cooked w butter / **Uncle Ben's** Stuff'n Such | 205 |
| Corn bread, prepared: ½ cup cooked wo butter / **Uncle Ben's** Stuff'n Such | 129 |
| Cube: 1 oz / **Pepperidge Farm** | 110 |
| Pork-flavored, mix, prepared w butter: ½ cup / **Stove Top** | 170 |
| Sage, prepared: ½ cup cooked w butter / **Uncle Ben's** Stuff'n Such | 198 |
| Sage, prepared: ½ cup cooked wo butter / **Uncle Ben's** Stuff'n Such | 124 |
| Seasoned: 1 oz / **Pepperidge Farm** | 110 |
| Seasoned: 1 oz / **Pepperidge Farm** Pan Style | 110 |
| Seasoned white bread: 1 oz / **Mrs. Cubbinson's** | 101 |
| w rice, prepared w butter: ½ cup / **Stove Top** | 180 |

## CROUTONS

¼ cup unless noted

| | |
|---|---|
| Artificial bacon / **Bel Air** | 40 |
| Caesar Salad / **Brownberry** | 45 |
| Cheddar cheese: 1 oz / **Pepperidge Farm** | 130 |
| Cheese / **Brownberry** | 45 |
| Cheese and garlic / **Bel Air** | 50 |
| Cheese-garlic: 1 oz / **Pepperidge Farm** | 140 |
| Croutettes: .7 oz dry mix / **Kellogg's** | 70 |
| Garlic / **Bel Air** | 40 |
| Italian cheese / **Bel Air** | 50 |
| Onion and garlic / **Brownberry** | 45 |
| Onion-garlic: 1 oz / **Pepperidge Farm** | 140 |
| Plain / **Bel Air** | 30 |
| Plain: 1 oz / **Pepperidge Farm** | 140 |
| Seasoned / **Bel Air** | 45 |
| Seasoned / **Brownberry** | 45 |
| Seasoned: 1 oz / **Pepperidge Farm** | 140 |
| Toasted / **Brownberry** "Buttery" | 45 |

# Butter and Margarine

CALORIES

## Butter

| | CALORIES |
|---|---|
| Regular: ½ cup (¼ lb stick) | 815 |
|         1 tbsp | 100 |
| Whipped: ½ cup | 540 |
|         1 tbsp | 65 |

## Margarine

Imitation: 1 tbsp

| | CALORIES |
|---|---|
| Mazola diet | 50 |
| Mrs. Filbert's diet soft | 50 |
| Parkay diet | 50 |
| Weight Watchers | 50 |

Regular and Soft: 1 tbsp

| | CALORIES |
|---|---|
| Blue Bonnet | 100 |
| Blue Bonnet Diet | 50 |
| Blue Bonnet Soft | 100 |
| Chiffon | 100 |
| Chiffon Soft | 100 |
| Coldbrook | 100 |
| Coldbrook Soft | 100 |
| Dalewood | 100 |
| Empress | 100 |
| Empress Soft | 100 |
| Fleischmann's | 100 |
| Fleischmann's Diet | 50 |
| Fleischmann's Parve | 100 |
| Fleischmann's Soft | 100 |
| Holiday | 100 |

|  | CALORIES |
|---|---|
| Mazola | 100 |
| Meadowlake | 100 |
| Mrs. Filbert's | 100 |
| Mrs. Filbert's Soft | 100 |
| Nucoa | 100 |
| Nucoa Soft | 90 |
| Parkay | 100 |
| Swift Allsweet | 100 |
| Spread: 1 tbsp | |
| Blue Bonnet | 80 |
| Coldbrook | 80 |
| Fleischmann's | 80 |
| Mrs. Filbert's Spread 25 | 64 |
| Parkay light | 70 |
| Whipped: 1 tbsp | |
| Blue Bonnet Whipped stick and Soft | 70 |
| Chiffon Soft | 70 |
| Fleischmann's Soft | 70 |
| Mrs. Filbert's Soft | 70 |

# Cakes

## FROZEN DESSERT CAKES

|  | CALORIES |
|---|---|
| **1 whole cake unless noted** | |
| Banana / Pepperidge Farm | 1120 |
| Banana / Sara Lee | 1442 |
| Banana nut, layer / Sara Lee | 1864 |
| Black Forest / Sara Lee | 1624 |
| Boston Creme / Pepperidge Farm | 1080 |
| Cheesecake | |
|    Mrs. Smith's | 1230 |
|    Cream cheese, small / Sara Lee | 861 |
|    Cream cheese, large / Sara Lee | 1440 |
|    Cream cheese, cherry / Sara Lee | 1284 |
|    Cream cheese, French / Sara Lee | 2192 |
|    Cream cheese, French, strawberry / | |
|      Sara Lee | 2064 |
|    Cream cheese, strawberry / Sara Lee | 1284 |
| Chocolate / Pepperidge Farm | 1240 |
| Chocolate / Sara Lee | 1377 |
| Chocolate Bavarian / Sara Lee | 2280 |
| Chocolate 'n Cream / Sara Lee | 1672 |
| Chocolate fudge / Pepperidge Farm | 1800 |
| Chocolate fudge / Pepperidge Farm Half Cakes | 900 |
| Chocolate, German / Pepperidge Farm | 1600 |
| Chocolate, German / Sara Lee | 1229 |
| Coconut / Pepperidge Farm | 1800 |
| Coconut / Pepperidge Farm Half Cakes | 900 |
| Crumbcake, blueberry / Stouffer's | 210 |

CALORIES

| | |
|---|---:|
| Crumbcake, chocolate chip / Stouffer's | 227 |
| Crumbcake, French / Sara Lee | 172 |
| Crumbcake, French / Stouffer's | 200 |
| Cupcake, cream-filled / Stouffer's | 240 |
| Cupcake, yellow / Stouffer's | 190 |
| Devil's food / Pepperidge Farm | 1800 |
| Devil's food / Sara Lee | 1496 |
| Double chocolate, layer / Sara Lee | 1712 |
| Golden / Pepperidge Farm Half Cakes | 900 |
| Golden / Sara Lee | 1442 |
| Golden, layer / Pepperidge Farm | 1800 |
| Lemon Bavarian / Sara Lee | 2176 |
| Lemon coconut / Pepperidge Farm | 1120 |
| Mandarin orange / Sara Lee | 1648 |
| Orange / Sara Lee | 1442 |
| Pound cake | |
|     Plain / Sara Lee | 1320 |
|     Plain: 1 oz / Stouffer's | 125 |
|     Apple nut / Pepperidge Farm | |
|       Old Fashioned | 1300 |
|     Banana nut / Sara Lee | 1170 |
|     Butter / Pepperidge Farm | |
|       Old Fashioned | 1300 |
|     Carrot / Pepperidge Farm | |
|       Old Fashioned | 1600 |
|     Chocolate / Pepperidge Farm | |
|       Old Fashioned | 1300 |
|     Chocolate / Sara Lee | 1220 |
|     Chocolate Swirl / Sara Lee | 1300 |
|     Family size / Sara Lee | 1905 |
|     Home style / Sara Lee | 1090 |
|     Raisin / Sara Lee | 1270 |
| Cherry shortcake / Mrs. Smith's | 2340 |
| Strawberry 'n Cream / Sara Lee | 1704 |
| Strawberry shortcake / Mrs. Smith's | 1830 |
| Strawberry shortcake / Sara Lee | 1544 |
| Vanilla / Pepperidge Farm | 1900 |
| Walnut / Sara Lee | 1688 |

## MIXES

**Prepared according to package directions:**
**1 whole cake unless noted**

Angel food

| | |
|---|---:|
| Betty Crocker | 1560 |
| Betty Crocker One-Step | 1680 |
| Duncan Hines | 1680 |
| Pillsbury | 1680 |
| Chocolate / Betty Crocker | 1680 |
| Confetti / Betty Crocker | 1800 |
| Lemon custard / Betty Crocker | 1680 |
| Raspberry / Pillsbury | 1680 |
| Strawberry / Betty Crocker | 1800 |

| | |
|---|---:|
| Apple raisin / Duncan Hines | 2280 |
| Apple raisin, spicy / Duncan Hines Moist and Easy | 1620 |
| Applesauce raisin / Betty Crocker Snackin' Cake | 1800 |
| Banana / Betty Crocker | 3240 |
| Banana / Duncan Hines Supreme | 2400 |
| Banana / Pillsbury Plus | 3120 |
| Banana nut / Duncan Hines Moist and Easy | 1800 |
| Banana walnut / Betty Crocker Snackin' Cake | 1800 |

Bundt cake

| | |
|---|---:|
| Chocolate macaroon / Pillsbury | 3960 |
| Fudge nut crown / Pillsbury | 3480 |
| Lemon blueberry / Pillsbury | 3360 |
| Marble / Pillsbury | 3960 |
| Pound / Pillsbury | 3720 |
| Triple fudge / Pillsbury | 3600 |

| | |
|---|---:|
| Butter / Duncan Hines | 3240 |
| Butter / Pillsbury Plus | 2680 |
| Butter brickle / Betty Crocker | 3120 |
| Butter fudge / Duncan Hines | 3240 |
| Butter pecan / Betty Crocker | 3120 |
| Cheesecake / Pillsbury No Bake | 3120 |

| | CALORIES |
|---|---|
| Cheesecake / Jell-O | 2000 |
| Cheesecake / Royal | 1840 |
| Cherry / Duncan Hines | 2280 |
| Cherry chip / Betty Crocker | 2280 |
| Chocolate / Betty Crocker Pudding Cake | 1380 |
| Chocolate / Duncan Hines | 2400 |
| Chocolate almond / Betty Crocker Snackin' Cake | 1890 |
| Chocolate chip / Betty Crocker Snackin' Cake | 1980 |
| Chocolate chip / Duncan Hines | 1710 |
| Chocolate chip, double / Duncan Hines | 1620 |
| Chocolate, dark / Pillsbury Plus | 3120 |
| Chocolate fudge / Betty Crocker | 3240 |
| Chocolate fudge / Betty Crocker Snackin' Cake | 1980 |
| Chocolate, German / Betty Crocker | 3240 |
| Chocolate, German / Pillsbury Plus | 3120 |
| Chocolate, milk / Betty Crocker | 3120 |
| Chocolate, sour cream / Betty Crocker | 3240 |
| Chocolate, sour cream / Duncan Hines | 2400 |
| Chocolate, Swiss / Duncan Hines | 2400 |
| Chocolate w chocolate frosting / Betty Crocker Stir n' Frost | 1680 |
| Coconut pecan / Betty Crocker Snackin' Cake | 1980 |
| Cupcake / Flako | 150 |
| Date nut / Betty Crocker Snackin' Cake | 1890 |
| Devil's food / Betty Crocker | 3240 |
| Devil's food / Duncan Hines | 2400 |
| Devil's food / Pillsbury Plus | 3240 |
| Fudge marble / Duncan Hines | 2400 |
| Fudge marble / Pillsbury Plus | 3240 |
| Gingerbread / Betty Crocker | 1890 |
| Gingerbread: 3-in square / Pillsbury | 190 |
| Lemon | |
|     Betty Crocker | 3240 |
|     Betty Crocker Pudding Cake | 1380 |
|     Duncan Hines | 2400 |
|     Pillsbury Plus | 3240 |
|     w lemon frosting / Betty Crocker Stir n' Frost | 1380 |

CALORIES

| | |
|---|---|
| Lemon chiffon / **Betty Crocker** | 2280 |
| Marble / **Betty Crocker** | 3360 |
| Orange / **Betty Crocker** | 3240 |
| Orange / **Duncan Hines** | 2400 |
| Pineapple / **Duncan Hines** | 2400 |
| Pineapple upside-down w topping / **Betty Crocker** | 2430 |
| Pound / **Betty Crocker** | 2280 |
| Spice / **Betty Crocker** | 3240 |
| Spice / **Duncan Hines** | 2400 |
| Spice w vanilla frosting / **Betty Crocker** Stir n' Frost | 1620 |
| Spice raisin / **Betty Crocker** Snackin' Cake | 1800 |
| Strawberry / **Betty Crocker** | 3240 |
| Strawberry / **Duncan Hines** | 2400 |
| Strawberry / **Pillsbury** | 3120 |
| Streusel cake | |
|     Cinnamon / **Pillsbury** | 4080 |
|     Devil's food / **Pillsbury** | 3960 |
|     Fudge marble / **Pillsbury** | 4080 |
|     German chocolate / **Pillsbury** | 3960 |
|     Lemon / **Pillsbury** | 4200 |
| White | |
|     **Betty Crocker** | 2400 |
|     **Duncan Hines** | 2280 |
|     **Pillsbury Plus** | 3000 |
|     Sour cream / **Betty Crocker** | 2400 |
| Yellow | |
|     **Betty Crocker** | 3240 |
|     **Betty Crocker** Butter Recipe | 2880 |
|     **Duncan Hines** | 2400 |
|     **Pillsbury Plus** | 3120 |
|     w chocolate frosting / **Betty Crocker** Stir n' Frost | 1380 |

## COFFEE CAKES

CALORIES

**1 whole cake**

| | |
|---|---:|
| Almond, frozen / **Sara Lee** | 1352 |
| Almond, frozen / **Sara Lee** Coffee Ring | 1106 |
| Apple, frozen / **Sara Lee** Danish | 1176 |
| Apple cinnamon, mix, prepared / **Pillsbury** | 1880 |
| Blueberry, frozen / **Sara Lee** Coffee Ring | 1080 |
| Blueberry, frozen / **Sara Lee** Danish | 1136 |
| Butter pecan, mix, prepared / **Pillsbury** | 2480 |
| Butter streusel, frozen / **Sara Lee** | 1393 |
| Cherry, frozen / **Sara Lee** Danish | 1050 |
| Cinnamon streusel, mix, prepared / **Pillsbury** | 2000 |
| Cinnamon streusel, frozen / **Sara Lee** | 1232 |
| Coffee cake, mix, prepared / **Aunt Jemima** Easy Mix | 1360 |
| Maple crunch, frozen / **Sara Lee** Coffee Ring | 1157 |
| Pecan, small, frozen / **Sara Lee** | 764 |
| Pecan, large, frozen / **Sara Lee** | 1320 |
| Raspberry, frozen / **Sara Lee** Coffee Ring | 1090 |
| Sour cream, mix, prepared / **Pillsbury** | 2160 |

## SNACK CAKES

| | |
|---|---:|
| Big Wheels: 1 cake / **Hostess** | 170 |
| Brownie, small / **Hostess** | 150 |
| Brownie, large / **Hostess** | 240 |
| Choco-Diles: 1 cake / **Hostess** | 250 |
| Creamies, chocolate: 1 pkg / **Tastykake** | 256 |
| Creamies, spice: 1 pkg / **Tastykake** | 272 |
| Crumb cake: 1 cake / **Hostess** | 130 |
| Cupcakes | |
|     Buttercream filled: 1 pkg / **Tastykake** Cup | 240 |
|     Chocolate: 1 cake / **Hostess** | 160 |
|     Chocolate: 3½ oz / **Rainbo** | 350 |
|     Chocolate: 1 pkg / **Tastykake** | 200 |
|     Chocolate, cream filled: 1 pkg / **Tastykake** | 244 |
|     Orange: 1 cake / **Hostess** | 150 |
| Devil Dog's: 1 piece / **Drake's** | 171 |

CALORIES

| | |
|---|---|
| Ding Dongs: 1 cake / Hostess | 170 |
| Donuts: 1 donut unless noted | |
|     Hostess plain | 110 |
|     Hostess Crunch | 100 |
|     Hostess Enrobed | 130 |
|     Cinnamon / Hostess | 110 |
|     Powdered / Hostess | 110 |
|     Sugar: 2½ oz / Rainbo Gem | 310 |
| Filled Twins: 3 oz / Rainbo | 300 |
| Funny Bones: 1¼ oz cake / Drake's | |
|     Family Pkg | 164 |
| Ho Ho's: 1 cake / Hostess | 120 |
| Juniors, chocolate: 1 pkg / Tastykake | 307 |
| Juniors, coconut: 1 pkg / Tastykake | 330 |
| Juniors, Koffee Kake: 1 pkg / Tastykake | 313 |
| Juniors, lemon: 1 pkg / Tastykake | 297 |
| Koffee Kake, cream filled: 1 pkg / Tastykake | 247 |
| Krimpets, butterscotch: 1 pkg / Tastykake | 192 |
| Krimpets, jelly: 1 pkg / Tastykake | 168 |
| Krimpies, chocolate: 1 pkg / Tastykake | 252 |
| Krimpies, vanilla: 1 pkg / Tastykake | 239 |
| Macaroon, fudge: 1 cake / Hostess | 210 |
| Oatmeal cake, creme filled: 2 oz / Frito-Lay | 257 |
| Oatmeal raisin: 1 pkg / Tastykake Bars | 267 |
| Orange Treats: 1 pkg / Tastykake | 229 |
| Pound, marble: 1 cake / Drake's | 186 |
| Pound, plain: 1 cake / Drake's | 181 |
| Pound, raisin: 1 cake / Drake's | 323 |
| Ring Ding: 1 piece / Drake's | 366 |
| Ring Ding Jr: 1⅓ oz cake / Drake's Family Pkg | 186 |
| Sno Balls: 1 cake / Hostess | 140 |
| Suzy Q / Hostess | 240 |
| Suzy Q, chocolate: 1 cake / Hostess | 225 |
| Tandy Takes, chocolate: 1 pkg / Tastykake | 181 |
| Tandy Takes, peanut butter: 1 pkg / Tastykake | 190 |
| Tasty Klairs, chocolate: 1 pkg / Tastykake | 435 |
| Teens, chocolate: 1 pkg / Tastykake | 225 |
| Tempty, chocolate cream: 1 pkg / Tastykake | 196 |

CANDY

| | CALORIES |
|---|---|
| Tempty, lemon: 1 pkg / **Tastykake** | 259 |
| Tiger Tails: 1 cake / **Hostess** | 430 |
| Twinkies: 1 cake / **Hostess** | 140 |
| Twinkies, devil's food: 1 cake / **Hostess** | 140 |
| Yankee Doodles: 1 cake / **Drake's** | 125 |
| Yodels: ⅞ oz cake / **Drake's** | 134 |

# Candy

| | CALORIES |
|---|---|
| Breath candy: 1 piece | |
|     Breath Savers, sugar free / **Life Savers** | 7 |
|     **Certs** Clear | 8 |
|     **Certs** Pressed | 6 |
|     **Chewels** | 10 |
|     **Clorets** Mints | 6 |
|     **Dentyne** Dynamints | 2 |
|     **Trident** Mints | 8 |
| Butter mints: 1 piece / **Kraft** | 8 |
| Butterscotch: 1 piece / **Rothchilds** | 19 |
| Caramels: 1 piece / **Kraft** | 35 |
| Caramel Nip: 1¾ oz / **Pearson** | 220 |
| Chocolate and chocolate-covered bars: | |
|   1 oz unless noted | |
|     **Ghirardelli** | 150 |
|     w almonds / **Ghirardelli** | 154 |
|     **Hershey's** | 160 |
|     w almonds / **Hershey's** | 160 |
|     **Nestlé's** | 150 |
|     w almonds / **Nestlé's** | 150 |
|     Baby Ruth: 1 bar | 260 |
|     Butterfinger: 1 bar | 220 |
|     Choco'Lite / **Nestlé's** | 150 |
|     Choc-O-Roon: 2 oz / **Frito-Lay** | 286 |

**CALORIES**

| | |
|---|---:|
| Chunky, regular | 130 |
| Chunky, pecan | 130 |
| Crisp / **Ghirardelli** | 150 |
| Crunch / **Nestlé's** | 150 |
| Forever Yours | 128 |
| Golden Almond / **Hershey's** | 160 |
| Kit Kat: 1.1 oz | 160 |
| Krackel | 160 |
| Marathon | 132 |
| Mars Almond | 138 |
| Milky Way | 130 |
| Mint / **Ghirardelli** | 158 |
| Mr. Goodbar: 1.3 oz | 210 |
| $100,000 / **Nestlé's** | 140 |
| Rally: 1.5 oz | 210 |
| Reggie: 1 bar | 290 |
| Snickers | 130 |
| Snik Snak Sticks | 150 |
| Special Dark Bar: 1.2 oz / **Hershey's** | 190 |
| 3 Musketeers | 123 |
| Tootsie Roll | 116 |
| Chocolate and chocolate-covered bits | |
|     Hershey-ets: 1.1 oz | 140 |
|     Kisses: 1 oz / **Hershey's** | 150 |
|     M & M's, plain: 1 oz | 140 |
|     M & M's, peanut: 1 oz | 144 |
|     Raisinets: 1 oz | 115 |
|     Rolo: 1 piece | 28 |
| Chocolate Parfait: 1¾ oz / **Pearson** | 240 |
| Chocolate Toffee: 1 piece / **Rothchilds** | 22 |
| Coffee Nip: 1¾ oz / **Pearson** | 220 |
| Coffioca: 1¾ oz / **Pearson** | 240 |
| Cough drops: 1 drop / **Beech-Nut** | 10 |
| Cough drops: 1 drop / **Pine Bros.** | 8 |
| Good and Plenty: 1 box | 136 |
| Good 'n Fruity: 1 box | 136 |
| Hard candies | |
|     **Life Savers**, all flavors: 1 drop | 9 |

| | |
|---|---:|
| **Life Savers** Sugar Nothings, | |
| all flavors: 1 tablet | 8 |
| Licorice Nip: 1¾ oz / **Pearson** | 220 |
| Lollipops: 1 lollipop | |
| Fruit: .35 oz size / **Life Savers** | 44 |
| Fruit: .5 oz size / **Life Savers** | 63 |
| Swirled: .35 oz size / **Life Savers** | 44 |
| Swirled: .5 oz size / **Life Savers** | 63 |
| Vanilla: .35 oz size / **Life Savers** | 44 |
| Vanilla: .5 oz size / **Life Savers** | 63 |
| Marshmallow: 1 piece / **JETS** | 24 |
| Marshmallows, miniature: 12 pieces / **Kraft** | 24 |
| Mint: 1 drop / **Life Savers** | 7 |
| Mint Parfait: 1¾ oz / **Pearson** | 240 |
| Peanut Bar: 1 oz / **Munch** | 150 |
| Peanut Butter Bar: 1¾ oz / **Frito-Lay** | 274 |
| Peanut Butter Cup: 1 piece / **Reese's** | 95 |
| Peanut candy, canned: 1 oz / **Planters** | |
| Old Fashioned | 140 |
| Sour Bites: 1 tablet / **Life Savers** | 4 |
| Starburst Fruit Chews: 1 oz | 114 |
| Toffee: 1 piece / **Rothchilds** Creamy | 22 |

## DIETETIC CANDY

| | |
|---|---:|
| Chocolate bars | |
| Almond: ¾ oz bar / **Estee** | 110 |
| Almond: 1 section of 3 oz bar / **Estee** | 37 |
| Bittersweet: 1 section of 3 oz bar / **Estee** | 38 |
| Crunch: ⅝ oz bar / **Estee** | 90 |
| Crunch: 1 section of 2½ oz bar / **Estee** | 30 |
| Fruit and nut: 1 section of 3 oz pkg / **Estee** | 37 |
| Milk: ¾ oz bar / **Estee** | 110 |
| Milk: 1 section of 3 oz pkg / **Estee** | 37 |
| Chocolates, boxed: 1 piece | |
| Peanut butter cups / **Estee** | 45 |
| Raisins, chocolate covered / **Estee** | 6 |
| T.V. Mix / **Estee** | 9 |
| **Estee-Ets**, plain / 1 piece | 6 |

|  | CALORIES |
|---|---|
| **Estee-Ets,** peanut / 1 piece | 7 |
| Gum drops, fruit: 1 piece / **Estee** | 3 |
| Gum drops, licorice: 1 piece / **Estee** | 3 |
| Hard candies: 1 piece | |
|     Assorted / **Estee** | 12 |
|     Cough / **Estee** | 12 |
|     Creme / **Estee** | 12 |
|     Peppermint / **Estee** | 12 |
| Mint candies: 1 piece | |
|     Assorted / **Estee** 5 Pak | 4 |
|     Assorted fruit / **Estee** 5 Pak | 4 |
|     Peppermint / **Estee** | 4 |
|     Sour cherry / **Estee** | 4 |
|     Sour lemon / **Estee** | 4 |
|     Sour orange / **Estee** | 4 |
|     Spearmint / **Estee** | 4 |

# Cereals

## DRY READY-TO-SERVE

|  | CALORIES |
|---|---|
| **Measurements vary according to what companies consider appropriate one-serving sizes. The servings generally are one ounce in weight.** | |
| All-bran: ⅓ cup / **Kellogg's** | 70 |
| Alpha-Bits: 1 cup / **Post** | 110 |
| Apple Jacks: 1 cup / **Kellogg's** | 110 |
| Boo Berry: 1 cup / **General Mills** | 110 |
| Bran, plain, added sugar, defatted wheat germ: ½ cup | 90 |

CALORIES

| | |
|---|---|
| Bran, plain, added sugar, malt extract: | |
| ½ cup | 75 |
| Bran Buds: ⅓ cup / Kellogg's | 70 |
| Bran Chex: ⅔ cup / Ralston Purina | 110 |
| Bran Flakes 40%: ⅔ cup / Kellogg's | 90 |
| Bran Flakes 40%: ⅔ cup / Post | 90 |
| Buc Wheats: ¾ cup / General Mills | 110 |
| Cap'n Crunch: ¾ cup | 121 |
| Cap'n Crunch's Crunchberries: ¾ cup | 120 |
| Cap'n Crunch's Peanut Butter: ¾ cup | 127 |
| Cheerios: 1¼ cup / General Mills | 110 |
| Chocolate Crazy Cow: 1 cup / General Mills | 110 |
| Cocoa Krispies: ¾ cup / Kellogg's | 110 |
| Cocoa Pebbles: ⅞ cup / Post | 120 |
| Cocoa Puffs: 1 cup / General Mills | 110 |
| Concentrate: ⅓ cup / Kellogg's | 110 |
| Cookie Crisp, chocolate chip: 1 cup / | |
| Ralston Purina | 110 |
| Cookie Crisp, vanilla wafer: 1 cup / | |
| Ralston Purina | 110 |
| Corn Chex: 1 cup / Ralston Purina | 110 |
| Corn flakes: 1 cup / General Mills Country | 110 |
| Corn flakes: 1 cup / Kellogg's | 110 |
| Corn flakes: 1¼ cup / Post Toasties | 110 |
| Corn flakes: 1 cup / Ralston Purina | 110 |
| Corn flakes: 1 cup / Safeway | 110 |
| Corn flakes, sugar-coated: ⅔ cup / | |
| Kellogg's Frosted | 110 |
| Corn Total: 1 cup / General Mills | 110 |
| Corny-Snaps: 1 cup / Kellogg's | 120 |
| Count Chocula: 1 cup / General Mills | 110 |
| Country Morning: ⅓ cup / Kellogg's | 130 |
| Country Morning w raisins and dates: | |
| ⅓ cup / Kellogg's | 130 |
| Cracklin' Bran: ⅓ cup / Kellogg's | 110 |
| Crispy Rice: 1 cup / Ralston Purina | 110 |
| Family Style: ½ cup / C.W. Post | 140 |
| Family Style w raisins: ½ cup / C.W. Post | 130 |

| | CALORIES |
|---|---|
| Franken Berry: 1 cup / **General Mills** | 110 |
| Froot Loops: 1 cup / **Kellogg's** | 110 |
| Frosty O's: 1 cup / **General Mills** | 110 |
| Fruit Brute: 1 cup / **General Mills** | 110 |
| Fruity Pebbles: ⅞ cup / **Post** | 120 |
| Golden Grahams: 1 cup / **General Mills** | 110 |
| Grape-Nuts: ¼ cup / **Post** | 110 |
| Granola: 1 oz / **Nature Valley** | 130 |
| Granola w cinnamon and raisins: 1 oz / **Nature Valley** | 130 |
| Granola w coconut and honey: 1 oz / **Nature Valley** | 130 |
| Granola w fruit and nuts: 1 oz / **Nature Valley** | 130 |
| Grape-Nut Flakes: ⅞ cup / **Post** | 100 |
| **Heartland**, plain: 1 oz | 120 |
| **Heartland**, coconut: 1 oz | 130 |
| **Heartland**, raisin: 1 oz | 120 |
| Honeycomb: 1⅓ cup / **Post** | 110 |
| Kaboom: 1 cup / **General Mills** | 110 |
| King Vitaman: ¾ cup | 120 |
| Kix: 1½ cup / **General Mills** | 110 |
| Life: ⅔ cup | 105 |
| Lucky Charms: 1 cup / **General Mills** | 110 |
| Mini-Wheats: about 5 biscuits / **Kellogg's** | 100 |
| Mini-Wheats, frosted: about 4 biscuits / **Kellogg's** | 110 |
| Oat flakes, fortified: ⅔ cup / **Post** | 110 |
| Pep: ¾ cup / **Kellogg's** | 100 |
| Product 19: ¾ cup / **Kellogg's** | 110 |
| **Quaker** 100% Natural: ¼ cup | 139 |
| **Quaker** 100% Natural w apples and cinnamon: ¼ cup | 135 |
| **Quaker** 100% Natural w raisins and dates: ¼ cup | 134 |
| Quisp: 1⅙ cup | 121 |
| Raisin bran: ¾ cup / **Kellogg's** | 120 |
| Raisin bran: ½ cup / **Post** | 90 |
| Raisin bran: ½ cup / **Ralston Purina** | 100 |

| | CALORIES |
|---|---|
| Raisin bran: ½ cup / **Safeway** | 100 |
| Rice: 1 cup / **Safeway** Crispy Rice | 110 |
| Rice, frosted: 1 cup / **Kellogg's** | 110 |
| Rice, puffed: ½ oz / **Malt-O-Meal** | 50 |
| Rice, puffed: 1 cup / **Quaker** | 55 |
| Rice Chex: 1⅛ cup / **Ralston Purina** | 110 |
| Rice Krinkles, frosted: ⅞ cup / **Post** | 110 |
| Rice Krispies: 1 cup / **Kellogg's** | 110 |
| Safeway Tasteeos: 1¼ cup | 110 |
| Special K: 1¼ cup / **Kellogg's** | 110 |
| Strawberry Crazy Cow: 1 cup / **General Mills** | 110 |
| Sugar Corn Pops: 1 cup / **Kellogg's** | 110 |
| Sugar Frosted Flakes: ¾ cup / **Ralston Purina** | 110 |
| Sugar Smacks: ¾ cup / **Kellogg's** | 110 |
| Super Sugar Crisp: ⅞ cup / **Post** | 110 |
| Toasty O's: 1 oz | 110 |
| Total: 1 cup / **General Mills** | 110 |
| Trix: 1 cup / **General Mills** | 110 |
| Wheat, puffed: ½ oz / **Malt-O-Meal** | 50 |
| Wheat, puffed: 1 cup / **Quaker** | 54 |
| Wheat, shredded: 1 biscuit / **Quaker** | 52 |
| Wheat Chex: ⅔ cup / **Ralston Purina** | 110 |
| Wheaties: 1 cup / **General Mills** | 110 |

## TO BE COOKED

**Measurements vary**

| | |
|---|---|
| Barley, pearled: ¼ cup uncooked (1 cup cooked) / **Quaker** Scotch Brand | 172 |
| Barley, pearled: ¼ cup uncooked (¾ cup cooked) / **Quaker** Scotch Brand Quick | 172 |
| Farina: 1 cup cooked / **H-O** Cream Enriched | 120 |
| Farina: ⅔ cup / **Pillsbury** | 80 |
| Farina: ⅔ cup prepared w milk and salt / **Pillsbury** | 200 |
| Farina: 1/6 cup uncooked / **Quaker** Hot 'n Creamy | 101 |

CALORIES

| | |
|---|---|
| Grits: ¼ cup uncooked / Albers | 150 |
| Grits: 1 packet / Quaker Instant Grits Product | 79 |
| Grits: 1/6 cup uncooked / 3-Minute Brand Quick | 100 |
| Grits, hominy, white: 3 tbsp / Aunt Jemima Quick Enriched | 101 |
| Grits, hominy, white: 3 tbsp / Aunt Jemima Regular | 101 |
| Grits, hominy, white: 3 tbsp / Quaker Quick | 101 |
| Grits, hominy, white: 3 tbsp / Quaker Regular | 101 |
| Grits w artificial cheese flavor: 1 packet / Quaker Instant Grits Product | 104 |
| Grits w imitation bacon bits: 1 packet / Quaker Instant Grits Product | 101 |
| Grits w imitation ham bits: 1 packet / Quaker Instant Grits Product | 99 |
| Malt-O-Meal Chocolate: 1 oz uncooked (about ¾ cup cooked) | 100 |
| Malt-O-Meal Quick: 1 oz uncooked (about ¾ cup cooked) | 100 |

Oats and oatmeal

| | |
|---|---|
| H-O Old Fashioned: ¾ cup cooked | 140 |
| H-O Quick: ¾ cup cooked | 130 |
| Harvest Quick: 1 oz uncooked | 110 |
| Quaker Old Fashioned: ⅓ cup uncooked | 109 |
| Quaker Quick: ⅓ cup uncooked | 109 |
| Ralston Purina: 1 oz uncooked | 110 |
| Ralston Purina Quick: 1 oz uncooked | 110 |
| Safeway Quick: ⅓ cup uncooked | 100 |
| 3-Minute Brand Quick: 1 oz uncooked | 110 |
| Instant: 1 packet / H-O | 105 |
| Instant: ½ cup uncooked / H-O | 130 |
| Instant: ¾ cup cooked / H-O Regular | 130 |
| Instant: 1 packet / H-O Sweet and Mellow | 150 |
| Instant: 1 packet / Quaker Regular | 105 |
| Instant: 1 packet / 3-Minute Brand Stir 'n Eat | 110 |

CALORIES

| | |
|---|---:|
| Instant w apple and brown sugar: 1 packet / **3-Minute Brand Stir 'n Eat** | 120 |
| Instant w apples and cinnamon: 1 packet / **Quaker** | 134 |
| Instant w bran and raisins: 1 packet / **Quaker** | 153 |
| Instant w cinnamon and spice: 1 packet / **Quaker** | 176 |
| Instant w maple and brown sugar: 1 packet / **H-O** | 165 |
| Instant w maple and brown sugar: 1 packet / **Quaker** | 163 |
| Instant w raisins and spice: 1 packet / **H-O** | 165 |
| Instant w raisins and spice: 1 packet / **Quaker** | 159 |
| Ralston: 1 oz uncooked / **Ralston Purina** | 100 |
| Ralston: 1 oz uncooked / **Ralston Purina** Instant | 100 |
| Rye: ¼ cup uncooked / **Con Agra** Cream of Rye | 90 |
| Whole wheat: ⅓ cup uncooked (⅔ cup cooked) / **Quaker** Pettijohns | 100 |

# Cheese

CALORIES

**1 oz unless noted**

American

| | |
|---|---:|
| Pimento / **Borden** | 105 |
| Processed / **Borden** | 105 |
| Processed / **Borden** Made In Wisconsin | 104 |

CALORIES

| | |
|---|---|
| Processed: 1 slice / **Borden** Single Slices | 67 |
| Processed / **Kraft** Singles | 90 |
| Sliced: 1 slice / **Lucerne** 24 Single Slices | 53 |
| Sliced: 1 slice / **Safeway** | 73 |
| American-flavored, processed, single wrap slices / **Kraft** Light 'n Lively | 60 |
| Blue / **Borden Bleu** | 105 |
| Blue / **Casino** | 100 |
| Brick / **Casino** | 110 |
| Brick, slices / **Kraft** | 110 |
| Brie, Danish / **Tiny Dane** | 100 |
| Camembert / **Borden** | 85 |
| Cheddar / **Borden** Longhorn | 113 |
| Cheddar / **Borden** Wisconsin Old Fashioned | 113 |
| Cheddar / **Kraft** Cracker Barrel | 110 |
| Colby / **Borden** | 111 |
| Colby, low sodium / **Swift Pauly** | 110 |
| Farmer's | |
|     **Dutch Garden** | 100 |
|     **Friendship** | 38 |
|     **Wispride** | 100 |
|     Salt free / **Friendship** | 38 |
|     Bulk: ½ cup / **Breakstone** | 200 |
|     Midget: ½ cup / **Breakstone** | 150 |
| Fondue / **Swiss Knight** | 60 |
| Gouda / **Borden** Dutch Maid | 86 |
| Gruyere / **Borden** | 101 |
| Gruyere, plain / **Swiss Knight** | 100 |
| Liederkranz / **Borden** | 86 |
| Limburger / **Borden** Dutch Maid | 97 |
| Limburger / **Mohawk Valley** | 100 |
| Monterey Jack / **Borden** | 103 |
| Monterey Jack / **Casino** | 100 |
| Monterey Jack / **Kraft** | 100 |
| Mozzarella / **Borden** | 96 |
| Muenster, slices / **Kraft** | 100 |
| Pimento / **Borden** Made In Wisconsin | 104 |
| Pizza / **Borden** | 85 |

CALORIES

| | |
|---|---|
| Provolone / **Borden** | 93 |
| Provolone, sharp / **Casino** | 90 |
| Provolone, slices / **Kraft** | 90 |
| Ricotta / **Borden** | 42 |
| Romano / **Casino** | 110 |
| Roquefort / **Borden** | 105 |
| Scamorze / **Kraft** | 70 |
| Skim milk cheese, low fat / | |
|   **Swift Pauly** Slim Line | 60 |
| Swiss | |
|   Natural / **Borden** | 104 |
|   Natural / **Borden** Imported Switzerland | 104 |
|   Natural / **Borden** Imported Finland | 104 |
|   Natural / **Kraft** | 100 |
|   Processed / **Borden** | 101 |
|   Processed / **Borden** Made In Wisconsin | 100 |

## COTTAGE CHEESE

**½ cup unless noted**

| | |
|---|---|
| Creamed | |
|   **Borden** | 121 |
|   **Friendship** / 4 oz | 120 |
|   **Lucerne** | 120 |
|   **Meadow Gold** | 120 |
|   w chives / **Borden** | 117 |
|   w chives / **Lucerne** | 120 |
|   w fruit salad: 4 oz / **Friendship** | |
|     Calorie Meter | 120 |
|   w fruit salad / **Lucerne** | 150 |
|   w pineapple / **Borden** | 107 |
|   w pineapple: 4 oz / **Friendship** | 140 |
|   w pineapple / **Lucerne** | 150 |
|   w vegetable salad / **Borden** | 119 |
|   w vegetable salad: 4 oz / **Friendship** | |
|     Garden Salad | 120 |
| Dry cottage cheese | |
|   **Borden** | 100 |

CALORIES

| | |
|---|---|
| **Lucerne** | 80 |
| Pot style / **Breakstone** | 110 |

Low-fat

| | |
|---|---|
| **Borden** Lite Line | 90 |
| **Breakstone** | 90 |
| **Friendship** Calorie Meter / 4 oz | 100 |
| **Friendship** Pot Style / 4 oz | 100 |
| **Lucerne** Lowfat | 100 |
| **Viva** Lowfat | 100 |
| **Weight Watchers** Lowfat | 90 |
| wo salt: 4 oz / **Friendship** Calorie Meter | 90 |
| Skim milk, large curd / **Breakstone** | 90 |

## CREAM AND NEUFCHATEL CHEESE

**1 oz**

Cream cheese

| | |
|---|---|
| **Borden** | 105 |
| **Philadelphia** Brand | 100 |
| **Lucerne** | 100 |
| w chives / **Borden** | 96 |
| w pimento / **Borden** | 74 |
| Imitation / **Philadelphia** Brand | 50 |

Cream cheese, whipped

| | |
|---|---|
| **Philadelphia** Brand | 100 |
| w bacon and horseradish / **Philadelphia** Brand | 90 |
| w blue cheese / **Philadelphia** Brand | 100 |
| w chives / **Philadelphia** Brand | 90 |
| w onion / **Philadelphia** Brand | 90 |
| w pimento / **Philadelphia** Brand | 90 |
| w smoked salmon / **Philadelphia** Brand | 90 |

Neufchatel cheese

| | |
|---|---|
| **Calorie-wise** | 70 |
| w bacon and horseradish / **Kraft** | 70 |
| w blue cheese / **Kraft** | 70 |
| w clams / **Kraft** | 70 |
| w dill pickles / **Kraft** | 70 |
| w garlic and onions / **Kraft** | 70 |

CALORIES

| | |
|---|---|
| w olive and pimento / **Borden** | 81 |
| w onions / **Kraft** | 70 |
| w pimento / **Borden** | 82 |
| w pineapple / **Kraft** | 70 |
| w relish / **Borden** | 81 |

### GRATED AND SHREDDED CHEESE

**1 oz (= about ⅓ cup or about 5½ tbsp)**

| | |
|---|---|
| American, grated / **Borden** | 30 |
| Parmesan, grated / **Borden** | 130 |
| Parmesan, grated / **Kraft** | 130 |
| Parmesan, grated / **Lucerne** | 110 |
| Parmesan and Romano, grated / **Borden** | 143 |
| Romano / **Kraft** | 130 |

### CHEESE FOODS

**1 oz unless noted**

| | |
|---|---|
| American | |
|     **Borden** | 92 |
|     **Lucerne** / 1 slice | 60 |
|     **Lucerne** 10 Single Slices / 1 slice | 72 |
|     **Safeway** / 1 slice | 100 |
|     **Swift Pauly** | 90 |
| Blue / **Borden** Blue Brand | 82 |
| Blue / **Borden** Vera Blue | 91 |
| Blue / **Wispride** Cold Pack | 100 |
| Cheddar flavor / **Wispride** Cold Pack | 100 |
| Pimento | |
|     **Borden** | 91 |
|     **Lucerne** / 1 slice | 60 |
|     **Safeway** / 1 slice | 75 |
|     **Swift Pauly** | 90 |
| Sweet Munchee / **Swift Pauly** | 100 |
| Swiss | |
|     **Borden** | 91 |

|  | CALORIES |
|---|---|
| **Lucerne** 10 Single Slices / 1 slice | 72 |
| **Swift Pauly** | 90 |
| **Wispride** Cold Pack | 100 |

## CHEESE SPREADS

**1 oz**

|  |  |
|---|---|
| American / **Borden** | 85 |
| American w bacon / **Borden** | |
|   Cheese 'N Bacon | 80 |
| Blue / **Roka** | 80 |
| Cheddar flavor, processed / **Wispride** | 80 |
| **Cheez Whiz** | 75 |
| w garlic / **Borden** | 82 |
| Limburger / **Borden** | 82 |
| Smoke-flavored / **Borden** | 80 |
| Smoke-flavored / **Squeez-A-Snak** | 83 |
| Velveeta, processed / **Kraft** | 80 |

## WELSH RAREBIT

|  |  |
|---|---|
| Canned: 1 cup / **Snow's** | 384 |
| Frozen: 5 oz / **Green Giant** Boil-in-Bag | |
|   Toast Toppers | 220 |
| w sherry, canned: 1 cup / **Snow's** | 324 |

# Chewing Gum

|  | CALORIES |
|---|---|
| **1 stick or piece** | |
| **Adams** Sour | 9 |
| **Beech-Nut** | 9 |
| **Beechies** | 6 |

CALORIES

Bubble
    Bubble Yum 27
    Bubblicious 25
    Care Free, all flavors 8
    Fruit Stripe 10
    Orbit 8
    Trident Stick 7
    Dietetic / Estee 3
Chiclets 6
Clorets 6
Dentyne 5
Freshen-Up 10
Fruit, dietetic / Estee 3
Fruit Stripe 9
Orbit, all flavors 8
Peppermint, dietetic / Estee 3
Spearmint, dietetic / Estee 3
Trident 5
Wrigley's, all flavors 10

# Chinese Foods

CALORIES

| | |
|---|---|
| Apple-cinnamon roll, frozen: 1 roll / La Choy | 38 |
| Bamboo shoots, canned: 8½ oz / Chun King | 48 |
| Bamboo shoots, canned: 8 oz / La Choy | 23 |
| Bean sprouts, canned: 16 oz / Chun King | 80 |
| Bean sprouts, canned: 1 cup / La Choy | 23 |
| Chop suey | |
|     Beef, frozen: 32 oz / Banquet | |
|     Buffet Supper | 418 |
|     Beef, frozen: 7 oz / Banquet Cookin' Bag | 73 |
|     Vegetables, canned: 1 cup / La Choy | 53 |

Chow mein, canned: 1 cup unless noted
| | |
|---|---|
| Beef / La Choy | 72 |
| Beef / La Choy Bi-Pack | 83 |
| Chicken / La Choy | 68 |
| Chicken / La Choy Bi-Pack | 101 |
| Chicken / La Choy 50 oz | 93 |
| Meatless / La Choy | 47 |
| Meatless / La Choy 50 oz | 46 |
| Mushroom / La Choy Bi-Pack | 85 |
| Pepper oriental / La Choy | 89 |
| Pepper oriental / La Choy Bi-Pack | 89 |
| Pork / La Choy Bi-Pack | 120 |
| Shrimp / La Choy | 61 |
| Shrimp / La Choy Bi-Pack | 110 |
| Vegetables: 16 oz can / Chun King | 88 |

Chow mein, frozen
| | |
|---|---|
| Beef: 1 cup / La Choy | 97 |
| Chicken: 32 oz / Banquet Buffet Supper | 345 |
| Chicken: 7 oz / Banquet Cookin' Bag | 89 |
| Chicken: 1 cup / La Choy | 108 |
| Chicken wo noodles: 9 oz / Green Giant Boil-in-Bag | 130 |
| Shrimp: 1 cup / La Choy | 73 |

| | |
|---|---|
| Egg rolls, chicken, frozen: 1 roll / La Choy | 30 |
| Egg rolls, lobster, frozen: 1 roll / La Choy | 27 |
| Fried rice, chicken, canned: 1 cup / La Choy | 418 |
| Fried rice, Chinese style, canned: 1 cup / La Choy | 414 |
| Fried rice and pork, frozen: 1 cup / La Choy | 216 |

Noodles, canned: 1 cup
| | |
|---|---|
| Chow mein / La Choy | 306 |
| Ramen-beef / La Choy | 225 |
| Ramen-chicken / La Choy | 202 |
| Ramen-oriental / La Choy | 207 |
| Rice / La Choy | 260 |
| Wide chow mein / La Choy | 298 |

| | |
|---|---|
| Pea pods, frozen: 1 pkg / La Choy | 90 |
| Pepper oriental, frozen: 1 cup / La Choy | 110 |

CALORIES

| | |
|---|---|
| Sweet and sour pork, frozen: 1 cup / La Choy | 245 |
| Vegetables, mixed Chinese, canned: | |
| 1 cup / La Choy | 35 |
| Water chestnuts, canned: 8½ oz / Chun King | 119 |
| Won ton, frozen: 1 cup / La Choy | 92 |

# Chips, Crisps and Similar Snacks

CALORIES

**1 oz unless noted**

| | |
|---|---|
| Cheddar Bitz / Frito-Lay | 129 |
| Cheese Doodles / Old London | 133 |
| Cheese Pixies / Wise | 158 |
| Chee.tos / Frito-Lay | 160 |
| Cheez Balls / Planters | 160 |
| Cheez Curls / Planters | 160 |
| Corn chips | |
| Fritos | 156 |
| Granny Goose | 157 |
| Old London | 150 |
| Old London Dipsy Doodles | 150 |
| Planters | 170 |
| Wise | 166 |
| Barbecue-flavored / Fritos | 150 |
| Barbecue-flavored / Wise | 160 |
| Corn Nuggets, toasted: 1⅜ oz / Frito-Lay | 176 |
| Fiesta chips / Granny Goose | 147 |
| Funyuns | 138 |
| Jalapeno Corn Toots / Granny Goose | 161 |

CALORIES

| | |
|---|---|
| Munchos / Frito-Lay | 154 |
| Onion-flavored rings / Old London | 136 |
| Onion-flavored rings / Wise | 126 |
| Potato chips | |
|     Frito-Lay | 158 |
|     Frito-Lay Natural Style | 157 |
|     Frito-Lay Ruffles | 155 |
|     Granny Goose | 161 |
|     Planters Stackable | 150 |
|     Pringles | 150 |
|     Pringles Country Style | 160 |
|     Pringles Extra Rippled | 150 |
|     Wise | 160 |
|     Wise Ridgies | 160 |
|     Barbecue-flavored / Granny Goose | 159 |
|     Barbecue-flavored / Frito-Lay | 157 |
|     Barbecue-flavored / Wise | 160 |
|     Green onion-flavored / Granny Goose | 160 |
|     Onion-garlic-flavored / Wise | 160 |
|     Sour cream-and-onion-flavored / Frito-Lay | 155 |
| Potato sticks, canned: 1½ oz / O & C | 231 |
| Potato sticks / Wise Julienne | 136 |
| Puffs-Crunchy, cheese-flavored / Chee.tos | 156 |
| Rinds, fried | |
|     Bacon / Wise Bakon Delites | 166 |
|     Bacon, barbecue-flavored / Wise | |
|       Bakon Delites | 160 |
|     Pork / Baken-Ets | 140 |
|     Pork / Granny Goose | 152 |
| Snack Sticks | |
|     Lightly salted / Pepperidge Farm | 120 |
|     Pumpernickel / Pepperidge Farm | 110 |
|     Sesame / Pepperidge Farm | 120 |
|     Whole wheat / Pepperidge Farm | 110 |
| Taco chips / Old London | 129 |
| Tortilla chips | |
|     Doritos | 137 |
|     Granny Goose | 139 |

| | CALORIES |
|---|---|
| **Planters** Nacho | 130 |
| **Planter** Taco | 130 |
| Nacho cheese flavor / **Doritos** | 141 |
| Taco flavor / **Doritos** | 142 |
| Wheat chips, imitation bacon-flavored / **Bakon-snacks** | 150 |

# Chocolate and Chips

| | CALORIES |
|---|---|
| **For Baking: 1 oz unless noted** | |
| Chips | |
| Butterscotch-flavored / **Nestlé's** Morsels | 150 |
| Chocolate: ¼ cup / **Hershey's** | 230 |
| Chocolate / **Nestlé's** Morsels | 150 |
| Chocolate-flavored / **Baker's** | 130 |
| Chocolate, semi-sweet / **Ghirardelli** | 150 |
| Chocolate, semi-sweet / **Hershey's** | 150 |
| Chocolate, semi-sweet / **Hershey's** Mini | 150 |
| Chocolate, semi-sweet / **Nestlé's** Morsels | 150 |
| Peanut butter-flavored / **Reese's** | 150 |
| Choco-bake / **Nestlé's** | 170 |
| Chocolate / **Ghirardelli** Eagle Bar | 151 |
| Chocolate, ground / **Ghirardelli** | 163 |
| Chocolate, solid | |
| **Ghirardelli** Milk Chocolate Blocks | 150 |
| **Hershey's** | 190 |
| German's sweet / **Baker's** | 140 |
| Semi-sweet / **Baker's** | 130 |
| Unswt / **Baker's** | 140 |

# Cocktails

## ALCOHOLIC

| Canned: 2 fl oz | CALORIES |
|---|---|
| Apricot Sour / Party Tyme | 66 |
| Banana Daiquiri / Party Tyme | 66 |
| Daiquiri / Party Tyme | 65 |
| Gimlet / Party Tyme | 82 |
| Gin and Tonic / Party Tyme | 55 |
| Mai Tai / Party Tyme | 65 |
| Manhattan / Party Tyme | 74 |
| Margarita / Party Tyme | 66 |
| Martini / Party Tyme | 82 |
| Pina Colada / Party Tyme | 63 |
| Rum and Cola / Party Tyme | 55 |
| Scotch Sour / Party Tyme | 65 |
| Screwdriver / Party Tyme | 69 |
| Tom Collins / Party Tyme | 58 |
| Vodka Martini / Party Tyme | 72 |
| Vodka Tonic / Party Tyme | 55 |

## NONALCOHOLIC MIXES

| Dry: 1 packet | |
|---|---|
| Alexander / Holland House | 69 |
| Banana Daiquiri / Holland House | 66 |
| Bloody Mary / Holland House | 56 |
| Daiquiri / Holland House | 69 |
| Gimlet / Holland House | 69 |
| Grasshopper / Holland House | 69 |

CALORIES

| | |
|---|---|
| Mai Tai / Holland House | 69 |
| Margarita / Holland House | 69 |
| Mint Julep / Holland House | 67 |
| Pina Colada / Holland House | 66 |
| Pink Squirrel / Holland House | 69 |
| Screwdriver / Holland House | 69 |
| Strawberry Margarita / Holland House | 62 |
| Strawberry Sting / Holland House | 74 |
| Tequilla Sunrise / Holland House | 63 |
| Tom Collins / Holland House | 69 |
| Vodka Sour / Holland House | 65 |
| Wallbanger / Holland House | 65 |
| Whiskey Sour / Holland House | 69 |

**Liquid: 1 fl oz unless noted**

| | |
|---|---|
| Amaretto / Holland House | 79 |
| Apricot Sour / Holland House | 48 |
| Black Russian / Holland House | 92 |
| Blackberry Sour / Holland House | 50 |
| Bloody Mary / Holland House Regular | 10 |
| Bloody Mary / Holland House Extra Tangy | 10 |
| Bloody Mary / Holland House Smooth 'n Spicy | 6 |
| Cocktail Host / Holland House | 47 |
| Collins Mixer: 8 fl oz / Canada Dry | 80 |
| Cream of Coconut / Holland House Coco Casa | 117 |
| Daiquiri / Holland House | 51 |
| Dry Martini / Holland House | 10 |
| Gimlet / Holland House | 40 |
| Mai Tai / Holland House | 33 |
| Manhattan / Holland House | 29 |
| Margarita / Holland House | 39 |
| Old Fashioned / Holland House | 36 |
| Pina Colada / Holland House | 60 |
| Strawberry Sting / Holland House | 35 |
| Tom Collins / Holland House | 67 |
| Whiskey Sour: 8 fl oz / Canada Dry | 90 |
| Whiskey Sour / Holland House | 55 |
| Whiskey Sour / Holland House Low Calorie | 9 |

# Cocoa

|  | CALORIES |
|---|---|
| Coca: 1 oz / **Hershey's** | 120 |
| Cocoa: 1 tbsp / **Marvel** | 30 |
| Cocoa, chocolate flavor: ¾ oz / **Nestlé's** | 70 |
| Cocoa | |
|    Mix: 1 oz / **Hershey's** | 110 |
|    Mix: 3 tbsp / **Hershey's** Instant | 80 |
|    Mix: 3 tbsp, prepared w 8 oz milk / | |
|      **Hershey's** Instant | 240 |
|    Mix: 1 oz / **Nestlé's** | 110 |
|    Mix: 1 oz / **Ovaltine** | 120 |
|    Mix: .69 oz / **Ovaltine** Reduced Calorie | 80 |
|    Mix, all flavors, instant: 1 oz / **Carnation** | 112 |

# Coconut

|  | CALORIES |
|---|---|
| Fresh | |
|    In shell: 1 coconut | 1373 |
|    Meat: 1 piece (2 x 2 x ½ in) | 156 |
|    Meat, shredded or grated: 1 cup | 277 |
|    Cream, (liquid from grated meat): 1 cup | 815 |
|    Milk, (liquid from mixture of grated | |
|      meat and water): 1 cup | 605 |
|    Water, (liquid from coconuts): 1 cup | 53 |

CALORIES

Canned or packaged: ¼ cup
| | |
|---|---|
| Plain / **Baker's** Angel Flake | 90 |
| Plain / **Baker's** Premium Shred | 100 |
| Plain / **Baker's** Southern Style | 90 |
| Plain, shredded / **Durkee** | 70 |
| Cookie-coconut / **Baker's** | 140 |

# Coffee

CALORIES

All coffee has about
    2 calories per cup for ground roasted
    4 calories per cup for instant and
       instant freeze-dried

| | |
|---|---|
| **Chase & Sanborn:** 1 cup | 2 |
| **Decaf** Instant: 1 tsp | 4 |
| **General Foods International:** 6 fl oz | |
| Cafe Francais, swtd, prepared | 60 |
| Cafe Vienna, swtd, prepared | 60 |
| Orange Cappuccino, swtd, prepared | 60 |
| Suisse Mocha, swtd, prepared | 60 |
| **Nescafé** Instant: 1 tsp | 4 |
| **Nescafé** Instant, freeze-dried, decaffeinated: 1 tsp | 4 |
| **Postum** (cereal beverage), instant: 6 fl oz | 10 |
| **Taster's Choice** Instant, freeze-dried: 1 tsp | 4 |
| **Taster's Choice** Instant, freeze dried, decaffeinated: 1 tsp | 4 |

# Condiments

CALORIES

| | |
|---|---|
| **A.1** Sauce / 1 tbsp | 12 |
| Catsup: 1 tbsp / **Del Monte** | 15 |
| Catsup: 1 tbsp / **Tillie Lewis** | 20 |
| Chili sauce: 1 tbsp / **Heinz** | 17 |
| Chutney: 1 tbsp / **Major Grey's** | 53 |
| Horseradish: 1 tbsp | 2 |
|     Cream style | 5 |
|     Oil style | 10 |
| Horseradish, raw: ¼ lb | 70 |
| Hot sauce: 1 tsp / **Frank's** | 12 |
| Mustard, prepared | |
|     Brown: 1 tbsp / **French's** Brown 'n Spicy | 15 |
|     Brown: 1 tsp / **Mr. Mustard** | 11 |
|     Cream salad: 1 tbsp / **French's** | 10 |
|     Dijon: 1 tsp / **Grey Poupon** | 5 |
|     w horseradish: 1 tbsp / **French's** | 15 |
|     w onion: 1 tbsp / **French's** | 25 |
|     Yellow: 1 tbsp / **French's** Medford | 16 |
| Sauce Diable: 1 tbsp / **Escoffier** | 20 |
| Sauce Robert: 1 tbsp / **Escoffier** | 19 |
| Seafood cocktail: ¼ cup / **Del Monte** | 70 |
| Seafood cocktail: 2 oz / **Pfeiffer** | 100 |
| Soy sauce: 1 tbsp / **La Choy** | 8 |
| Steak sauce: 1 tbsp / **Steak Supreme** | 20 |
| Taco sauce: 1 tbsp / **Ortega** | 21 |
| Taco sauce: 1 oz / **Old El Paso** | 8 |
| Tartar sauce: 1 tbsp | |
|     **Best Foods** | 70 |
|     **Hellmann's** | 70 |
|     **Seven Seas** | 80 |

| | CALORIES |
|---|---|
| Tartar sauce, mix: 1 pkg / **Lawry's** | 64 |
| Vinegar: 1 fl oz | |
|     Champagne / **Regina** | 1 |
|     Red wine / **Regina** | 1 |
|     Red wine w garlic / **Regina** | 1 |
| Wine, cooking | |
|     Marsala: 1 fl oz / **Holland House** | 35 |
|     Red: 1 fl oz / **Holland House** | 25 |
|     Sauterne: ¼ cup / **Regina** | 2 |
|     Sherry: 1 fl oz / **Holland House** | 40 |
|     Sherry: ¼ cup / **Regina** | 19 |
|     White: 1 fl oz / **Holland House** | 25 |
| Worcestershire: 1 tbsp / **French's** | 10 |
| Worcestershire, hickory smoke-flavored: | |
|   1 tbsp / **French's** Smoky | 10 |

*See also* Sauces, Seasonings

# Cookies

| | CALORIES |
|---|---|
| **1 piece as packaged unless noted** | |
| Adelaide / **Pepperidge Farm** | 53 |
| Angel puffs / **Stella D'Oro** Dietetic | 17 |
| Angelica Goodies / **Stella D'Oro** | 100 |
| Anginetti / **Stella D'Oro** | 28 |
| Animal crackers | |
|     **Keebler** | 12 |
|     **Sunshine** | 10 |
|     Iced / **Sunshine** | 26 |
|     Barnum's Animals / **Nabisco** | 12 |
| Anisette sponge / **Stella D'Oro** | 50 |
| Anisette toast / **Stella D'Oro** | 46 |

CALORIES

| | |
|---|---|
| Applesauce / Sunshine | 86 |
| Applesauce, iced / Sunshine | 86 |
| Arrowroot / Sunshine | 16 |
| Assortment | |
|     Stella D'Oro Hostess with the Mostest | 39 |
|     Stella D'Oro Lady Stella | 37 |
| Aunt Sally, iced / Sunshine | 96 |
| Big Treat / Sunshine | 153 |
| Biscos / Nabisco | 44 |
| Bordeaux / Pepperidge Farm | 37 |
| Breakfast Treats / Stella D'Oro | 100 |
| Brown sugar / Pepperidge Farm | 50 |
| Brussels / Pepperidge Farm | 57 |
| Butter-flavored / Nabisco | 23 |
| Butter-flavored / Sunshine | 23 |
| Buttercup / Keebler | 24 |
| Cameo creme sandwich / Nabisco | 68 |
| Capri / Pepperidge Farm | 85 |
| Chessman / Pepperidge Farm | 43 |
| Chinese dessert cookies / Stella D'Oro | 170 |
| Chip-A-Roos / Sunshine | 63 |
| Chocolate brownie / Pepperidge Farm | 57 |
| Chocolate chip | |
|     Estee Dietetic | 30 |
|     Keebler Old Fashioned | 80 |
|     Keebler Rich 'n Chips | 73 |
|     Pepperidge Farm | 43 |
| Chocolate chip coconut / Sunshine | 80 |
| Chocolate fudge sandwich / Sunshine | 72 |
| Chocolate-strawberry wafers, dietetic, single serving pkg: 1 pkg / Estee | 90 |
| Cinnamon sugar / Pepperidge Farm | 53 |
| Cinnamon toast / Sunshine | 13 |
| Coconut Bar / Keebler | 62 |
| Coconut Bar / Sunshine | 47 |
| Coconut cookies / Stella D'Oro Dietetic | 47 |
| Coconut Chocolate Drop / Keebler | 75 |
| Coconut macaroons / Nabisco | 87 |

CALORIES

| | |
|---|---|
| Como Delight / **Stella D'Oro** | 150 |
| Cream Lunch / **Sunshine** | 45 |
| Crescents, almond-flavored / **Nabisco** | 34 |
| Cup Custard, chocolate / **Sunshine** | 70 |
| Cup Custard, vanilla / **Sunshine** | 71 |
| Danish Wedding / **Keebler** | 31 |
| Date-Nut Granola / **Pepperidge Farm** | 53 |
| Devilsfood / **Keebler** | 64 |
| Dixie Vanilla / **Sunshine** | 60 |
| Egg biscuits | |
|     **Stella D'Oro** | 42 |
|     **Stella D'Oro** Dietetic | 40 |
|     Anise / **Stella D'Oro** Roman | 131 |
|     Rum and brandy / **Stella D'Oro** Roman | 131 |
|     Sugared / **Stella D'Oro** | 60 |
|     Vanilla / **Stella D'Oro** Roman | 131 |
| Egg Jumbo / **Stella D'Oro** | 43 |
| Fig bar: 2 oz / **Frito-Lay** | 189 |
| Fig bar / **Keebler** | 71 |
| Fig bar / **Sunshine** | 45 |
| French vanilla creme / **Keebler** | 93 |
| Fudge Chip / **Pepperidge Farm** | 57 |
| Fudge Stick / **Keebler** | 42 |
| Fudge Stripes / **Keebler** | 57 |
| German chocolate / **Keebler** | 85 |
| Ginger snap | |
|     **Keebler** | 24 |
|     **Nabisco** | 29 |
|     **Sunshine** | 24 |
| Gingerman / **Pepperidge Farm** | 33 |
| Golden bars / **Stella D'Oro** | 110 |
| Golden Fruit / **Sunshine** | 61 |
| Graham crackers | |
|     **Sunshine** Sweet-Tooth | 45 |
|     Chocolate-covered / **Keebler** Deluxe | 42 |
|     Cinnamon: smallest piece when broken on | |
|       score line / **Keebler** Crisp | 17 |
|     Crumbs: 1 bag / **Sunshine** | 420 |

| | |
|---|---|
| Honey: smallest piece when broken on score line / Keebler | 17 |
| Honey / Nabisco Honey Maid | 30 |
| Honey: 1 entire piece / Sunshine | 60 |
| Hydrox / Sunshine | 48 |
| Hydrox, mint / Sunshine | 48 |
| Hydrox, vanilla / Sunshine | 50 |
| Irish oatmeal / Pepperidge Farm | 50 |
| Keebies / Keebler | 51 |
| Kichel / Stella D'Oro Dietetic | 8 |
| Krisp Kreem, chocolate / Keebler | 32 |
| Krisp Kreem, strawberry / Keebler | 31 |
| Krisp Kreem, vanilla / Keebler | 31 |
| Lady Joan / Sunshine | 47 |
| Lady Joan, iced / Sunshine | 42 |
| LaLanne Sesame / Sunshine | 15 |
| LaLanne Soya / Sunshine | 16 |
| Lemon / Sunshine | 76 |
| Lemon Coolers / Sunshine | 29 |
| Lemon nut crunch / Pepperidge Farm | 60 |
| Lemon Thins, dietetic / Estee | 25 |
| Lido / Pepperidge Farm | 95 |
| Love Cookies / Stella D'Oro Dietetic | 110 |
| Mallopuffs / Sunshine | 63 |
| Mandel toast / Stella D'Oro | 54 |
| Margherite combination / Stella D'Oro | 73 |
| Margherite, vanilla / Stella D'Oro | 73 |
| Marigold sandwich / Keebler | 91 |
| Milano / Pepperidge Farm | 63 |
| Mint Milano / Pepperidge Farm | 70 |
| Molasses crisps / Pepperidge Farm | 30 |
| Molasses and spice / Sunshine | 67 |
| Nassau / Pepperidge Farm | 75 |
| 'Nilla wafers / Nabisco | 18 |
| Nutter Butter / Nabisco | 69 |
| Oatmeal | |
| Sunshine | 58 |
| Almond / Pepperidge Farm | 53 |

| | CALORIES |
|---|---|
| Iced / **Keebler** Old Fashioned | 81 |
| Iced / **Sunshine** | 69 |
| Marmalade / **Pepperidge Farm** | 53 |
| Peanut butter / **Sunshine** | 79 |
| Raisin / **Nabisco** | 77 |
| Raisin / **Pepperidge Farm** | 57 |
| Raisin, dietetic / **Estee** | 30 |
| Opera Creme Sandwich / **Keebler** | 82 |
| Orbit Creme Sandwich / **Sunshine** | 51 |
| Oreo / **Nabisco** | 50 |
| Orleans / **Pepperidge Farm** | 33 |
| Peanut / **Pepperidge Farm** | 47 |
| Peanut butter / **Keebler** Old Fashioned | 81 |
| Peanut butter wafers / **Sunshine** | 33 |
| Peanut creme patties / **Nabisco** | 34 |
| Pecan Sandies / **Keebler** | 85 |
| Penguin / **Keebler** | 93 |
| Penguin, peanut butter / **Keebler** | 91 |
| Pfeffernusse / **Stella D'Oro** Spice Drops | 44 |
| Pirouette / **Pepperidge Farm** | 40 |
| Pirouette, chocolate-laced / **Pepperidge Farm** | 40 |
| Pitter Patter / **Keebler** | 84 |
| Raisin bar, iced / **Keebler** | 80 |
| Raisin Bran / **Pepperidge Farm** | 53 |
| Raisin fruit biscuit / **Nabisco** | 56 |
| Royal Nuggets / **Stella D'Oro** Dietetic | 1 |
| St. Moritz / **Pepperidge Farm** | 47 |
| Sandwich | |
|     **Estee** Dietetic | 50 |
|     Assortment / **Nabisco** Pride | 55 |
|     Creme, Swiss / **Nabisco** | 52 |
|     Creme, chocolate fudge / **Keebler** | 99 |
|     Creme, lemon / **Keebler** | 80 |
|     Creme, vanilla / **Keebler** | 82 |
|     Lemon / **Estee** Dietetic | 60 |
| Scotties / **Sunshine** | 39 |
| Sesame cookies / **Stella D'Oro** Regina | 49 |
| Sesame cookies / **Stella D'Oro** Regina Dietetic | 43 |

| | |
|---|---|
| Shortbread / **Pepperidge Farm** | 65 |
| Shortbread, almond / **Keebler** Spiced Windmill | 61 |
| Shortbread, pecan / **Nabisco** | 77 |
| Social Tea Biscuit / **Nabisco** | 21 |
| Social Tea Sandwich / **Nabisco** | 51 |
| Sorrento cookies / **Stella D'Oro** | 57 |
| Sprinkles / **Sunshine** | 57 |
| Sugar / **Keebler** Old Fashioned | 78 |
| Sugar / **Pepperidge Farm** | 53 |
| Sugar / **Sunshine** | 86 |
| Sugar Rings / **Nabisco** | 68 |
| Sunflower Raisin / **Pepperidge Farm** | 53 |
| Swedish Kremes / **Keebler** | 98 |
| Swiss Fudge / **Stella D'Oro** | 64 |
| Tahiti / **Pepperidge Farm** | 85 |
| Taste of Vienna / **Stella D'Oro** | 85 |
| Toy Cookies / **Sunshine** | 13 |
| Vanilla snaps / **Nabisco** | 13 |
| Vanilla thins, dietetic / **Estee** | 25 |
| Vienna Finger sandwich / **Sunshine** | 71 |
| Wafers | |
|      Assorted, dietetic / **Estee** | 35 |
|      Brown edge / **Nabisco** | 28 |
|      Chocolate, dietetic / **Estee** | 25 |
|      Peanut butter-chocolate, dietetic / **Estee** | 90 |
|      Spiced / **Nabisco** | 40 |
|      Sugar / **Biscos** | 18 |
|      Sugar / **Sunshine** | 43 |
|      Sugar, lemon / **Sunshine** | 44 |
|      Vanilla / **Keebler** | 19 |
|      Vanilla / **Sunshine** | 15 |
|      Vanilla, dietetic / **Estee** | 25 |
| Yum Yums / **Sunshine** | 83 |
| Zanzibar / **Pepperidge Farm** | 37 |
| Zuzu Ginger Snaps / **Nabisco** | 16 |

## COOKIE MIXES AND DOUGH

CALORIES

| | |
|---|---:|
| Bar, date, mix, prepared: 1/32 pkg / **Betty Crocker** | 60 |
| Bar, Vienna, mix, prepared: 1/24 pkg/ **Betty Crocker** | 90 |
| Brownies | |
|    Chocolate chip butterscotch, mix, prepared: 1/16 pkg / **Betty Crocker** | 130 |
|    Fudge, mix, prepared: 1/24 pkg / **Betty Crocker** Family Size | 130 |
|    Fudge, mix, prepared: 1/16 pkg / **Betty Crocker** Regular Size | 120 |
|    Fudge, mix, prepared: 1/24 pkg / **Betty Crocker** Supreme | 120 |
|    Fudge, mix, prepared: 1 brownie / **Duncan Hines** Double Fudge | 140 |
|    Fudge, mix, prepared: 1½-in square / **Pillsbury** | 65 |
|    Fudge, mix, prepared: 1½-in square / **Pillsbury** Family Size | 70 |
|    Fudge, refrigerator, to bake: 1/16 pkg / **Pillsbury** | 110 |
|    German chocolate, mix, prepared: 1/16 pkg / **Betty Crocker** | 150 |
|    Walnut, mix, prepared: 1/16 pkg / **Betty Crocker** | 140 |
|    Walnut, mix, prepared: 1/24 pkg / **Betty Crocker** Family Size | 140 |
|    Walnut, mix, prepared: 1½-in square / **Pillsbury** | 75 |
|    Walnut, mix, prepared: 1½-in square / **Pillsbury** Family Size | 75 |
| Butterscotch nut, refrigerator, to bake: 1/36 pkg / **Pillsbury** | 53 |
| Chocolate chip, mix, prepared: 1/36 pkg / **Betty Crocker** Big Batch | 75 |
| Chocolate chip, refrigerated: 1 cookie / **Merico** | 55 |

| | |
|---|---|
| Chocolate chip, refrigerator, to bake: 1/36 pkg / **Pillsbury** | 53 |
| Fudge, refrigerator, to bake: 1/30 pkg / **Pillsbury** | 83 |
| Fudge chip, mix, prepared: 1 cookie / **Quaker** | 75 |
| Ginger, refrigerator, to bake: 1/36 pkg / **Pillsbury** Spicy | 53 |
| Macaroon, coconut, mix, prepared: 1/24 pkg / **Betty Crocker** | 80 |
| Oatmeal, mix, prepared: 1/36 pkg / **Betty Crocker** Big Batch | 70 |
| Oatmeal, mix, prepared: 1 cookie / **Quaker** | 65 |
| Oatmeal chocolate chip, refrigerator, to bake: 1/36 pkg / **Pillsbury** | 56 |
| Oatmeal raisin, refrigerator, to bake: 1/36 pkg / **Pillsbury** | 60 |
| Peanut butter, mix, prepared: 1/36 pkg / **Betty Crocker** Big Batch | 70 |
| Peanut butter, mix, prepared: 1 cookie / **Quaker** | 75 |
| Peanut butter, refrigerator: 1 cookie / **Merico** | 60 |
| Peanut butter, refrigerator, to bake: 1/36 pkg / **Pillsbury** | 53 |
| Sugar, mix, prepared: 1/36 pkg / **Betty Crocker** Big Batch | 65 |
| Sugar, mix, prepared: 1 cookie / **Quaker** | 80 |
| Sugar, refrigerator: 1 cookie / **Merico** | 50 |
| Sugar, refrigerator, to bake: 1/36 pkg / **Pillsbury** | 63 |

# Corn Starch

|  | CALORIES |
|---|---|
| **1 tbsp** | |
| Argo | 35 |
| Duryea's | 35 |
| Kingsford's | 35 |

# Crackers

|  | CALORIES |
|---|---|
| **1 cracker unless noted** | |
| Butter-Flavor Thins / Keebler | 17 |
| Cheese filled: 1½ oz / Frito-Lay | 203 |
| Cheese Peanut Butter Snax / Keebler | 14 |
| Cheez-Its: 1 piece / Sunshine | 6 |
| Che-zo / Keebler | 5 |
| Club: smallest piece when broken on score line / Keebler | 15 |
| Flings Curls / Nabisco | 10 |
| Gold Fish | |
|     Cheddar cheese: 1 oz / Pepperidge Farm | 140 |
|     Lightly salted: 1 oz / Pepperidge Farm | 140 |
|     Parmesan cheese: 1 oz / Pepperidge Farm | 140 |
|     Pizza: 1 oz / Pepperidge Farm | 140 |
|     Pretzel: 1 oz / Pepperidge Farm | 120 |
|     Sesame-garlic: 1 oz / Pepperidge Farm | 140 |

CALORIES

| | |
|---|---|
| Taco: 1 oz / **Pepperidge Farm** | 140 |
| Thins, cheddar cheese: 4 thins / | |
| **Pepperidge Farm** | 70 |
| Thins, lightly salted: 4 thins / | |
| **Pepperidge Farm** | 70 |
| Thins, rye: 4 thins / **Pepperidge Farm** | 70 |
| Thins, wheat: 4 thins / **Pepperidge Farm** | 70 |
| Hi-Ho / **Sunshine** | 18 |
| Kavli Flatbread: 1 wafer | 35 |
| Matzos: 1 sheet or 1 cracker | |
| American / **Manischewitz** | 122 |
| Egg Matzo / **Manischewitz** | 132 |
| Egg 'n' Onion / **Manischewitz** | 113 |
| Onion Tams / **Manischewitz** | 13 |
| Regular Matzo / **Manischewitz** | 109 |
| Tam Tams / **Manischewitz** | 14 |
| Tasteas / **Manischewitz** | 116 |
| Thin Tea / **Manischewitz** | 111 |
| Thins / **Manischewitz** | 90 |
| Whole Wheat / **Manischewitz** | 124 |
| Melba Toast: 1 piece | |
| Garlic rounds / **Old London** | 9 |
| Onion rounds / **Old London** | 10 |
| Pumpernickel / **Old London** | 17 |
| Rye, salted / **Old London** | 17 |
| Rye, unsalted / **Old London** | 18 |
| Sesame, rounds / **Old London** | 10 |
| Wheat, salted / **Old London** | 17 |
| Wheat, unsalted / **Old London** | 18 |
| White / **Old London** | 17 |
| White, unsalted / **Old London** | 17 |
| White rounds, salted / **Old London** | 9 |
| Mixed Suites, green onion: 1 oz / | |
| **Pepperidge Farm** | 140 |
| Mixed Suites, pretzel-cheese: 1 oz / | |
| **Pepperidge Farm** | 130 |
| Mixed Suites, sesame-cheese: 1 oz / | |
| **Pepperidge Farm** | 140 |

| | CALORIES |
|---|---|
| Oyster / Keebler Crax | 3 |
| Oyster / Keebler Zesta Crax | 2 |
| Oyster / Sunshine | 3 |
| Peanut butter: 1½ oz / Frito-Lay | 214 |
| Ritz / Nabisco | 16 |
| Ritz Cheeze / Nabisco | 17 |
| Ry Krisp: 1 triple cracker | 23 |
| Ry Krisp, seasoned: 1 triple cracker | 26 |
| Saltines and soda crackers | |
|   Export soda: smallest piece when broken on score line / Keebler | 25 |
|   Krispy / Sunshine | 11 |
|   Milk Lunch Biscuit / Keebler | 27 |
|   Premium / Nabisco | 12 |
|   Premium, unsalted tops / Nabisco | 12 |
|   Royal Lunch / Nabisco | 54 |
|   Sea toast / Keebler | 62 |
|   Sunshine | 20 |
|   Uneeda, unsalted / Nabisco | 22 |
|   Waldorf, low sodium / Keebler | 16 |
|   Zesta / Keebler | 12 |
|   Zesta, unsalted / Keebler | 14 |
| Shapies, cheese-flavored / Nabisco | 9 |
| Shapies, cheese-flavored shells / Nabisco | 10 |
| Sip 'N Chips, cheese-flavored / Nabisco | 9 |
| Sociables / Nabisco | 10 |
| Toast | |
|   Bacon / Keebler | 15 |
|   Cheese / Keebler | 16 |
|   Onion / Keebler | 18 |
|   Rye: smallest piece when broken on score line / Keebler | 17 |
|   Sesame / Keebler | 16 |
|   Wheat / Keebler | 16 |
| Town House / Keebler | 18 |
| Triangle Thins / Nabisco | 8 |
| Triscuit / Nabisco | 21 |
| Twigs / Nabisco | 14 |

CALORIES

| | |
|---|---|
| Waverly Wafers / **Nabisco** | 18 |
| Wheat Thins / **Nabisco** | 9 |
| Zweiback / **Nabisco** | 31 |

# Cream

CALORIES

Half and half (cream and milk, 11.7% fat)
| | |
|---|---|
| 1 cup | 324 |
| 1 tbsp | 20 |

Light, coffee or table (20.6% fat)
| | |
|---|---|
| 1 cup | 506 |
| 1 tbsp | 32 |

Light whipping (31.3% fat)
| | |
|---|---|
| 1 cup (about 2 cups whipped) | 717 |
| 1 tbsp | 45 |

Heavy whipping (37.6% fat)
| | |
|---|---|
| 1 cup (about 2 cups whipped) | 838 |
| 1 tbsp | 53 |
| whipping, in aerosol can: 1 whipped oz / **Lucerne** Real Cream Topping | 20 |

## NON-DAIRY CREAMERS

Dry
| | |
|---|---|
| **Carnation Coffee-Mate** / 1 packet | 17 |
| **Coffee Tone** / 1 tsp | 12 |
| **Cremora** / 1 tsp | 12 |

Liquid
| | |
|---|---|
| **Coffee Tone** Freezer Pack / 1 tbsp | 20 |
| **Lucerne** Cereal Blend / ½ cup | 150 |
| Powdered: 1 tsp / **Pet** | 10 |

## SOUR CREAM

|  | CALORIES |
|---|---|
| **Lucerne** / 2 tbsp | 59 |
| 1 cup | 475 |
| **Lucerne,** half and half / 2 tbsp | 42 |
| 1 cup | 335 |
| **Sealtest** / 2 tbsp | 57 |
| 1 cup | 456 |
| **Sealtest,** half and half / 2 tbsp | 41 |
| 1 cup | 328 |
| Imitation sour cream / **Borden's** Zest 2 tbsp | 49 |
| 1 cup | 388 |
| Imitation sour cream / **Pet** 1 tbsp | 25 |

# Dessert Mixes

| | CALORIES |
|---|---|
| Apple cinnamon, prepared: ⅔ cup / **Pillsbury Appleasy** | 200 |
| Apple caramel, prepared: ½ cup / **Pillsbury Appleasy** | 160 |
| Apple raisin, prepared: ⅔ cup / **Pillsbury Appleasy** | 215 |

# Diet Bars

| | CALORIES |
|---|---|
| All flavors: 1 bar / **Pillsbury** Figurines | 137 |
| All flavors: 1 stick / **Pillsbury** Food Sticks | 45 |
| Cinnamon: 1 bar / **Carnation** Slender Bars | 137 |
| Chocolate: 1 bar / **Carnation** Slender Bars | 137 |
| Vanilla: 1 bar / **Carnation** Slender Bars | 137 |

# Dinners

## FROZEN DINNERS

| | CALORIES |
|---|---|
| Beans and beef patties: 11 oz / Swanson "TV" | 500 |
| Beans w franks: 10¾ oz / Banquet | 591 |
| Beans w franks: 10¾ oz / Morton | 530 |
| Beans w franks: 11¼ oz / Swanson "TV" | 550 |
| Beef | |
|     Banquet / 11 oz | 312 |
|     La Choy | 342 |
|     Morton / 10 oz | 270 |
|     Swanson 3 Course / 15 oz | 490 |
|     Swanson "TV" / 11½ oz | 370 |
| Beef, chopped: 11 oz / Banquet | 443 |
| Beef, chopped: 11 oz / Morton | 340 |
| Beef, sirloin, chopped: 10 oz / Swanson "TV" | 460 |
| Beef, sliced: 14 oz / Morton Country Table | 540 |
| Beef, sliced: 17 oz / Swanson Hungry-Man | 540 |
| Beef steak, chopped: 18 oz / Swanson Hungry-Man | 730 |
| Beef tenderloin: 9½ oz / Morton Steak House Dinner | 920 |
| Chicken / La Choy | 354 |
| Chicken, boneless: 10 oz / Morton | 240 |
| Chicken, boneless: 19 oz / Swanson Hungry-Man | 730 |
| Chicken breast: 15 oz / Weight Watchers | 330 |
| Chicken croquette: 10¼ oz / Morton | 410 |
| Chicken, fried | |
|     Banquet / 11 oz | 530 |
|     Banquet Man Pleaser / 17 oz | 1026 |

CALORIES

| | |
|---|---|
| Morton / 11 oz | 470 |
| Morton Country Table / 15 oz | 710 |
| Swanson Hungry-Man / 12 oz | 620 |
| Swanson Hungry-Man / 15¾ oz | 910 |
| Swanson Hungry-Man Barbecue-flavored / 16 ½ oz | 760 |
| Swanson 3 Course / 15 oz | 630 |
| Swanson "TV" / 11½ oz | 570 |
| Barbecue-flavored: 12 oz / Swanson Hungry-Man | 550 |
| Barbecue-flavored: 11¼ oz / Swanson "TV" | 530 |
| Crispy fried: 10¾ oz / Swanson "TV" | 650 |
| w whipped potatoes: 7 oz / Swanson "TV" | 360 |
| Chicken w dumplings: 12 oz / Banquet | 282 |
| Chicken w dumplings: 11 oz / Morton | 280 |
| Chicken w noodles: 12 oz / Banquet | 374 |
| Chicken w noodles: 10¼ oz / Morton | 260 |
| Chicken oriental style: 16 oz / Weight Watchers | 320 |
| Chop suey, beef: 12 oz / Banquet | 282 |
| Chow mein, chicken: 12 oz / Banquet | 282 |
| Enchilada / El Chico | 680 |
| Enchilada, beef: 12 oz / Banquet | 479 |
| Enchilada, beef: 15 oz / Swanson "TV" | 570 |
| Enchilada, cheese: 12 oz / Banquet | 459 |
| Fish: 8¾ oz / Banquet | 382 |
| Fish: 9 oz / Morton | 270 |
| Fish 'n' Chips: 15¾ oz / Swanson Hungry-Man | 760 |
| Fish 'n' Chips: 10¼ oz / Swanson "TV" | 450 |
| Flounder: 16 oz / Weight Watchers | 240 |
| German style: 11¾ oz / Swanson "TV" | 430 |
| Haddock: 8¾ oz / Banquet | 419 |
| Haddock: 16 oz / Weight Watchers | 250 |
| Ham: 10 oz / Banquet | 369 |
| Ham: 10 oz / Morton | 440 |
| Ham: 10¼ oz / Swanson "TV" | 380 |

CALORIES

| | |
|---|---|
| Hash, corned beef: 10 oz / **Banquet** | 372 |
| Italian style: 11 oz / **Banquet** | 446 |
| Italian style: 13 oz / **Swanson "TV"** | 420 |
| Lasagna and meat: 17¾ oz / **Swanson** Hungry-Man | 740 |
| Macaroni and beef: 12 oz / **Banquet** | 394 |
| Macaroni and beef: 10 oz / **Morton** | 260 |
| Macaroni and beef: 12 oz / **Swanson "TV"** | 400 |
| Macaroni and cheese: 12 oz / **Banquet** | 326 |
| Macaroni and cheese: 11 oz / **Morton** | 320 |
| Macaroni and cheese: 12½ oz / **Swanson "TV"** | 390 |
| Meat loaf: 11 oz / **Banquet** | 412 |
| Meat loaf: 11 oz / **Morton** | 340 |
| Meat loaf: 15 oz / **Morton** Country Table | 480 |
| Meat loaf: 10¾ oz / **Swanson "TV"** | 530 |
| Meatballs: 11¾ oz / **Swanson "TV"** | 400 |
| Mexican style: 16 oz / **Banquet** | 608 |
| Mexican style combination: 12 oz / **Banquet** | 571 |
| Mexican / **El Chico** | 820 |
| Mexican style combination: 16 oz / **Swanson "TV"** | 600 |
| Noodles and chicken: 10¼ oz / **Swanson "TV"** | 390 |
| Pepper oriental / **La Choy** | 349 |
| Perch, ocean: 8¾ oz / **Banquet** | 434 |
| Perch, ocean: 16 oz / **Weight Watchers** | 320 |
| Polynesian style: 13 oz / **Swanson "TV"** | 490 |
| Pork, loin of: 11¼ oz / **Swanson "TV"** | 470 |
| Queso / **El Chico** | 810 |
| Rib eye: 9 oz / **Morton** Steak House Dinner | 820 |
| Salisbury steak | |
|     **Banquet** / 11 oz | 390 |
|     **Morton** / 11 oz | 290 |
|     **Morton** Country Table / 15 oz | 430 |
|     **Swanson** Hungry-Man / 17 oz | 870 |
|     **Swanson** 3 Course / 16 oz | 490 |
|     **Swanson "TV"** / 11½ oz | 500 |
| Saltillo / **El Chico** | 790 |

CALORIES

| | |
|---|---:|
| Shrimp / La Choy | 325 |
| Sirloin, chopped: 9½ oz / Morton Steak House Dinner | 760 |
| Sirloin strip: 9½ oz / Morton Steak House Dinner | 920 |
| Sole: 16 oz / Weight Watchers | 240 |
| Spaghetti and meatballs: 11½ oz / Banquet | 450 |
| Spaghetti and meatballs: 11 oz / Morton | 360 |
| Spaghetti and meatballs: 18½ oz / Swanson Hungry-Man | 660 |
| Spaghetti and meatballs: 12½ oz / Swanson "TV" | 410 |
| Swiss steak: 10 oz / Swanson "TV" | 350 |
| Turbot: 16 oz / Weight Watchers | 490 |
| Turkey | |
|      Banquet / 11 oz | 293 |
|      Banquet Man Pleaser / 19 oz | 620 |
|      Morton / 11 oz | 350 |
|      Morton Country Table / 15 oz | 600 |
|      Swanson Hungry-Man / 19 oz | 740 |
|      Swanson 3 Course / 16 oz | 520 |
|      Swanson "TV" / 11½ oz | 360 |
|      Breast: 10 oz / Weight Watchers | 400 |
| Veal Parmagian: 11 oz / Banquet | 421 |
| Veal Parmigiana: 10¼ oz / Morton | 330 |
| Veal Parmigiana: 20½ oz / Swanson Hungry-Man | 910 |
| Veal Parmigiana: 12¼ oz / Swanson "TV" | 520 |
| Western: 11 oz / Banquet | 417 |
| Western Round-Up: 11¾ oz / Morton | 410 |
| Western style: 17¾ oz / Swanson Hungry-Man | 890 |
| Western style: 11¾ oz / Swanson "TV" | 460 |

## DINNER MIXES

| | |
|---|---:|
| Ann Page Beef Noodle Dinner / 1/5 prepared dinner | 330 |

CALORIES

| | |
|---|---|
| **Ann Page** Cheeseburger Macaroni Dinner / 1/5 prepared dinner | 360 |
| **Ann Page** Chili Tomato Dinner / 1.6 oz before preparation | 150 |
| **Ann Page** Hash Dinner / 1/5 prepared dinner | 300 |
| **Ann Page** Italian Style Dinner / 2 oz before preparation | 210 |
| **Ann Page** Potato Stroganoff Dinner / 1/5 prepared dinner | 320 |
| Dinner Mexicana, Taco Casserole: 1 pkg before preparation / **McCormick** | 655 |
| Dinner Mexicana, Taco Casserole: 1 pkg before preparation / **Schilling** | 655 |
| Dinner Mexicana, Tamale Pie: 1 pkg before preparation / **McCormick** | 860 |
| Dinner Mexicana, Tamale Pie: 1 pkg before preparation / **Schilling** | 860 |
| Hamburger Helper: 1/5 prepared dinner | |
|     Beef Noodle / **Betty Crocker** | 320 |
|     Beef Romanoff / **Betty Crocker** | 340 |
|     Cheeseburger Macaroni / **Betty Crocker** | 360 |
|     Chili Tomato / **Betty Crocker** | 330 |
|     Hamburger Hash / **Betty Crocker** | 300 |
|     Hamburger Pizza Dish / **Betty Crocker** | 340 |
|     Hamburger Stew / **Betty Crocker** | 290 |
|     Lasagne / **Betty Crocker** | 330 |
|     Potato Stroganoff / **Betty Crocker** | 330 |
|     Rice Oriental / **Betty Crocker** (6½ oz pkg) | 300 |
|     Rice Oriental / **Betty Crocker** (8 oz pkg) | 340 |
|     Spaghetti / **Betty Crocker** | 330 |
| Tuna Helper: 1/5 prepared dinner | |
|     Dumplings and noodles / **Betty Crocker** | 230 |
|     Noodles / **Betty Crocker** | 280 |
|     Noodles w cheese sauce / **Betty Crocker** | 230 |

# Dips

CALORIES
**(Ready to serve unless noted)**

| | |
|---|---|
| Bacon and horseradish: 1 oz | |
|     **Borden** | 79 |
|     **Kraft** Ready | 71 |
|     **Kraft** Teez | 57 |
|     **Lucerne** | 63 |
| Bacon and smoke flavor: 1 oz / **Sealtest** | |
|   Dip 'n Dressing | 47 |
| Barbecue: 1 oz / **Borden's** Western Bar BQ | 48 |
| Bean, chili / **Lucerne** | 51 |
| Bean, Jalapeno: 1 oz | |
|     **Fritos** | 36 |
|     **Gebhardt** | 30 |
|     **Granny Goose** | 37 |
|     **Lucerne** | 36 |
| Blue cheese: 1 oz | |
|     **Granny Goose** Chip-Dip | 108 |
|     **Kraft** Ready | 69 |
|     **Kraft** Teez | 51 |
|     **Lucerne** Bleu Tang | 67 |
|     **Sealtest** Dip 'n Dressing | 49 |
| Casino Dip 'n Dressing: 1 oz / **Sealtest** | 44 |
| Chipped beef: 1 oz / **Sealtest** Dip 'n Dressing | 46 |
| Clam: 1 oz | |
|     **Kraft** Ready | 66 |
|     **Kraft** Teez | 45 |
|     **Lucerne** | 34 |
|     and lobster / **Borden** | 60 |
| Dill pickle: 1 oz / **Kraft** Ready | 67 |
| Garden Spice: 1 oz / **Borden** | 66 |
| Garlic: 1 oz / **Granny Goose** Chip-Dip | 101 |
| Garlic: 1 oz / **Kraft** Teez | 47 |
| Garlic: 1 oz / **Lucerne** | 58 |
| Green chili: 1 oz / **Borden** | 55 |

CALORIES

| | |
|---|---|
| Green Goddess: 1 oz / **Kraft** Teez | 46 |
| Green onion: 1 oz / **Granny Goose** Chip-Dip | 105 |
| Green onion, mix: ½ oz pkg / **Lawry's** | 50 |
| Guacamole: 1 oz / **Lucerne** | 83 |
| Guacamole, mix: ½ oz pkg / **Lawry's** | 60 |
| Hickory-smoke flavor: 1 oz / **Lucerne** | 60 |
| Onion: 1 oz unless noted | |
|     **Borden** | 48 |
|     **Kraft** Ready | 68 |
|     French / **Kraft** Teez | 43 |
|     French / **Lucerne** | 58 |
|     French / **Sealtest** Dip 'n Dressing | 47 |
|     and garlic / **Sealtest** Dip 'n Dressing | 46 |
|     mix: ½ oz pkg / **Lawry's** | 48 |
| Tasty Tartar: 1 oz / **Borden** | 48 |

# Eggs

Chicken egg
    Raw, hard-cooked or poached
        Extra large                                        94
        Large                                              82
        Medium                                             72
    Raw, white only
        Extra large                                        19
        Large                                              17
        Medium                                             15
        1 cup                                             124
    Raw, yolk only
        Extra large                                        66
        Large                                              59
        Medium                                             52
    Fried
        Extra large                                       112
        Large                                              99
        Medium                                             86
    Scrambled
        Extra large                                       126
        Large                                             111
        Medium                                             97
Duck, raw: 1 egg                                          134
Goose, raw: 1 egg                                         266
Turkey, raw: 1 egg                                        135

## EGG MIXES AND SEASONINGS

Egg, imitation, frozen: ¼ cup / **Morningstar**
**Farms** Scramblers                                       64

CALORIES

| | |
|---|---|
| Egg, imitation, mix: ½ pkg / **Eggstra** | 50 |
| Egg, imitation, refrigerated: ¼ cup / | |
| No-Fat **Egg Beaters** | 40 |
| Omelet, prepared: 1 pkg / **Durkee** Puffy | 604 |
| Omelet, dry mix: 1 pkg / **Durkee** Puffy | 112 |
| Omelet, bacon, prepared: 1 pkg / **Durkee** | 620 |
| Omelet, bacon, dry mix: 1 pkg / **Durkee** | 128 |
| Omelet, cheese, prepared: 1 pkg / **Durkee** | 617 |
| Omelet, cheese, dry mix: 1 pkg / **Durkee** | 125 |
| Omelet, cheese: 1¼ oz pkg / **McCormick** | 130 |
| Omelet, cheese: 1¼ oz pkg / **Schilling** | 130 |
| Omelet, Western: 1 pkg prepared w | |
| water only / **Durkee** | 170 |
| Omelet, Western: 1 pkg prepared w eggs / | |
| **Durkee** | 604 |
| Omelet, Western, dry mix: 1 pkg / **Durkee** | 110 |
| Omelet, Western: 1¼ oz pkg / **McCormick** | 115 |
| Omelet, Western: 1¼ oz pkg / **Schilling** | 115 |
| Scrambled: 1 pkg / **Durkee** | 124 |
| Scrambled w bacon: 1 pkg / **Durkee** | 181 |

# Fish and Seafood

## FRESH

| | |
|---|---:|
| Abalone, raw: 3½ oz | 98 |
| Abalone, canned: 3½ oz | 80 |
| Bass, black sea, raw, whole: 1 lb | 165 |
| Bass, striped, raw: 4 oz | 120 |
| Bass, striped, oven fried: 1 oz | 56 |
| Bass, white, raw: 4 oz | 110 |
| Bluefish | |
|     Baked or broiled: 1 fillet (3½" x 3" x ½") | 200 |
|     Baked or broiled w butter or margarine: 1 oz | 180 |
|     Fried: 1 fillet (3½" x 3" x ½") | 310 |
| Catfish, raw, meat only: 3½ oz | 103 |
| Caviar, sturgeon, granular: 1 tbsp | 42 |
| Caviar, sturgeon, pressed: 1 tbsp | 54 |
| Clams, hard or round, raw, meat only: 1 pint (1 lb) | 363 |
| Clams, 4 cherrystone or 5 little neck clams | 56 |
| Clams, soft, raw, meat only: 1 pint (1 lb) | 345 |
| Cod, raw: 4 oz | 90 |
| Cod, broiled: 4 oz | 195 |
| Crab, cooked, pieces: 1 cup | 144 |
| Crab, cooked, flaked: 1 cup | 116 |
| Crayfish, freshwater, raw, meat only: 3½ oz | 72 |
| Eel, raw: 4 oz | 183 |
| Flounder, raw, whole: 1 lb | 120 |
| Flounder, raw: 4 oz | 90 |
| Frog legs, raw, meat only: 3½ oz | 73 |

CALORIES

| | |
|---|---|
| Haddock, raw: 4 oz | 90 |
| Haddock, fried: 3½ oz | 165 |
| Halibut, raw: 4 oz | 115 |
| Halibut, steak, broiled (4″ x 3″ x ½″) | 255 |
| Lobster, northern, cooked pieces: 1 cup | 138 |
| Lobster, whole, steamed, meat only: 3½ oz | 95 |
| Mackerel, Atlantic, whole, raw: 1 lb | 470 |
| Mackerel, Atlantic, raw: 4 oz | 220 |

Oysters, raw

| | |
|---|---|
|     Eastern: 1 cup (13-19 Selects) or (27-44 Standards) | 158 |
|     Pacific and Western: 1 cup (about 4-6 medium) or (6-9 small) | 218 |
|     Cooked, fried: 4 Select (medium) | 108 |
| Perch, ocean, Atlantic (redfish), raw, meat only: 3½ oz | 88 |
| Perch, ocean, Pacific, raw, meat only: 3½ oz | 95 |
| Pike, northern, raw, meat only: 3½ oz | 88 |
| Pompano, raw, meat only: 4 oz | 188 |
| Rockfish, oven steamed: 4 oz | 120 |
| Roe, carp, cod, haddock, shad: 3½ oz | 130 |

Salmon

| | |
|---|---|
|     Fresh, raw Atlantic: 4 oz | 245 |
|     Fresh, raw Chinook: 4 oz | 251 |
|     Fresh, raw Pink: 4 oz | 134 |
|     Broiled or baked w butter or margarine: 1 oz | 52 |
|     Smoked: 1 oz | 50 |
| Shad, raw: 4 oz | 192 |
| Shad, baked w butter or margarine: 1 lb | 912 |
| Scallops, bay and sea, raw: 4 oz | 92 |
| Scallops, bay and sea, steamed: 4 oz | 127 |
| Shrimp, raw, peeled: 4 oz | 103 |
| Shrimp, french fried: 1 oz | 64 |
| Snails, raw: 1 oz | 26 |
| Sole, raw: 4 oz | 90 |
| Squid, raw, edible portion only: 3½ oz | 84 |
| Sturgeon, cooked, steamed: 1 oz | 45 |
| Sturgeon, smoked: 1 oz | 42 |

CALORIES

| | |
|---|---:|
| Swordfish, raw: 4 oz | 135 |
| Swordfish, broiled w butter or margarine: 3½ oz | 174 |
| Turbot, raw: 4 oz | 165 |
| Turtle, green, raw, meat only: 3½ oz | 89 |
| Whitefish, raw: 4 oz | 175 |
| Whitefish, smoked: 4 oz | 175 |

## CANNED AND FROZEN

Clams
| | |
|---|---:|
| Chopped or minced, canned: 6 oz can, drained / **Doxsee** | 84 |
| Chopped or minced, canned: 8 oz can, drained / **Doxsee** | 112 |
| Chopped or minced, canned: 10½ oz can, drained / **Doxsee** | 147 |
| Chopped or minced, canned: ½ cup / **Snow's** | 60 |
| Fried, frozen: 5 oz / **Howard Johnson's** | 395 |
| Fried, frozen: 2½ oz / **Mrs. Paul's** | 270 |
| Cakes, frozen: 1 cake / **Mrs. Paul's** Thins | 155 |
| Deviled, frozen: 1 cake / **Mrs. Paul's** | 180 |
| Sticks, frozen: 1 stick / **Mrs. Paul's** | 48 |
| In cocktail sauce: 4 oz jar / **Sau-Sea** | 99 |

Crab
| | |
|---|---:|
| Canned: 6½ oz can / **Gold Seal** Fancy | 185 |
| Canned: 7½ oz can / **Icy Point** | 215 |
| Canned: 7½ oz can / **Pillar Rock** | 215 |
| King, in cocktail sauce: 4 oz jar / **Sau-Sea** | 107 |
| King, frozen: 8 oz / **Ship Ahoy** | 211 |
| King, frozen: 6 oz / **Wakefield's** | 158 |
| Cakes, frozen: 1 cake / **Mrs. Paul's** Thins | 160 |
| Deviled, frozen: 1 cake / **Mrs. Paul's** | 160 |
| Deviled, frozen: 3½ oz / **Mrs. Paul's** Miniatures | 220 |

Fish, frozen
| | |
|---|---:|
| Cakes: 1 cake / **Mrs. Paul's** | 105 |
| Cakes: 1 cake / **Mrs. Paul's** Beach Haven | 110 |
| Cakes: 1 cake / **Mrs. Paul's** Thins | 160 |

CALORIES

| | |
|---|---:|
| Fillets, buttered: 1 fillet (2½ oz) /<br>  **Mrs. Paul's** | 155 |
| Fillets. fried: 1 fillet (2 oz) /<br>  **Mrs. Paul's** | 110 |
| Fillets in light batter: 1 fillet /<br>  **Mrs. Paul's** | 140 |
| Fillets in light batter, fried: 1 fillet /<br>  **Mrs. Paul's** Supreme | 220 |
| In light batter: 3 oz / **Mrs. Paul's**<br>  Miniatures | 150 |
| Sticks: 1 stick / **Mrs. Paul's** | 37 |
| Sticks, in light batter, fried: 1 stick /<br>  **Mrs. Paul's** | 57 |
| Flounder fried, frozen: 1 fillet (2 oz) /<br>  **Mrs. Paul's** | 110 |
| Flounder w lemon butter, frozen: 4½ oz /<br>  **Mrs. Paul's** | 150 |
| Gefilte fish. canned or in jars:<br>  1 piece unless noted | |
|   **Manischewitz** (4 piece, 12 oz jar) | 53 |
|   **Manischewitz** (8 piece, 24 oz jar) | 53 |
|   **Manischewitz** (24 piece. 4 lb jar) | 48 |
|   **Manischewitz**, sweet (4 piece, 12 oz jar) | 65 |
|   **Manischewitz**, sweet (8 piece. 24 oz jar) | 65 |
|   **Manischewitz**, sweet (24 piece, 4 lb jar) | 59 |
|   **Mother's** (4 piece, 12 oz jar) | 41 |
|   **Mother's** (4 piece, 1 lb jar) | 55 |
|   **Mother's** (5 piece, 27 oz jar) | 74 |
|   **Mother's** (6 piece, 15 oz jar), unsalted | 34 |
|   **Mother's** (6 piece, 1 lb jar) | 37 |
|   **Mother's** (6 piece, 24 oz jar) | 55 |
|   **Mother's** (8 piece, 24 oz jar) | 41 |
|   **Mother's** (8 piece, 2 lb jar) | 55 |
|   **Mother's** (12 piece, 2 lb jar) | 37 |
|   **Rokeach** (in liquid broth): 1 oz | 14 |
|   **Rokeach** Old Vienna (in jellied broth): 1 oz | 19 |
|   Fishlets, 24 oz jar / **Manischewitz** | 8 |

Whitefish and pike, 4 piece, 12 oz jar /
  **Manischewitz** — 49
Whitefish and pike, 8 piece, 24 oz jar /
  **Manischewitz** — 49
Whitefish and pike, 24 piece, 4 lb jar /
  **Manischewitz** — 44
Whitefish and pike, sweet, 4 piece, 12
  oz jar / **Manischewitz** — 64
Whitefish and pike, sweet, 8 piece, 24
  oz jar / **Manischewitz** — 64
Whitefish and pike, sweet, 24 piece, 4 lb
  jar / **Manischewitz** — 58
Haddock, fried, frozen: 1 fillet (2 oz) /
**Mrs. Paul's** — 115
Herring, in jars
  Pickled: 6 oz jar, drained / **Vita** Bismark — 238
  Pickled: 8½ oz jar / **Vita** Cocktail — 365
  Pickled: 8¾ oz jar / **Vita** Lunch — 372
  Pickled: 8¾ oz jar, drained / **Vita** Matjes — 220
  Pickled: 8¾ oz jar, drained / **Vita**
    Party Snacks — 345
  Pickled: 8¾ oz jar, drained / **Vita**
    Tastee Bits — 283
  Pickled, in cream sauce, 8⅓ oz jar /
    **Vita** — 407
Oysters wo shell, canned: ½ cup / **Bumblebee** — 86
Perch, fried, frozen: 1 fillet (2 oz) / **Mrs. Paul's** — 125
Salmon, canned
  Blueback: 3¾ oz can / **Icy Point** — 181
  Blueback: 7¾ oz can / **Icy Point** — 376
  Coho steak: 3¾ oz can / **Icy Point** — 162
  Pink: 7¾ oz / **Del Monte** — 310
  Red: 1 lb can / **Icy Point** — 775
  Red: 3¾ oz can / **Pillar Rock** — 181
  Red: 7¾ oz can / **Pillar Rock** — 376
  Red: 1 lb can / **Pillar Rock** — 775
  Red sockeye: ½ cup / **Bumblebee** — 143
  Red sockeye: 7¾ oz / **Del Monte** — 340

Sardines, in mustard sauce: 1 oz / **Underwood**    52
Sardines, in soya bean oil: 1 oz / **Underwood**    62
Sardines, in tomato sauce, canned:
  7½ oz / **Del Monte**    330
Sardines. in tomato sauce: 1 oz / **Underwood**    45
Scallops fried, frozen: 3½ oz / **Mrs. Paul's**    210
Scallops, in light batter, fried, frozen: 3½ oz /
  **Mrs. Paul's**    200
Seafood. combination, fried, frozen: 9 oz /
  **Mrs. Paul's** Platter    510
Seafood croquettes, frozen: 1 cake / **Mrs. Paul's**    180
Shrimp
    Baby, solids and liquids: 4½ oz can /
     **Bumblebee**    90
    Fancy, tiny: 4½ oz can, drained /
     **Icy Point**    148
    Fancy, tiny: 4½ oz can, drained /
     **Pillar Rock**    148
    Fried, frozen: 3 oz / **Mrs. Paul's**    170
    Fried, frozen: 4 oz / **Sau-Sea**
     Shrimp Fries    240
    Frozen, in bag, cooked: 2 oz / **Sau-Sea**    36
    Cakes, frozen: 1 cake / **Mrs. Paul's**    150
    Cakes, frozen: 1 cake / **Mrs. Paul's** Thins    155
    Sticks, frozen: 1 stick / **Mrs. Paul's**    47
    In cocktail sauce: 4 oz jar / **Sau-Sea**
     Shrimp Cocktail    107
Sole w lemon butter, frozen: 4½ oz /
  **Mrs. Paul's**    160
Tuna, canned
    In oil, drained:
     ½ cup / **Bumblebee**    167
    In water, undrained:
     1 cup / **Bumblebee**    300
    Light, chunk, in oil, drained:
     6½ oz / **Del Monte**    450
    Light, chunk, in oil:
     3¼ oz can / **Chicken of The Sea**    224
      drained    192

| | |
|---|---:|
| Light, chunk, in oil: | |
|   6½ oz can / **Chicken of The Sea** | 447 |
|     drained | 384 |
| Light, chunk in oil: | |
|   9¼ oz can / **Chicken of The Sea** | 636 |
|     drained | 543 |
| Light, chunk, in oil: | |
|   12½ oz can / **Chicken of The Sea** | 860 |
|     drained | 738 |
| Light, chunk, in oil: | |
|   5 oz can drained / **Gold Seal** | 278 |
| Light, chunk, in oil: | |
|   5 oz can drained / **Icy Point** | 278 |
| Light, chunk, in oil: | |
|   5 oz can drained / **Pillar Rock** | 278 |
| Light, chunk, in oil: | |
|   5 oz can drained / **Snow Mist** | 278 |
| Light, grated, in oil: | |
|   6¼ oz can / **Van Camp** | 440 |
|     drained | 415 |
| Light, solid, in oil: | |
|   3½ oz can / **Chicken of The Sea** | 220 |
|     drained | 153 |
| Light, solid, in oil: | |
|   7 oz can / **Chicken of The Sea** | 440 |
|     drained | 305 |
| White, flake, in oil: | |
|   5 oz can drained / **Gold Seal** | 278 |
| White, solid, in oil: | |
|   5.1 oz can drained / **Gold Seal** | 290 |
| White, solid, in oil: | |
|   5.1 oz can drained / **Icy Point** | 290 |
| White, solid, in oil: | |
|   5.1 oz can drained / **Pillar Rock** | 290 |
| White, solid, in vegetable oil: | |
|   3½ oz can / **Chicken of The Sea** | 254 |
|     drained | 164 |

White, solid, in vegetable oil:
  6½ oz can / **Chicken of The Sea**          413
    drained                                     324
White, solid, in vegetable oil:
  7 oz can / **Chicken of The Sea**            507
    drained                                     328
White, solid, in vegetable oil:
  9¼ oz can / **Chicken of The Sea**           588
    drained                                     461
White, solid, in vegetable oil:
  12½ oz can / **Chicken of The Sea**          794
    drained                                     623
White, solid, in vegetable oil:
  13 oz can / **Chicken of The Sea**           942
    drained                                     609
White, solid, in water:
  7 oz can / **Chicken of The Sea**            230
    drained                                     216

## FISH AND SEAFOOD ENTREES, FROZEN

Crepes, clam: 5½ oz / **Mrs. Paul's**                   280
Crepes, crab: 5½ oz / **Mrs. Paul's**                   240
Crepes, scallop: 5½ oz / **Mrs. Paul's**                220
Crepes, shrimp: 5½ oz / **Mrs. Paul's**                 250
Croquette, shrimp w Newburg sauce:
  12 oz / **Howard Johnson's**                          478
Fish Au Gratin: 5 oz / **Mrs. Paul's**                  250
Fish Au Gratin: 4 oz / **Mrs. Paul's Party Pak**        200
Fish 'n' Chips: 1 entree / **Swanson "TV"**             290
Fish 'n' Chips, in light batter, fried: 7 oz /
  **Mrs. Paul's**                                       370
Fish Parmesan: 5 oz / **Mrs. Paul's**                   220
Fish Parmesan: 4 oz / **Mrs. Paul's Party Pak**         150
Flounder w chopped broccoli, cauliflower, red
  peppers: 8½ oz / **Weight Watchers**                  160
Haddock au Groton: 10 oz / **Howard Johnson's**         318
Haddock w stuffing and spinach: 8¾ oz /
  **Weight Watchers**                                   180

CALORIES

| | |
|---|---|
| Perch, ocean w chopped broccoli: 8½ oz / Weight Watchers | 190 |
| Scallops w butter and cheese: 7 oz / Mrs. Paul's | 260 |
| Shrimp and Scallops Mariner: 1 pkg / Stouffer's 10¼ oz | 400 |
| Sole w peas, mushrooms, lobster sauce: 9½ oz / Weight Watchers | 200 |
| Tuna, creamed w peas: 5 oz / Green Giant Boil-in-Bag Toast Toppers | 140 |
| Turbot w peas, carrots: 8 oz / Weight Watchers | 280 |

# Flavorings, Sweet

CALORIES

**1 tsp unless noted**

| | |
|---|---|
| Almond extract, pure / Durkee | 13 |
| Almond extract, pure / Ehlers | 5 |
| Anise extract, imitation / Durkee | 16 |
| Anise extract, pure / Ehlers | 12 |
| Banana extract, imitation / Durkee | 15 |
| Banana extract, imitation / Ehlers | 7 |
| Black walnut flavor, imitation / Durkee | 4 |
| Brandy extract, imitation / Durkee | 15 |
| Brandy extract, imitation / Ehlers | 18 |
| Cherry extract, imitation / Ehlers | 8 |
| Chocolate extract / Durkee | 7 |
| Coconut flavor, imitation / Durkee | 8 |
| Coconut extract, imitation / Ehlers | 13 |
| Lemon extract, imitation / Durkee | 17 |
| Lemon extract, pure / Ehlers | 14 |
| Maple extract, imitation / Durkee | 6 |
| Maple extract, imitation / Ehlers | 9 |

CALORIES

| | |
|---|---:|
| Mocha extract, imitation / **Durkee** | 14 |
| Orange extract, imitation / **Durkee** | 16 |
| Orange extract, pure / **Ehlers** | 14 |
| Peppermint extract, imitation / **Durkee** | 15 |
| Peppermint extract, pure / **Ehlers** | 12 |
| Pineapple extract, pure / **Ehlers** | 13 |
| Raspberry extract, imitation / **Ehlers** | 10 |
| Rum extract, imitation / **Durkee** | 14 |
| Rum extract, imitation / **Ehlers** | 11 |
| Strawberry extract, imitation / **Durkee** | 12 |
| Strawberry extract, imitation / **Ehlers** | 13 |
| Vanilla extract, imitation / **Durkee** | 3 |
| Vanilla extract, pure / **Durkee** | 8 |

# Flour and Meal

## FLOUR

CALORIES

**1 cup unless noted**

| | |
|---|---:|
| Biscuit mix / **Bisquick** | 480 |
| Buckwheat, dark, sifted | 326 |
| Buckwheat, light, sifted | 340 |
| Carob | 252 |
| Corn | 431 |
| Corn: 1 lb | 1669 |
| Lima bean, sifted | 432 |
| Peanut, defatted | 223 |
| Rye | |
|     Light | 314 |
|     Medium | 308 |
|     Medium / **Pillsbury** | 420 |

CALORIES

| | |
|---|---|
| Dark | 419 |
| Wheat / **Pillsbury** Bohemian | 400 |
| Soybean | |
| Full fat | 295 |
| Low fat | 313 |
| Defatted | 326 |
| Tortilla, corn: ⅓ cup / **Quaker's** Masa Harina | 137 |
| Tortilla, wheat: ⅓ cup / **Quaker's** Masa Trigo | 149 |
| Wheat | |
| All purpose | 499 |
| Bread | 500 |
| Cake or pastry | 430 |
| Gluten | 529 |
| Self-rising | 440 |
| Whole wheat | 400 |
| Whole wheat / **Pillsbury** | 400 |
| White | |
| **Ballard** | 400 |
| **Peavey Family** High Altitude Hungarian | 400 |
| **Peavey Family** Occident | 400 |
| **Peavey Family** King Midas | 400 |
| **Pillsbury** All Purpose | 400 |
| Cake, self-rising / **Presto** | 400 |
| Cake / **Softasilk** | 412 |
| Self-rising: ¼ cup / **Aunt Jemima** | 109 |
| Self-rising / **Ballard** | 380 |
| Self-rising / **Pillsbury** | 380 |
| Unbleached / **Pillsbury** | 400 |

## MEAL

| | |
|---|---|
| Almond, partially defatted: 1 oz | 116 |
| Corn | |
| White or yellow, whole ground unbolted, dry: 1 cup | 433 |
| White: 1 oz (2 tbsp and 2 tsp) / **Albers** | 100 |
| White: about 3 tbsp / **Aunt Jemima** Enriched | 102 |
| White: about 3 tbsp / **Quaker** Enriched | 102 |

CALORIES

White, bolted, mix: 1/6 cup / **Aunt Jemima**      99
White, bolted, self-rising: 1/6 cup /
  **Aunt Jemima**                                  99
White, self-rising: 1/6 cup / **Aunt Jemima**      98
Yellow: 1 oz (2 tbsp and 2 tsp) / **Albers**      100
Yellow: about 3 tbsp / **Aunt Jemima**
  Enriched                                        102
Yellow: about 3 tbsp / **Quaker** Enriched        102
Crackermeal: 1 cup / **Sunshine**                 400
Matzo meal: 1 cup / **Manischewitz**              438

# Frostings

CALORIES

**Ready to spread: 1 can unless noted**

Cake and cookie decorator, all colors:

1 tbsp / **Pillsbury**                             70
Butter pecan / **Betty Crocker**                 2040
Cherry / **Betty Crocker**                       2040
Chocolate / **Betty Crocker**                    2040
Chocolate fudge / **Pillsbury**                  1920
Chocolate nut / **Betty Crocker**                1920
Dark Dutch fudge / **Betty Crocker**             1920
Double Dutch / **Pillsbury**                     1920
Lemon / **Betty Crocker** Sunkist                2040
Lemon / **Pillsbury**                            1920
Milk chocolate / **Betty Crocker**               1920
Milk chocolate / **Pillsbury**                   1920
Orange / **Betty Crocker**                       2040
Sour cream, chocolate / **Betty Crocker**        2040
Sour cream, vanilla / **Pillsbury**              1920
Sour cream, white / **Betty Crocker**            1920

CALORIES

| | |
|---|---|
| Strawberry / Pillsbury | 1920 |
| Vanilla / Betty Crocker | 2040 |
| Vanilla / Pillsbury | 2040 |

**1 pkg: prepared**

| | |
|---|---|
| Banana / Betty Crocker Chiquita | 1800 |
| Butter Brickle / Betty Crocker | 1800 |
| Butter pecan / Betty Crocker | 1800 |
| Caramel / Pillsbury Rich 'n Easy | 2040 |
| Cherry / Betty Crocker | 1800 |
| Chocolate / Betty Crocker Lite | 1200 |
| Chocolate fudge / Betty Crocker | 1920 |
| Chocolate fudge / Pillsbury Rich 'n Easy | 2040 |
| Coconut almond / Pillsbury | 2040 |
| Coconut pecan / Betty Crocker | 1320 |
| Coconut pecan / Pillsbury | 1800 |
| Dark chocolate fudge / Betty Crocker | 1800 |
| Double Dutch / Pillsbury Rich n' Easy | 2040 |
| Lemon / Betty Crocker Sunkist | 1800 |
| Lemon / Pillsbury Rich 'n Easy | 2040 |
| Milk chocolate / Betty Crocker | 1800 |
| Milk chocolate / Pillsbury Rich n' Easy | 2040 |
| Sour cream chocolate / Betty Crocker | 1800 |
| Sour cream white / Betty Crocker | 1800 |
| Strawberry / Pillsbury Rich 'n Easy | 2040 |
| Vanilla / Betty Crocker Lite | 1200 |
| Vanilla / Pillsbury Rich 'n Easy | 2040 |
| White, creamy / Betty Crocker | 1920 |
| White, fluffy / Betty Crocker Lite | 720 |
| White, fluffy / Pillsbury | 840 |

# Fruit

## FRESH

| | CALORIES |
|---|---|
| Acerola cherries: 10 fruits | 23 |
| **Apples** | |
| w skin: 1 small (about 4 per lb) | 61 |
| w skin: 1 medium (about 3 per lb) | 80 |
| w skin: 1 large (about 2 per lb) | 123 |
| Peeled: 1 small (about 4 per lb) | 53 |
| Peeled: 1 medium (about 3 per lb) | 70 |
| Peeled: 1 large (about 2 per lb) | 107 |
| **Apricots** | |
| Raw, halves: 1 cup | 79 |
| Raw, halves: 1 lb | 231 |
| Raw, whole: 3 apricots | 55 |
| Raw, whole (12 per lb): 1 lb | 217 |
| **Avocados** | |
| California: ½ average | 185 |
| California, cubed: 1 cup | 257 |
| California, puree: 1 cup | 393 |
| Florida: ½ average | 196 |
| Florida, cubed: 1 cup | 192 |
| Florida, puree: 1 cup | 294 |
| **Bananas** | |
| 1 small, 7¾ in | 81 |
| 1 medium, 8¾ in | 101 |
| 1 large, 9¾ in | 116 |
| Mashed: 1 cup | 191 |
| Red: 1 banana, 7¼ in | 118 |
| Red, sliced: 1 cup | 135 |
| Sliced: 1 cup | 128 |
| Dehydrated or flakes: 1 tbsp | 21 |
| Dehydrated or flakes: 1 cup | 340 |
| Blackberries (including dewberries, boysenberries, youngberries), raw: 1 cup | 84 |
| Blueberries, raw: 1 cup | 90 |

| | |
|---|---|
| Blueberries, raw: 1 lb | 281 |
| Cherries | |
|     Raw, sour, red: 1 cup | 60 |
|     Raw, sour, red: 1 lb | 237 |
|     Raw, sweet: 1 cup | 82 |
|     Raw, sweet: 1 lb | 286 |
| Cranberries, raw, chopped: 1 cup | 51 |
| Cranberries, raw, whole: 1 cup | 44 |
| Figs, raw, whole: 1 small | 32 |
| Figs, raw, whole: 1 medium | 40 |
| Figs, raw, whole: 1 large | 52 |
| Gooseberries, raw: 1 cup | 59 |
| Grapefruit: half, 3½-in diam | 40 |
| Grapefruit, sections: 1 cup | 94 |
| Grapes | |
|     Concord, Delaware, Niagara, Catawba, Scuppernong: 10 grapes | 18 |
|     Flame Tokay, Emperor: 10 grapes | 38 |
|     Ribier: 10 grapes | 45 |
|     Thompson Seedless, Malaga, Muscat: 10 grapes | 34 |
| Lemons, wedge: 1 from large lemon | 7 |
| Lemons, whole fruit: 1 large | 29 |
| Limes, raw: 1 lime | 19 |
| Loganberries, raw: 1 cup | 89 |
| Loquats, raw: 10 fruits | 59 |
| Lychees, raw: 10 fruits | 58 |
| Mangoes, raw, whole: 1 fruit | 152 |
| Muskmelons | |
|     Canteloupes, cubed, diced or balls: 1 cup | 48 |
|     Canteloupes: half, 5-in diam | 82 |
|     Casaba, cubed, diced or balls: 1 cup | 46 |
|     Casaba, whole about 6 lbs: 1 melon | 367 |
|     Honeydew, cubed, diced or balls: 1 cup | 56 |
|     Honeydew, whole about 5¼ lbs: 1 melon | 495 |
| Nectarines, raw, 2½-in diam: 1 nectarine | 88 |
| Oranges | |
|     California navels (winter): 1 small | 45 |

CALORIES

| | |
|---|---|
| California navels (winter): 1 medium | 71 |
| California navels (winter): 1 large | 87 |
| California navels, sections: 1 cup | 77 |
| Valencias (summer): 1 small | 50 |
| Valencias (summer): 1 medium | 62 |
| Valencias (summer): 1 large | 96 |
| Valencias, sections: 1 cup | 92 |
| Florida: 1 small | 57 |
| Florida: 1 medium | 71 |
| Florida: 1 large | 89 |
| Florida, sections: 1 cup | 87 |
| Papaws, raw, whole: 1 papaw | 83 |
| Papayas, raw, cubed, ½-in pieces: 1 cup | 55 |
| Papayas, raw, whole, about 1 lb: 1 papaya | 119 |

Peaches

| | |
|---|---|
| Raw, pared, sliced: 1 cup | 65 |
| Raw, whole, peeled: 1 small (about 4 per lb) | 38 |
| Raw, whole, peeled: 1 large (about 2½ per lb) | 58 |
| Raw, whole, peeled: 1 lb | 150 |

Pears

| | |
|---|---|
| Raw, sliced or cubed: 1 cup | 101 |
| Raw, whole, Bartlett: 1 pear (about 2½ per lb) | 100 |
| Raw, whole, Boscs: 1 pear (about 3 per lb) | 86 |
| Raw, whole, D'Anjous: 1 pear (about 2 per lb) | 122 |
| Persimmons raw, Japanese or kaki: 1 persimmon | 129 |
| Persimmons, raw, native: 1 persimmon | 31 |
| Pineapple, raw, diced pieces: 1 cup | 81 |
| Pineapple, raw, sliced: 1 slice, ¾-in thick | 44 |

Plums

| | |
|---|---|
| Raw, whole, Damson: 10 plums, 1-in diam | 66 |
| Raw, whole, Damson: 1 lb | 272 |
| Raw, Japanese and hybrid: 1 plum, 2⅛-in diam | 32 |

| | |
|---|---:|
| Raw, Japanese and hybrid: 1 lb | 299 |
| Prune type, raw: 1 plum, 1½-in diam | 21 |
| Prune type, raw: 1 lb | 320 |
| Pomegranate: 1 pomegranate, 3⅜-in diam | 97 |
| Raspberries, raw, black: 1 cup | 98 |
| Raspberries, raw, red: 1 cup | 70 |
| Rhubarb, raw, diced: 1 cup | 20 |
| Rhubarb, cooked w sugar: 1 cup | 381 |
| Strawberries, raw, whole berries: 1 cup | 55 |
| Tangerines, raw, whole fruit: 1 large, 2½-in diam | 46 |
| Watermelon | |
| Raw: 1 lb | 118 |
| Raw, diced pieces: 1 cup | 42 |
| Raw, slice, 10-in diam by 1-in thick | 111 |
| Raw, wedge, 4 in x 8 in radius | 111 |

## CANNED AND FROZEN

| | |
|---|---:|
| Applesauce in cans or jars | |
| **Del Monte** / ½ cup | 85 |
| **Mott's** Natural Style / 8 oz | 90 |
| **S and W Nutradiet** / ½ cup | 48 |
| **Stokely-Van Camp** / 1 cup | 180 |
| **Tillie Lewis** / ½ cup | 60 |
| **Town House** / 8 oz | 170 |
| Unswt: ½ cup / **S and W Nutradiet** | 48 |
| Apricots: 1 cup unless noted | |
| Halves / **Del Monte** | 200 |
| Halves / **Stokely-Van Camp** | 220 |
| Halves / **Tillie Lewis** | 120 |
| Halves, in heavy syrup / **Libby's** | 200 |
| Halves, in heavy syrup / **Town House** | 220 |
| Halves, in light syrup / **Scotch Buy** | 160 |
| Halves, in light syrup / **Town House** | 160 |
| Whole / **Del Monte** | 200 |
| Whole, in heavy syrup / **Town House** | 201 |
| Swt: 4 halves / **S and W Nutradiet** | 40 |

CALORIES

| | |
|---|---|
| Unswt: 4 halves / **S and W Nutradiet** | 38 |
| Swt, whole: 2 whole / **S and W Nutradiet** | 31 |
| Blackberries, canned, swt: ½ cup / **S and W Nutradiet** | 36 |
| Blueberries, unswt, frozen: ½ cup / **Seabrook Farms** | 45 |
| Boysenberries, canned, swt: ½ cup / **S and W Nutradiet** | 32 |
| Cherries, canned: 1 cup unless noted | |
|    **Tillie Lewis** | 120 |
|    Dark, sweet / **Del Monte** | 180 |
|    Dark, sweet / **S and W Nutradiet** | 106 |
|    Dark, sweet, in heavy syrup / **Libby's** | 200 |
|    Dark, sweet, pitted / **Del Monte** | 190 |
|    Light, sweet / **Del Monte** Royal Anne | 190 |
|    Light, sweet, in heavy syrup / **Libby's** | 200 |
|    Light, sweet, unswt: 14 whole / **S and W Nutradiet** Royal Anne | 47 |
|    Sour, pitted / **Stokely-Van Camp** | 100 |
| Cranberry orange, crushed: 2 oz / **Ocean Spray** | 100 |
| Cranberry orange relish: 2 oz / **Ocean Spray** | 100 |
| Cranberry sauce, jellied: 2 oz / **Ocean Spray** | 90 |
| Cranberry sauce, whole: 2 oz / **Ocean Spray** | 90 |
| Currants, canned: ½ cup / **Del Monte** Zante | 190 |
| Figs, whole, canned: 1 cup / **Del Monte** | 210 |
| Figs, whole, swt, canned: 6 whole / **S and W Nutradiet** | 49 |
| Figs, whole, unswt, canned: 6 whole / **S and W Nutradiet** | 52 |
| Fruit cocktail, canned: 1 cup | |
|    **Del Monte** | 170 |
|    **Libby's** Juice Pack | 150 |
|    **S and W Nutradiet** | 72 |
|    **Stokely-Van Camp** | 190 |
|    **Tillie Lewis** | 100 |
|    In heavy syrup / **Libby's** | 170 |

| | |
|---|---:|
| In heavy syrup / **Town House** | 170 |
| Unswt / **S and W Nutradiet** | 70 |
| Fruit mixed, canned: 5 oz / **Del Monte** | 100 |
| Fruit mixed, frozen: 5 oz / **Birds Eye** Quick Thaw | 130 |
| Fruit salad, canned: 1 cup / **Del Monte** Tropical | 200 |
| Fruits for salad, canned: 1 cup | |
| **Del Monte** | 170 |
| **Stokely-Van Camp** | 190 |
| In heavy syrup / **Libby's** | 180 |
| Swt / **S and W Nutradiet** | 70 |
| Unswt / **S and W Nutradiet** | 76 |
| Grapefruit sections, canned: 1 cup / **Tillie Lewis** | 90 |
| Grapefruit sections, in juice, canned: 1 cup / **Del Monte** | 90 |
| Grapefruit sections, in syrup, canned: 1 cup / **Del Monte** | 140 |
| Grapefruit sections, unswt, canned: ½ cup / **S and W Nutradiet** | 36 |
| Oranges, Mandarin, canned: 5½ oz / **Del Monte** | 100 |
| Oranges, Mandarin, canned: ½ cup / **Tillie Lewis** | 45 |
| Oranges, Mandarin, swt, canned: ½ cup / **S and W Nutradiet** | 27 |
| Oranges, Mandarin, unswt, canned: ½ cup / **S and W Nutradiet** | 27 |
| Peaches, canned: 1 cup unless noted | |
| **Stokely-Van Camp** | 190 |
| Cling / **Del Monte** | 170 |
| Cling / **Tillie Lewis** | 100 |
| Cling, diced: 5 oz can / **Del Monte** | 110 |
| Cling, in heavy syrup / **Libby's** | 170 |
| Cling, in heavy syrup / **Town House** | 190 |
| Cling, in light syrup / **Highway** | 140 |
| Cling, in light syrup / **Scotch Buy** | 140 |

CALORIES

| | |
|---|---|
| Cling, slices / Del Monte | 170 |
| Cling, slices, in heavy syrup / Town House | 190 |
| Cling, slices, in light syrup / Highway | 140 |
| Cling. slices, in swt juice / Libby's | |
|     Juice Pack | 150 |
| Cling, slices, swt / S and W Nutradiet | 50 |
| Cling. slices, unswt / S and W Nutradiet | 48 |
| Cling. unswt: 2 halves / S and W Nutradiet | 28 |
| Freestone, halves / Del Monte | 170 |
| Freestone, halves, in extra heavy syrup / | |
|     Town House | 260 |
| Freestone, mixed pieces, in heavy | |
|     syrup / Highway | 200 |
| Freestone, mixed pieces, in heavy | |
|     syrup / Scotch Buy | 200 |
| Freestone, slices / Del Monte | 170 |
| Freestone. slices, in extra heavy syrup / | |
|     Town House | 260 |
| Freestone, swt: ½ cup / S and W Nutradiet | 24 |
| Slices / Stokely-Van Camp | 180 |
| Spiced w pits: 7¼ oz / Del Monte | 150 |
| Peaches, frozen: 5 oz / Birds Eye Quick Thaw | 130 |
| Peaches, frozen, slices: ½ cup / Seabrook Farms | 106 |
| Pears, canned: 1 cup unless noted | |
|     Bartlett / Tillie Lewis | 100 |
|     Bartlett, halves / Del Monte | 160 |
|     Bartlett, halves, in light syrup / Highway | 160 |
|     Bartlett, halves, in light syrup / Scotch Buy | 140 |
|     Bartlett halves, in heavy syrup / Libby's | 170 |
|     Bartlett halves, in heavy syrup / | |
|     Town House | 190 |
|     Bartlett, slices / Del Monte | 160 |
|     Bartlett. slices, in heavy syrup / | |
|     Town House | 190 |
|     Halves / Stokely-Van Camp | 210 |
|     Halves, in swt juice / Libby's | |
|     Juice Pack | 150 |
|     Halves, swt: 2 halves / S and W Nutradiet | 28 |

CALORIES

| | |
|---|---|
| Quartered, swt / **S and W Nutradiet** | 52 |
| Quartered, unswt / **S and W Nutradiet** | 54 |
| Slices / **Stokely-Van Camp** | 200 |
| Pineapple, canned: 1 cup | |
| **Tillie Lewis** | 140 |
| Chunks, in juice / **Del Monte** | 140 |
| Chunks, in juice / **Dole** | 128 |
| Chunks, in juice, unswt / **Town House** | 140 |
| Chunks, in syrup / **Del Monte** | 190 |
| Chunks, in syrup / **Dole** | 168 |
| Chunks, in syrup / **Town House** | 190 |
| Chunks, swt / **S and W Nutradiet** | 98 |
| Crushed, in juice / **Del Monte** | 140 |
| Crushed, in juice, unswt / **Town House** | 140 |
| Crushed, in syrup / **Del Monte** | 190 |
| Crushed, in syrup / **Town House** | 190 |
| Slices, in juice / **Del Monte** | 140 |
| Slices, in juice, unswt / **Town House** | 140 |
| Slices, in syrup / **Del Monte** | 190 |
| Slices, in syrup / **Town House** | 190 |
| Slices, swt / **S and W Nutradiet** | 112 |
| Slices, unswt / **S and W Nutradiet** | 178 |
| Tidbits, in syrup / **Town House** | 190 |
| Tidbits, swt / **S and W Nutradiet** | 98 |
| Tidbits, unswt / **S and W Nutradiet** | 138 |
| Plums, canned: 1 cup | |
| **Del Monte** | 190 |
| **Libby's** | 210 |
| **S and W Nutradiet** | 100 |
| **Stokely-Van Camp** | 240 |
| **Tillie Lewis** | 140 |
| Prunes, stewed, canned: 1 cup / **Del Monte** | 230 |
| Raspberries, red, frozen: 5 oz / **Birds Eye** | |
| Quick Thaw | 140 |
| Strawberries | |
| Canned: 1 cup / **S and W Nutradiet** | 40 |
| Frozen: 5 oz / **Birds Eye** Quick Thaw | 110 |
| Halves, frozen: 5.3 oz / **Birds Eye** | 170 |

CALORIES

| | |
|---|---:|
| Slices, frozen: 5 oz / **Birds Eye** | 180 |
| Slices, frozen: ½ cup / **Seabrook Farms** | 140 |
| Whole, frozen: 4 oz / **Birds Eye** | 70 |
| Whole. frozen. unswt: ½ cup / **Seabrook Farms** | 42 |

## DRIED

**Uncooked**

| | |
|---|---:|
| Apples: 2 oz / **Del Monte** | 140 |
| Apples: 1 pkg / **Weight Watchers** Apple Snacks | 50 |
| Apricots: 2 oz / **Del Monte** | 140 |
| Currants: 1 cup / **Del Monte** Zanta | 410 |
| Dates, chopped: 1 cup / **Dromedary** | 493 |
| Dates, diced: 1 cup / **Bordo** | 660 |
| Dates, whole. pitted: 4 average / **Bordo** | 76 |
| Dates, whole pitted: 1 cup / **Dromedary** | 470 |
| Figs: 1 large (2 in x 1 in) | 60 |
| Fruits and peels, glazed: 4 oz / **Liberty** | 388 |
| Fruits: 1 pkg / **Weight Watchers** Fruit Snacks | 50 |
| Peaches: 2 oz / **Del Monte** | 140 |
| Pears: 2 oz / **Del Monte** | 150 |
| Prunes, w pits: 2 oz / **Del Monte** | 120 |
| Prunes, w pits: 2 oz / **Del Monte** Moist-pak | 120 |
| Prunes, pitted: 2 oz/ **Del Monte** | 140 |
| Raisins. muscat: 3 oz / **Del Monte** | 250 |
| Raisins, seedless, golden: 3 oz / **Del Monte** | 260 |
| Raisins, seedless, Thompson: 3 oz / **Del Monte** | 260 |

# Fruit Drinks and Fruit-Flavored Beverages

CALORIES

All flavors, mix, w sugar:
| | |
|---|---|
| 1 env / **Ann Page** Cheeri-Aid | 320 |

All flavors. mix. wo sugar:
| | |
|---|---|
| 1 env / **Ann Page** Cheeri-Aid | 32 |

All flavors, mix, prepared:
| | |
|---|---|
| 8 fl oz / **Funny Face** | 80 |

All flavors mix prepared, swt:
| | |
|---|---|
| 8 fl oz / **Kool-Aid** | 90 |

All flavors. mix, unswt:
| | |
|---|---|
| 8 fl oz prepared w sugar / **Kool-Aid** | 100 |
| Apple, canned: 8 fl oz / **Ann Page** | 120 |
| Apple. canned: 6 fl oz / **Hi-C** | 92 |
| Apple-grape, canned: 6 fl oz / **Mott's** "P.M." | 90 |
| Berry, canned: 8 fl oz / **Cragmont** Wild Berry | 120 |

Cherry
| | |
|---|---|
| Canned: 8 fl oz / **Ann Page** | 120 |
| Canned: 8 fl oz / **Cragmont** | 120 |
| Canned: 6 fl oz / **Hi-C** | 93 |
| Mix, prepared: 6 fl oz / **Hi-C** | 76 |
| Citrus cooler, canned: 8 fl oz / **Ann Page** | 120 |
| Citrus cooler, canned: 8 fl oz / **Cragmont** | 120 |
| Citrus cooler. canned: 6 fl oz / **Hi-C** | 93 |

Cranberry juice cocktail
| | |
|---|---|
| Bottled: 8 fl oz / **Ann Page** | 160 |
| Bottled: 6 fl oz / **Ocean Spray** | 110 |
| Bottled: 6 fl oz / **Ocean Spray** Low Calorie | 35 |
| Canned: 4 fl oz / **Seneca** | 79 |
| Canned: 6 fl oz / **Town House** | 110 |
| Canned and bottled: 6 fl oz / **Welch's** | 105 |

Cranberry-apple drink
| | |
|---|---|
| Bottled: 8 fl oz / **Ann Page** | 180 |

CALORIES

| | |
|---|---|
| Bottled: 6 fl oz / **Ocean Spray Cranapple** | 130 |
| Bottled: 6 fl oz / **Ocean Spray**<br>Low Calorie **Cranapple** | 30 |
| Canned: 6 fl oz / **Town House** | 132 |
| Cranberry-apricot drink, bottled:<br>6 fl oz / **Ocean Spray Cranicot** | 110 |
| Cranberry-grape drink, bottled:<br>6 fl oz / **Ocean Spray Crangrape** | 110 |
| Cranberry-prune drink, bottled:<br>6 fl oz / **Ocean Spray Cranprune** | 120 |
| Fruit, canned: 6 fl oz / **Mott's "A.M."**<br>Fruit Drink | 90 |
| Fruit, mix, prepared:<br>8 fl oz / **Hawaiian Punch** Red | 100 |
| Grape | |
| Bottled: 6 fl oz / **Sunshake** | 90 |
| Canned: 8 fl oz / **Ann Page** | 120 |
| Canned: 6 fl oz / **Hi-C** | 89 |
| Canned: 8 fl oz / **Cragmont** | 130 |
| Canned: 6 fl oz / **Welchade** | 90 |
| Canned: 6 fl oz / **Welchade** Red | 90 |
| Mix: 1 heaping tsp / **Ann Page**<br>Instant Breakfast Drink | 30 |
| Mix, prepared: 6 fl oz / **Hi-C** | 76 |
| Mix, prepared: 4 fl oz / **Tang** | 60 |
| Refrigerated: 6 fl oz / **Welch's** Juice Drink | 110 |
| Grapefruit, bottled: 6 fl oz /<br>**Ann Page** Ready-Made | 80 |
| Grapefruit, mix, prepared: 4 fl oz / **Tang** | 50 |
| Lemonade | |
| Frozen, reconstituted: 6 fl oz /<br>**Minute Maid** | 74 |
| Mix, prepared: 8 fl oz / **Country Time** | 90 |
| Mix, prepared: 6 fl oz / **Hi-C** | 76 |
| Mix, prepared: 6 fl oz /<br>**Minute Maid** Crystals | 80 |
| Mix, prepared: 6 fl oz / **Wyler's** | 66 |

| | |
|---|---:|
| Pink, mix, prepared: 8 fl oz / **Country Time** | 90 |
| Pink, mix, prepared: 6 fl oz / **Minute Maid** Crystals | 80 |
| Lemon-limeade. frozen, reconstituted: 6 fl oz / **Minute Maid** | 75 |
| Limeade, frozen, reconstituted: 6 fl oz / **Minute Maid** | 75 |
| Orange | |
|     Bottled: 6 fl oz / **A & P Ready-Made** | 80 |
|     Bottled: 6 fl oz / **Sunshake** | 90 |
|     Canned: 8 fl oz / **Ann Page** | 120 |
|     Canned: 8 fl oz / **Cragmont** | 130 |
|     Canned: 6 fl oz / **Hi-C** | 92 |
|     Canned: 6 fl oz / **Welchade** | 100 |
|     Frozen, reconstituted: 6 fl oz / **Birds Eye Orange Plus** | 100 |
|     Mix: 1 heaping tsp / **Ann Page** Instant Breakfast Drink | 30 |
|     Mix: 3 rounded tsp / **Town House** Instant Breakfast Drink | 100 |
|     Mix, prepared: 6 fl oz / **Hi-C** | 76 |
|     Mix, prepared: 4 fl oz / **Start** | 60 |
|     Mix, prepared: 4 fl oz / **Tang** | 60 |
| Orangeade, frozen. reconstituted: 6 fl oz / **Minute Maid** | 94 |
| Orange-pineapple, canned: 8 fl oz / **Ann Page** | 120 |
| Orange-pineapple. canned: 6 fl oz / **Hi-C** | 94 |
| Peach, canned: 6 fl oz / **Hi-C** | 90 |
| Peach, mix, prepared: 6 fl oz / **Hi-C** | 76 |
| Pineapple-grapefruit, canned: 6 fl oz / **Town House** Juice Drink | 90 |
| Pineapple-pink grapefruit, canned: 6 fl oz / **Dole** Drink | 91 |
| Pineapple-orange, canned: 8 fl oz / **Cragmont** | 130 |
| Punch | |
|     All flavors, canned: 8 fl oz / **Hawaiian Punch** | 120 |

CALORIES

| | |
|---|---|
| All flavors, frozen, reconstituted: | |
|    8 fl oz / **Hawaiian Punch** | 120 |
| All flavors, mix, prepared: | |
|    8 fl oz / **Hawaiian Punch** Shelf Concentrate | 120 |
| Florida punch, canned: 6 fl oz / **Hi-C** | 95 |
| Fruit, canned: 6 fl oz / **Welchade** | 100 |
| Tropical fruit, canned: 8 fl oz / **Ann Page** | 120 |
| Tropical, canned: 8 fl oz / **Cragmont** | 130 |
| Mix, prepared: 6 fl oz / **Hi-C** | 76 |
| Strawberry, canned: 6 fl oz / **Hi-C** | 89 |
| Tangerine, canned: 6 fl oz / **Hi-C** | 90 |
| Wild berry, canned: 8 fl oz / **Ann Page** | 120 |
| Wild berry, canned: 6 fl oz / **Hi-C** | 88 |

# Fruit Juices

## FRESH

CALORIES

**1 cup unless noted**

| | |
|---|---|
| Acerola cherry | 56 |
| Grapefruit | 96 |
| Lemon | 61 |
| Lemon: 1 tbsp | 4 |
| Lime: 1 tbsp | 4 |
| Orange | |
|    California navels | 120 |
|    Florida | 106 |
|    Valencias | 117 |
| Tangerine | 106 |

## BOTTLED, CANNED AND FROZEN

|  | CALORIES |
|---|---|
| **6 fl oz unless noted** | |
| Apple | |
| Bottled: 8 fl oz / **Ann Page** | 120 |
| Canned / **Mott's** | 80 |
| Canned / **Mott's** Natural Style | 80 |
| Canned / **Pillsbury** | 90 |
| Canned and bottled: 4 fl oz / **Seneca** | 61 |
| Canned from concentrate / **Welch's** | 90 |
| Apricot nectar | |
| Canned / **Del Monte** | 100 |
| Canned / **Libby's** | 110 |
| Canned: 4 fl oz / **Seneca** | 77 |
| Canned / **Town House** | 110 |
| Grape | |
| Bottled, canned and frozen concentrate: | |
| 4 fl oz / **Seneca** | 74 |
| Bottled / **Welch's** | 120 |
| Bottled, red / **Welch's** | 120 |
| Bottled, red / **Welch's** Sparkling | 120 |
| Bottled, white / **Welch's** | 120 |
| Bottled, white / **Welch's** Sparkling | 120 |
| Frozen, reconstituted / **Minute Maid** | 99 |
| Grapefruit | |
| Bottled / **Ocean Spray** | 70 |
| Canned: 4 fl oz / **Seneca** | 54 |
| Canned from concentrate / **Welch's** | 75 |
| Canned, swt / **Del Monte** | 80 |
| Canned, swt / **Libby's** | 100 |
| Canned, unswt / **Del Monte** | 70 |
| Canned, unswt / **Libby's** | 75 |
| Canned, unswt: 1 cup / **Treesweet** | 100 |
| Frozen, reconstituted / **Minute Maid** | 75 |
| Frozen, reconstituted: 1 cup / **Treesweet** | 100 |
| Grapefruit-orange, canned: 4 fl oz / **Seneca** | 59 |
| Lemon, bottled, reconstituted: 2 tbsp / **ReaLemon** | 8 |

CALORIES

Lemon, canned, reconstituted:
   1 tbsp / **Town House**     3
Lemon, frozen, reconstituted / **Minute Maid**     40
Orange
   Canned: 4 fl oz / **Seneca**     59
   Canned from concentrate / **Welch's**     90
   Canned, swt / **Del Monte**     70
   Canned, swt / **Libby's**     100
   Canned, unswt / **Del Monte**     80
   Canned, unswt / **Libby's**     90
   Canned, unswt: 1 cup / **Treesweet**     120
   Frozen, reconstituted / **Bright and Early**     90
   Frozen, reconstituted / **Minute Maid**     90
   Frozen, reconstituted / **Snow Crop**     90
   Frozen, reconstituted: 1 cup / **Treesweet**     120
   Imitation, frozen, reconstituted /
     **Birds Eye** Awake     90
Orange-grapefruit
   Canned, swt / **Del Monte**     80
   Canned, unswt / **Libby's**     80
   Canned, unswt / **Del Monte**     80
   Frozen, reconstituted / **Minute Maid**     76
Peach nectar, canned / **Del Monte**     100
Peach nectar, canned / **Libby's**     90
Pear nectar, canned / **Del Monte**     110
Pear nectar, canned / **Libby's**     100
Pineapple
   Canned / **Del Monte**     100
   Canned / **Dole**     93
   Canned: 4 fl oz / **Seneca**     68
   Canned, unswt / **Town House**     100
   Frozen, reconstituted / **Minute Maid**     92
Pineapple-grapefruit, canned / **Del Monte**     90
Pineapple-orange, frozen, reconstituted /
   **Minute Maid**     94
Pineapple-pink grapefruit, canned / **Del Monte**     90
Prune
   Bottled / **Ann Page**     140

|  | CALORIES |
|---|---|
| Bottled / **RealPrune** | 130 |
| Canned / **Del Monte** | 120 |
| Canned / **Mott's** | 140 |
| Canned / **Mott's** Prune Nectar | 100 |
| Canned: 4 fl oz / **Seneca** | 102 |
| Canned or bottled / **Sunsweet** | 123 |
| Canned / **Welch's** | 150 |
| Canned w pulp / **Mott's** | 120 |
| Tangerine, frozen, reconstituted / **Minute Maid** | 86 |

# Gelatin

| | CALORIES |
|---|---|
| All flavors, mix, prepared: ½ cup / **D-Zerta** | 8 |
| All flavors, mix, prepared:<br>½ cup / **Estee** Low Calorie | 40 |
| All flavors, mix, prepared: ½ cup / **Jell-O** | 80 |
| All flavors, mix, prepared: ½ cup / **Royal** | 80 |
| All flavors, unswt, mix, prepared:<br>½ cup / **Royal Sweet As You Please** | 6 |
| Orange-flavored, drinking: 1 env / **Knox** Gelatine | 70 |
| Unflavored: 1 pkg (¼ oz) / **Ann Page** | 24 |
| Unflavored: 1 env / **Knox** Gelatine | 25 |

# Gravies

| | CALORIES |
|---|---|
| **¼ cup unless noted** | |
| Au Jus | |
|     Mix, prepared: 1 env / **Ann Page** | 64 |
|     Mix, prepared / **Durkee** | 8 |
|     Mix w roasting bag:<br>        1 pkg / **Durkee** Roastin' Bag | 64 |
|     Mix, prepared / **French's** | 8 |
|     Mix, prepared / **French's** Pan Rich | 30 |
|     Mix, prepared: ½ cup / **McCormick** | 8 |

CALORIES

| | |
|---|---:|
| Mix, prepared: ½ cup / **Schilling** | 8 |
| Beef, canned: 1/5 can / **Ann Page** | 25 |
| Beef, canned: 2 oz / **Franco-American** | 30 |
| Beef, canned: ½ cup / **Howard Johnson's** | 51 |

Brown

| | |
|---|---:|
| Mix, prepared: 1 env / **Ann Page** | 80 |
| Mix, prepared / **Durkee** | 15 |
| Mix, prepared / **French's** | 20 |
| Mix, prepared / **French's** Pan Rich | 60 |
| Mix, prepared / **McCormick** | 26 |
| Mix, prepared / **McCormick** Lite | 10 |
| Mix, prepared / **Pillsbury** | 15 |
| Mix, prepared / **Schilling** | 26 |
| Mix, prepared / **Schilling** Lite | 10 |
| Mix, prepared: 1 fl oz / **Spatini** Family Style | 10 |
| Mix, prepared / **Weight Watchers** | 8 |
| Herb-flavored, mix, prepared / **McCormick** | 21 |
| Herb-flavored, mix, prepared / **Schilling** | 21 |
| w mushroom broth, canned: | |
| 1 oz / **Dawn Fresh** | 10 |
| w mushrooms, mix, prepared / **Durkee** | 15 |
| w mushrooms, mix, prepared / | |
| **Weight Watchers** | 12 |
| w onions, canned: 2 oz / | |
| **Franco-American** | 25 |
| w onions, mix, prepared / **Durkee** | 17 |
| w onions, mix, prepared / **Weight Watchers** | 13 |

Chicken

| | |
|---|---:|
| Canned: 2 oz / **Franco-American** | 50 |
| Mix, prepared: 1 env / **Ann Page** | 120 |
| Mix, prepared / **Durkee** | 22 |
| Mix, prepared / **Durkee** Creamy | 39 |
| Mix w roasting bag: | |
| 1 pkg / **Durkee** Roastin' Bag | 122 |
| Mix w roasting bag: | |
| 1 pkg / **Durkee** Roastin' Bag | |
| Italian Style | 144 |
| Mix, prepared / **French's** | 25 |

CALORIES

| | |
|---|---:|
| Mix, prepared / **French's** Pan Rich | 60 |
| Mix, prepared / **McCormick** | 21 |
| Mix, prepared / **McCormick** Lite | 10 |
| Mix, prepared / **Pillsbury** | 25 |
| Mix, prepared / **Schilling** | 21 |
| Mix, prepared / **Schilling** Lite | 10 |
| Mix, prepared / **Weight Watchers** | 10 |
| Mix, creamy w roasting bag: | |
|     1 pkg / **Durkee** Roastin' Bag | 242 |
| Chicken giblet, canned: 2 oz / **Franco-American** | 35 |
| Homestyle, mix, prepared / **Durkee** | 18 |
| Homestyle, mix, prepared / **French's** | 25 |
| Homestyle, mix, prepared / **Pillsbury** | 15 |
| Meatloaf, mix w roasting bag: | |
|     1 pkg / **Durkee** Roastin' Bag | 129 |
| Mushroom | |
|     Canned: 2 oz / **Franco-American** | 35 |
|     Mix, prepared: 1 env / **Ann Page** | 80 |
|     Mix, prepared / **French's** | 20 |
|     Mix, prepared / **McCormick** | 19 |
|     Mix, prepared / **Schilling** | 19 |
| Onion, mix, prepared: 1 env / **Ann Page** | 120 |
| Onion, mix, prepared / **Durkee** | 21 |
| Onion, mix, prepared / **French's** | 25 |
| Onion, mix, prepared / **French's** Pan Rich | 50 |
| Onion pot roast, mix w roasting bag: | |
|     1 pkg / **Durkee** Roastin' Bag | 124 |
| Pork, mix, prepared / **Durkee** | 18 |
| Pork, mix w roasting bag: 1 pkg / | |
|     **Durkee** Roastin' Bag | 130 |
| Pork, mix, prepared / **French's** | 20 |
| Pot roast stew, mix w roasting bag: | |
|     1 pkg / **Durkee** Roastin' Bag | 125 |
| Sparerib sauce, mix w roasting bag: | |
|     1 pkg / **Durkee** Roastin' Bag | 162 |
| Swiss steak, mix, prepared / **Durkee** | 11 |
| Swiss steak, mix w roasting bag: | |
|     1 pkg / **Durkee** Roastin' Bag | 115 |

CALORIES

Turkey giblet, canned:
  ½ cup / **Howard Johnson's**      55
Turkey, mix, prepared / **Durkee**      23
Turkey, mix, prepared / **French's**      25
Turkey, mix, prepared / **McCormick**      21
Turkey, mix, prepared / **Schilling**      21

# Health Foods

## Flour, Meal, Rice and Yeast

| | |
|---|---|
| Flour, soy: ¼ cup / **Loma Linda** | 115 |
| Meal, almond: 2 tbsp / **Roberts** | 114 |
| Meal, coconut: 2 tbsp / **Roberts** | 126 |
| Meal, millet seed: 2 tbsp / **Roberts** | 65 |
| Meal, sesame, 2 tbsp / **Roberts** | 111 |
| Meal, sunflower: 2 tbsp / **Roberts** | 106 |
| Rice, brown: ¼ cup raw / **Datetree** | 180 |
| Rice, brown: ¼ cup raw / **Roberts** | 180 |
| Yeast, brewer's: 1 rounded tbsp / **Datetree** | 49 |
| Yeast, brewer's: 1 rounded tbsp / **Roberts** | 49 |

## Granola Bars

| | |
|---|---|
| w cinnamon: 1 bar / **Nature Valley** | 110 |
| w coconut: 1 bar / **Nature Valley** | 120 |
| w oats and honey: 1 bar / **Nature Valley** | 110 |
| Peanut: 1 bar / **Nature Valley** | 120 |

## Seasonings and Gravy

| | |
|---|---|
| Gravy, mix, brown: | |
| 1/6 pkg / **Loma Linda** Gravy Quick | 15 |
| Seasoning, chicken: 1 tbsp / **Loma Linda** | 8 |

## Soy Milk

| | |
|---|---|
| Soyagen, all purpose: | |
| 1 cup prepared / **Loma Linda** | 140 |

Soyagen, carob:
1 cup prepared / **Loma Linda**                    140
Soyalac, concentrated:
6 fl oz prepared / **Loma Linda**                  120
Soyalac, powder:
6 fl oz prepared / **Loma Linda**                  120
I-Soyalac, concentrated:
6 fl oz prepared / **Loma Linda**                  120

## Soybeans and Legumes

Beans, brown, canned:
½ cup / **Loma Linda**                             122
Beans, in tomato sauce, canned:
½ cup / **Loma Linda**                             118
Garbanzo beans, canned:
½ cup / **Loma Linda**                             145
Lentils, canned: ¾ cup / **Loma Linda**            91
Soy beans
   Boston style, canned:
     ½ cup / **Loma Linda**                    141
   Cooking: ½ cup raw / **Datetree**               331
   Cooking: ½ cup raw / **Roberts**                331
   Dry roasted: 1 oz / **Soy Ahoy**                129
   Dry roasted: 1 oz / **Soy Town**                129
   Green, canned: ½ cup / **Loma Linda**           109
   Oil roasted: 1 oz / **Soy Ahoy**                145
   Oil roasted: 1 oz / **Soy Town**                145
   Roasted: ¼ cup / **Datetree**                   118
   Roasted: ¼ cup / **Roberts**                    118

## Spreads and Sandwich Fillings

Almond butter: 1 tbsp / **Roberts**                96
Cashew butter: 1 tbsp / **Roberts**                90
Marmalade, orange: 1 tbsp / **Datetree**           50
Mayonnaise: 1 tbsp / **Datetree**                  92
Peanut butter: 1 tbsp / **Datetree**               93
Peanut butter: 1 tbsp / **Roberts**                93

Preserves: 1 tbsp
    Blackberry / **Datetree** ............... 55
    Grape / **Datetree** ..................... 50
    Red raspberry / **Datetree** ........... 55
    Rose hip / **Datetree** ................. 50
    Strawberry / **Datetree** .............. 55
Sandwich filling:
    ½-in slice / **Loma Linda** Vegelona ... 154
Sandwich spread: 3 tbsp / **Loma Linda** ... 80
Sesame butter: 1 tbsp / **Roberts** ........ 93
Soy bean cheese:
    ½-in slice / **Loma Linda** Vegechee ... 106

## Sweets, Nuts and Snacks: Natural

Almonds, raw: ¼ cup / **Datetree** ........ 191
Almonds, raw: ¼ cup / **Roberts** ......... 191
Apricot chew: ¼ bar / **Datetree** ........ 92
Apricot chew: ¼ bar / **Roberts** ......... 92
Candy bridge mix: 1 piece / **Joan's Natural** ... 10
Cashews, raw: ¼ cup / **Datetree** ........ 180
Cashews, raw: ¼ cup / **Roberts** ......... 180
Coconut shreds: 2 tbsps / **Datetree** ..... 119
Coconut shreds: 2 tbsps / **Roberts** ...... 119
Date 'n' seed chew: ¼ bar / **Roberts** .... 92
Fruit 'n' nut bar:
    1 section of 4 oz bar / **Joan's Natural** ... 74
Fruit 'n' nut chew: ¼ bar / **Datetree** ... 92
Fruit 'n' nut chew: ¼ bar / **Roberts** .... 92
Honey-sesame bar:
    1 section of 4 oz bar / **Joan's Natural** ... 78
Milk bar:
    1 section of 4 oz bar / **Joan's Natural** ... 78
Peanut butter-carob bar:
    1 section of 4 oz bar / **Joan's Natural** ... 79
Peanut butter cups: 1 piece / **Joan's Natural** ... 40
Peanutettes: 1 peanut / **Joan's Natural** ... 7
Pistachio nuts, natural: ¼ cup / **Datetree** ... 149

Protein, bar:
¼ bar / **Roberts** Hi Protein Bar                                92
Raisin nut mix: ½ cup / **Datetree**                            228
Raisin nut mix: ½ cup / **Roberts**                             228
Raisin 'n' peanut chew: ¼ bar / **Roberts**           97
Raisins, coated: 1 raisin / **Joan's Natural**          4
Rose hip chew: ¼ bar / **Datetree**                            97
Rose hip chew: ¼ bar / **Roberts**                              97
Seeds
    Millet: ¼ cup / **Datetree**                               144
    Millet: ¼ cup / **Roberts**                                144
    Pepitas: ¼ cup / **Datetree**                            177
    Pumpkin: ¼ cup / **Datetree**                         177
    Pumpkin: ¼ cup / **Roberts**                          177
    Sesame: ¼ cup / **Datetree**                            280
    Sesame: ¼ cup / **Roberts**                             280
    Squash, dry, hulled: 1 oz                             165
    Sunflower: 1 oz / **Frito Lay**                         181
    Sunflower: 1 oz / **Granny Goose**               174
    Sunflower, dry roasted: 1 oz / **Planters**    160
    Sunflower, unsalted: 1 oz / **Planters**        170
    Sunflower, raw or roasted:
       ¼ cup / **Datetree**                                 179
    Sunflower, raw or roasted:
       ¼ cup / **Roberts**                                  179
    Sunflower, whole: 1 oz / **Granny Goose**    159
Sesame carob chew: ¼ bar / **Datetree**              97
Sesame carob chew: ¼ bar / **Roberts**                97
Sesame 'n' almond bar: ¼ bar / **Roberts**         97
Sesame 'n' cashew bar: ¼ bar / **Roberts**         97
Sesame 'n' coconut bar: ¼ bar / **Roberts**       97
Sesame 'n' fruit bar: ¼ bar / **Roberts**             97
Sesame 'n' honey bar: ¼ bar / **Roberts**           97

**Sweeteners**

Honey, tupelo: 1 tbsp / **Datetree**                          61
Honey, wildflower: 1 tbsp / **Datetree**                   61

Molasses, blackstrap: 1 tbsp / **Datetree**          43
Sugar, turbinado: 1 tsp / **Datetree**          15
Sugar, turbinado: 1 tsp / **Roberts**          15

## Wheat and Wheat Germ

Bulgur, club wheat: 1 cup dry          628
Bulgur, hard red winter wheat: 1 cup dry          602
Bulgur, white wheat: 1 cup dry          553
Wheat, oven cooked: ½ cup / **Loma Linda**          263
Wheat germ: ¼ cup / **Kretschmer** Regular          106
Wheat germ:
   ¼ cup / **Kretschmer** Sugar 'N Honey          107
Wheat germ, natural and toasted:
   2 tbsp / **Loma Linda**          80
Wheat germ, raw: 2 rounded tbsp / **Datetree**          58
Wheat germ, raw: ¼ cup / **Pillsbury**          115
Wheat germ, raw: 2 rounded tbsp / **Roberts**          58
Wheat germ, toasted: ¼ cup / **Pillsbury**          120

## Vegetarian meat substitutes (gluten base unless noted)

Bologna: ½-in slice / **Loma Linda**          190
Burgers:
   1 burger / **Loma Linda** Sizzle Burgers          180
Chicken (4-in diameter):
   ½-in slice / **Loma Linda**          180
Frankfurters:
   1 frank / **Loma Linda** Big Franks          110
Linketts: 1 link / **Loma Linda**          70
Little Links: 1 link / **Loma Linda**          45
Meatballs: 1 ball / **Loma Linda**          48
Nuteena (peanut-butter base):
   ½-in slice / **Loma Linda**          210
Proteena (gluten-peanut-butter base):
   ½-in slice / **Loma Linda**          160
Redi-Burger: ½-in slice / **Loma Linda**          150
Roast beef: ½-in slice / **Loma Linda**          200
Salami: ½-in slice / **Loma Linda**          210

| | |
|---|---|
| Sausage: 1 link / **Loma Linda** Breakfast Links | 47 |
| Sausage: | |
|   1 piece / **Loma Linda** Breakfast Sausage | 140 |
| Stew Pac: 2 oz / **Loma Linda** | 70 |
| Swiss Steak: 1 steak / **Loma Linda** | 140 |
| Tender Bits: 1 bit / **Loma Linda** | 20 |
| Tender Rounds: 1 round / **Loma Linda** | 47 |
| Turkey: ½-in slice / **Loma Linda** | 190 |
| Vegeburger: ½ cup / **Loma Linda** | 120 |
| Vegeburger, unsalted: ½ cup / **Loma Linda** | 120 |
| Vegelona: ½-in slice / **Loma Linda** | 160 |

# Ice Cream and Similar Frozen Products

|  | CALORIES |
|---|---|
| Frozen dessert: | |
| 5 fl oz / **Weight Watchers** Dietary | 100 |
| Frozen dessert: | |
| 6 fl oz / **Weight Watchers** Frosted Treat | 120 |
| Ice cream: ½ cup unless noted | |
| Black raspberry / **Breyers** | 130 |
| Black walnut / **Meadow Gold** | 160 |
| Butter almond / **Sealtest** | 160 |
| Butter almond, chocolate / **Breyers** | 160 |
| Butter brickle / **Sealtest** | 150 |
| Butter pecan / **Meadow Gold** | 150 |
| Butter pecan / **Sealtest** | 160 |
| Caramel pecan crunch / **Breyers** | 160 |
| Cherry nugget / **Sealtest** | 140 |
| Cherry-vanilla / **Breyers** | 140 |
| Cherry-vanilla / **Meadow Gold** | 140 |
| Cherry-vanilla / **Sealtest** | 130 |
| Chocolate / **Breyers** | 161 |
| Chocolate: 4 oz / **Howard Johnson's** | 260 |
| Chocolate / **Meadow Gold** | 140 |
| Chocolate / **Sealtest** | 140 |
| Chocolate / **Swift's** | 130 |
| Chocolate almond / **Breyers** | 180 |
| Chocolate almond / **Sealtest** | 160 |
| Chocolate chip / **Meadow Gold** | 150 |
| Chocolate chip / **Sealtest** | 150 |

CALORIES

| | |
|---|---|
| Chocolate Revel / Meadow Gold | 140 |
| Coconut / Sealtest | 160 |
| Coffee / Breyers | 140 |
| Coffee / Sealtest | 140 |
| Dutch chocolate almond / Breyers | 180 |
| Lemon / Sealtest | 140 |
| Maple walnut / Sealtest | 160 |
| Mint chocolate chip / Breyers | 170 |
| Peach / Meadow Gold | 130 |
| Peach / Sealtest | 130 |
| Pineapple / Sealtest | 130 |
| Southern pecan butterscotch / Breyers | 160 |
| Strawberry / Breyers | 130 |
| Strawberry: 4 oz / Howard Johnson's | 220 |
| Strawberry / Meadow Gold | 140 |
| Strawberry / Sealtest | 131 |
| Strawberry / Swift's | 120 |
| Vanilla / Breyers | 150 |
| Vanilla: 4 oz / Howard Johnson's | 247 |
| Vanilla / Meadow Gold | 140 |
| Vanilla / Meadow Gold Golden | 140 |
| Vanilla / Sealtest | 140 |
| Vanilla / Swift's | 130 |
| Vanilla, French / Sealtest | 140 |
| Vanilla-flavored cherry / Sealtest Royale | 140 |
| Vanilla-flavored red raspberry / Sealtest Royale | 140 |
| Vanilla fudge / Breyers | 156 |

Ice milk: ½ cup

| | |
|---|---|
| Banana-strawberry twirl / Sealtest Light N' Lively | 110 |
| Chocolate / Sealtest Light N' Lively | 100 |
| Chocolate / Swift Light'n Easy | 110 |
| Coffee / Sealtest Light N' Lively | 100 |
| Fudge Twirl / Sealtest Light N' Lively | 100 |
| Neapolitan / Sealtest Light N' Lively | 100 |
| Peach / Sealtest Light N' Lively | 100 |
| Strawberry / Sealtest Light N' Lively | 100 |

|  | CALORIES |
|---|---|
| Strawberry / **Swift Light'n Easy** | 100 |
| Vanilla / **Sealtest Light N' Lively** | 100 |
| Vanilla / **Swift Light'n Easy** | 110 |
| Sherbet: ½ cup unless noted | |
| Lemon / **Sealtest** | 130 |
| Lemon-lime / **Sealtest** | 130 |
| Lime / **Meadow Gold** | 120 |
| Lime / **Sealtest** | 130 |
| Orange: 4 oz / **Howard Johnson's** | 133 |
| Orange / **Meadow Gold** | 120 |
| Orange / **Sealtest** | 130 |
| Pineapple / **Meadow Gold** | 130 |
| Pineapple / **Sealtest** | 130 |
| Rainbow / **Sealtest** | 130 |
| Red raspberry / **Sealtest** | 130 |
| Strawberry / **Sealtest** | 130 |

## ICE CREAM BARS

**1 bar or piece**

| | |
|---|---|
| Almond, toasted / **Good Humor** | 220 |
| Banana: 2½ fl oz bar / **Fudgsicle** | 102 |
| Chocolate: 2½ fl oz bar / **Bi-Sicle** | 112 |
| Chocolate: 2½ fl oz bar / **Fudgsicle** | 102 |
| Chocolate eclair / **Good Humor** | 220 |
| **Creamsicle** / 2½ fl oz bar | 78 |
| **Dreamsicle** / 2½ fl oz bar | 70 |
| **Drumstick,** ice cream | 181 |
| **Drumstick,** ice milk | 163 |
| Ice Whammy, assorted flavors / **Good Humor** | 50 |
| Orange cream: 2 fl oz bar / **Sealtest** | 70 |
| Orange Treat: 3 fl oz bar / **Sealtest** | 90 |
| **Popsicle,** all fruit flavors / 3 fl oz | 70 |
| Sandwich / **Good Humor** | 200 |
| Strawberry Shortcake / **Good Humor** | 200 |
| Whammy Assorted Ice Cream / **Good Humor** | 100 |
| Whammy Chip Crunch / **Good Humor** | 110 |
| Vanilla, chocolate coated / **Good Humor** | 170 |

# Italian Foods

*See also* Pizza and Spaghetti

CALORIES

| | |
|---|---:|
| Cannelloni Florentine w veal, spinach, cheese and sauce, frozen: 13 oz / **Weight Watchers** | 450 |
| Eggplant Parmigiana, frozen: 4 oz / **Buitoni** | 208 |
| Eggplant Parmigiana, frozen: 13 oz / **Weight Watchers** | 280 |
| Lasagna | |
|     Canned: 10 oz / **Hormel** | 370 |
|     Canned: 7½ oz can / **Hormel Short Orders** | 270 |
|     Frozen: 4 oz / **Buitoni** 26 oz | 120 |
|     Frozen: 4 oz / **Buitoni** Family Size | 168 |
|     Frozen: 7 oz / **Green Giant** Oven Bake Entrees | 300 |
|     Frozen: 9 oz / **Green Giant** Boil-in-Bag Entrees | 310 |
|     Frozen: 10½ oz / **Stouffer's** | 385 |
|     Frozen: 1 entree / **Swanson** Hungry-Man | 540 |
|     Frozen w cheese, veal and sauce: 13 oz / **Weight Watchers** | 350 |
|     Frozen w meat sauce: 4 oz / **Buitoni** 14 oz | 168 |
|     Mix, prepared: 1/5 pkg / **Golden Grain** Stir-n-Serv | 140 |
| Manicotti, frozen w sauce: 4 oz / **Buitoni** | 176 |
| Manicotti, frozen wo sauce: 4 oz / **Buitoni** | 196 |
| Ravioli | |
|     Beef, in sauce, canned: 7½ oz / **Franco-American** | 220 |
|     Beef, in sauce, canned: 7½ oz / **Franco-American** Raviolos | 220 |
|     Cheese, canned: ½ can / **Buitoni** | 204 |
|     Cheese, frozen: 4 oz / **Buitoni** 12 Count Round | 272 |

CALORIES

| | |
|---|---:|
| Cheese, frozen: 4 oz / **Buitoni** 40 Count | 316 |
| Meat, canned: ½ can / **Buitoni** | 224 |
| Meat, frozen: 4 oz / **Buitoni** 40 Count | 340 |
| Meat, frozen: 4 oz / **Buitoni** Raviolettes | 340 |
| Ravioli Parmigiana, cheese, frozen: | |
|    4 oz / **Buitoni** | 152 |
| Ravioli Parmigiana, meat, frozen: | |
|    4 oz / **Buitoni** | 192 |
| Rotini in tomato sauce, canned: | |
|    7½ oz / **Franco-American** | 200 |
| Rotini and meatballs, in tomato sauce, canned: | |
|    7¼ oz / **Franco-American** | 230 |
| Sausage and peppers w rigati, frozen: | |
|    4 oz / **Buitoni** | 164 |
| Shells w sauce, frozen: 4 oz / **Buitoni** | 136 |
| Shrimp Marinara w shells, frozen: | |
|    4 oz / **Buitoni** | 116 |
| Spaghetti, in sauce w veal: | |
|    1 entree / **Swanson** "TV" 8¼ oz | 290 |
| Veal Parmigiana | |
|    Frozen: 5 oz / **Banquet** Cookin' Bag | 287 |
|    Frozen: 7 oz / **Green Giant** | |
|       Oven Bake Entrees | 310 |
|    Frozen w spaghetti twists: 4 oz / **Buitoni** | 160 |
|    Frozen w tomato sauce: | |
|       32 oz / **Banquet** Buffet Supper | 1563 |
|    Frozen w zucchini: | |
|       9½ oz / **Weight Watchers** | 230 |
| Ziti, baked w sauce, frozen: 4 oz / **Buitoni** | 136 |
| Ziti w veal and sauce, frozen: | |
|    13 oz / **Weight Watchers** | 350 |

# Jams, Jellies, Preserves, Butters, Marmalade

CALORIES

**Butters**

| | |
|---|---:|
| Apple: 1 tbsp / **Bama** | 31 |
| Apple, cider: 1 tsp / **Smucker's** | 13 |
| Apple, spiced: 1 tsp / **Smucker's** | 13 |
| Peach: 1 tsp / **Smucker's** | 15 |

**Jams**

| | |
|---|---:|
| All flavors: 1 tsp / **Ann Page** | 17 |
| All flavors: 1 tsp / **Kraft** | 16 |
| All flavors: 1 tsp / **Smucker's** | 18 |
| All flavors, imitation: | |
|   1 tsp / **Smucker's Slenderella** Low Calorie | 8 |
| Apricot: 1 tbsp / **Bama** | 51 |
| Apricot-pineapple, swt: | |
|   1 tbsp / **Diet Delight** | 21 |
| Blackberry, swt: 1 tbsp / **Diet Delight** | 21 |
| Blackberry, swt: 1 tbsp / **S and W Nutradiet** | 10 |
| Peach: 1 tbsp / **Bama** | 51 |
| Pear: 1 tbsp / **Bama** | 51 |
| Plum: 1 tbsp / **Bama** | 51 |
| Raspberry, swt: 1 tbsp / **Diet Delight** | 21 |
| Raspberry, art swt: 1 tbsp / **S and W Nutradiet** | 10 |
| Strawberry, swt: 1 tbsp / **Diet Delight** | 18 |
| Strawberry, art swt: | |
|   1 tbsp / **S and W Nutradiet** | 12 |
| Strawberry, imitation, art swt: | |
|   1 tsp / **Smucker's** | 1 |

CALORIES

Jellies

| | |
|---|---:|
| All flavors: 1 tsp / **Ann Page** | 17.5 |
| All flavors: 1 tbsp / **Bama** | 51 |
| All flavors: 1 tsp / **Empress** | 18 |
| All flavors: 1 tsp / **Kraft** | 16 |
| All flavors except low calorie: | |
|   1 tbsp / **Kraft** | 47 |
| All flavors: 1 tsp / **Smucker's** | 18 |
| All flavors, imitation: 1 tsp / **Smucker's** | |
|   **Slenderella** Low Calorie | 8 |
| Apple: 1 tbsp / **Kraft** Low Calorie | 22 |
| Apple, swt: 1 tbsp / **Diet Delight** | 22 |
| Apple, art swt: 1 tbsp / **S and W Nutradiet** | 13 |
| Blackberry-apple: 1 tbsp / **Kraft** | |
|   Low Calorie | 22 |
| Blackberry, imitation: ⅜ oz / **Smucker's** | |
|   Single Service | 4 |
| Cherry, imitation: ⅜ oz / **Smucker's** | |
|   Single Service | 4 |
| Grape: 1 tsp / **Home Brands** | 18 |
| Grape: 1 tbsp / **Kraft** Low Calorie | 22 |
| Grape, swt: 1 tbsp / **Diet Delight** | 21 |
| Grape, art swt: 1 tbsp / **S and W Nutradiet** | 10 |
| Grape, imitation: 1 tsp / **Kraft** Low Calorie | 6 |
| Grape, imitation, art swt: 1 tsp / **Smucker's** | 1 |
| Grape, imitation, art swt: ⅜ oz / | |
|   **Smucker's** Single Service | 4 |

Marmalade

| | |
|---|---:|
| All flavors: 1 tsp / **Ann Page** | 18 |
| Orange: 1 tbsp / **Bama** | 54 |
| Orange: 1 tbsp / **Kraft** | 54 |
| Orange: 1 tbsp / **Kraft** Low Calorie | 25 |
| Orange: 1 tsp / **Smucker's** | 18 |
| Orange, art swt: 1 tbsp / **S and W Nutradiet** | 11 |
| Orange, imitation: 1 tsp / **Smucker's** | |
|   **Slenderella** Low Calorie | 8 |

Preserves

| | |
|---|---:|
| All flavors: 1 tsp / **Ann Page** | 18 |

CALORIES

| | |
|---|---:|
| All flavors: 1 tsp / **Empress** | 18 |
| All flavors: 1 tsp / **Kraft** | 16 |
| All flavors: 1 tbsp / **Kraft** Regular | 55 |
| All flavors: 1 tsp / **Smucker's** | 18 |
| Apricot: 1 tbsp / **Bama** | 51 |
| Apricot-pineapple, art swt: 1 tbsp / **S and W Nutradiet** | 10 |
| Boysenberry, art swt: 1 tbsp / **S and W Nutradiet** | 11 |
| Cherry, art swt: 1 tbsp / **S and W Nutradiet** | 11 |
| Peach: 1 tbsp / **Bama** | 51 |
| Peach: 1 tbsp / **Kraft** Low Calorie | 25 |
| Pear: 1 tbsp / **Bama** | 51 |
| Plum: 1 tbsp / **Bama** | 51 |
| Raspberry, black: 1 tbsp / **Kraft** Low Calorie | 25 |
| Strawberry: 1 tsp / **Home Brands** | 18 |
| Strawberry, imitation: 1 tsp / **Kraft** Low Calorie | 6 |

Spreads

| | |
|---|---:|
| All fruit flavors: 1 tsp / **Smucker's** Low Sugar | 8 |
| All fruit flavors: 1 tsp / **Tillie Lewis** | 4 |

# Liqueurs and Brandies

| | CALORIES |
|---|---|
| **Brandies: 1 fl oz** | |
| **Leroux Deluxe** | 67 |
| Apricot / **Leroux** | 92 |
| Blackberry / **Leroux** | 91 |
| Blackberry / **Leroux Polish** type | 92 |
| Cherry / **Leroux** | 91 |
| Cherry / **Leroux Kirschwasser** | 80 |
| Coffee / **Leroux** | 91 |
| Ginger / **Leroux** | 76 |
| Peach / **Leroux** | 93 |
| Liqueurs: 1 fl oz | |
| Ancsone / **Leroux** | 86 |
| Anisette / **Leroux** | 89 |
| Apricot / **Leroux** | 85 |
| Aquavit / **Leroux** | 75 |
| Banana / **Leroux** | 92 |
| Blackberry / **Leroux** | 78 |
| Cherry / **Kijafa** | 49 |
| Cherry / **Leroux** | 80 |
| Cherry / **Leroux Cherry Karise** | 71 |
| Chocolate, cherry / **Cheri-Suisse** | 90 |
| Chocolate, minted / **Vandermint** | 90 |
| Chocolate, orange / **Sabra** | 91 |
| Claristine / **Leroux** | 114 |
| Coffee / **Pasha Turkish Coffee** | 97 |
| Creme de Cacao, brown / **Leroux** | 101 |
| Creme de Cacao, white / **Leroux** | 98 |
| Creme de Cafe / **Leroux** | 104 |

CALORIES

| | |
|---|---|
| Creme de Cassis / **Leroux** | 88 |
| Creme de Menthe, green / **Leroux** | 110 |
| Creme de Menthe, white / **Leroux** | 101 |
| Creme de Noya / **Leroux** | 108 |
| Curacao / **Leroux** | 88 |
| Gold-O-Mint / **Leroux** | 110 |
| Grenadine / **Leroux** | 81 |
| Kummel / **Leroux** | 75 |
| **Lochan Ora** Scotch | 89 |
| Maraschino / **Leroux** | 88 |
| Peach / **Leroux** | 85 |
| Peppermint Schnapps / **Leroux** | 87 |
| Raspberry / **Leroux** | 74 |
| Rock and Rye / **Leroux** | 91 |
| Rock and Rye–Irish Moss / **Leroux** | 110 |
| Sloe gin / **Leroux** | 74 |
| Strawberry / **Leroux** | 74 |
| Triple Sec / **Leroux** | 102 |

# Macaroni

|  | CALORIES |
|---|---|
| plain, cooked to firm stage "al dente": | |
|   1 cup | 192 |
| plain, cooked to tender stage: | |
|   1 cup | 155 |
| and beef, in tomato sauce, canned: | |
|   7½ oz / **Franco-American** Beefy Mac | 220 |
| and beef, frozen: | |
|   32 oz / **Banquet** Buffet Supper | 1000 |
| and beef w tomato sauce, frozen: | |
|   9 oz / **Green Giant** Boil-in-Bag Entrees | 240 |
| and beef w tomatoes, frozen: | |
|   ½ pkg / **Stouffer's** 11½ oz | 190 |
| and cheese | |
|   Canned: 7¼ oz / **Franco-American** | 180 |
|   Canned: 7½ oz can / **Hormel Short Orders** | 340 |
|   Frozen: 8 oz / **Banquet** | 279 |
|   Frozen: 32 oz / **Banquet** Buffet Supper | 1027 |
|   Frozen: 8 oz / **Banquet** Cookin' Bag | 261 |
|   Frozen: 9 oz / **Green Giant** Boil-in-Bag Entrees | 330 |
|   Frozen: 8 oz / **Green Giant** Oven Bake Entrees | 290 |
|   Frozen: 10 oz / **Howard Johnson's** | 541 |
|   Frozen: 19 oz / **Howard Johnson's** | 1028 |
|   Frozen: 1 pkg / **Morton** Casserole | 280 |
|   Frozen: ½ pkg / **Stouffer's** 12 oz | 260 |
|   Frozen / **Swanson** 7 oz | 230 |
|   Mix, dry: 1.8 oz / **Ann Page** | 190 |

CALORIES

| | |
|---|---:|
| Mix, prepared: ¼ pkg / **Betty Crocker** | 310 |
| Mix, prepared: 1 pouch / **Betty Crocker** Mug-O-Lunch | 240 |
| Mix, prepared: ¼ pkg / **Golden Grain** Macaroni and Cheddar | 200 |
| Mix, prepared: ¾ cup / **Kraft** | 280 |
| Mix, prepared: ½ cup / **Pennsylvania Dutch Brand** | 160 |
| and meatballs, in tomato sauce, canned: 7½ oz / **Franco-American** Meatball Mac | 220 |

# Mayonnaise

CALORIES

**1 tbsp**

| | |
|---|---:|
| **Ann Page** | 100 |
| **Best** | 100 |
| **Hellmann's** | 100 |
| **Kraft** Real | 100 |
| **Mrs. Filbert's** Real | 100 |
| **Nu Made** | 100 |
| **Piedmont** | 100 |
| **Sultana** | 100 |
| Flavored / **Durkee** Famous Sauce | 69 |
| Imitation | |
|    **Mrs. Filbert's** | 40 |
|    **Piedmont** | 50 |
|    **Weight Watchers** | 40 |
| Miracle Whip / **Kraft** | 70 |
| w relish / **Mrs. Filbert's** Relish Spread | 80 |

# Meat

## FRESH

|  | CALORIES |
|---|---|
| Beaver, roasted: 3 oz | 211 |
| Beef, ground, lean (10% fat), raw: 4 oz | 202 |
| Beef, ground, regular (21% fat), raw: 4 oz | 303 |
| Beef, roast, oven-cooked, no liquid added: | |
| relatively fat, such as rib: | |
| 3 oz lean and fat | 375 |
| 1.8 oz lean only | 125 |
| relatively lean, such as heel of round: | |
| 3 oz lean and fat | 165 |
| 2.7 oz lean only | 125 |
| Brains, all varieties, raw: 4 oz | 141 |
| Hamburger (ground beef), broiled: | |
| 3 lean oz | 185 |
| 3 regular oz | 245 |
| Heart | |
| Beef, lean, cooked: 4 oz | 212 |
| Beef, lean, raw: 4 oz | 122 |
| Calf, cooked: 4 oz | 235 |
| Calf, raw: 4 oz | 140 |
| Lamb, cooked: 4 oz | 294 |
| Lamb, raw: 4 oz | 183 |
| Kidney, beef, cooked: 4 oz | 285 |
| Kidney, beef, raw: 4 oz | 147 |
| Kidney, lamb, raw: 4 oz | 119 |
| Lamb,* cooked: | |
| Chop, 4.8 oz thick w bone, broiled | 400 |
| 4.0 oz lean and fat, broiled | 400 |
| 2.6 oz lean only, broiled | 140 |
| Leg, roasted: | |
| 3 oz lean and fat | 235 |

* Outer layer of fat on cut removed to within approx ½ in of lean.

|  |  |
|---|---|
| 2.5 oz lean only | 130 |
| Shoulder, roasted: | |
| 3 oz lean and fat | 285 |
| 2.3 oz lean only | 130 |
| **Liver** | |
| Beef, fried: 4 oz | 259 |
| Beef, raw: 4 oz | 158 |
| Calf, fried: 4 oz | 295 |
| Calf, raw: 4 oz | 158 |
| Lamb, broiled: 4 oz | 295 |
| Lamb, raw: 4 oz | 154 |
| **Pork, fresh,* cooked:** | |
| Chop, 3.5 oz thick w bone | 260 |
| 2.3 oz lean and fat | 260 |
| 1.7 lean only | 130 |
| Roast, oven-cooked, no liquid added: | |
| 3 oz lean and fat | 310 |
| 2.4 oz lean only | 175 |
| Cuts, simmered: | |
| 3 oz lean and fat | 320 |
| 2.2 oz lean only | 135 |
| Quail: 8 oz dressed, ready to cook | 343 |
| Rabbit, domesticated: 1 lb dressed, ready to cook | 581 |
| Rabbit, wild: 1 lb dressed, ready to cook | 490 |
| **Steak, broiled** | |
| relatively fat such as sirloin: | |
| 3 oz lean and fat | 330 |
| 2 oz lean only | 115 |
| relatively lean such as round: | |
| 3 oz lean and fat | 220 |
| 2.4 oz lean only | 130 |
| **Sweetbreads, 4 oz cooked** | |
| Beef | 362 |
| Calf | 190 |
| Lamb | 198 |
| Tongue, beef, cooked: 4 oz | 276 |

* Outer layer of fat on cut removed to within approx ½ in of lean.

CALORIES

| | |
|---|---|
| Tongue, calf, cooked: 4 oz | 181 |
| Tongue, lamb, cooked: 4 oz | 287 |
| Veal, med fat, cooked, bone removed: | |
|     Cutlet, 3 oz | 185 |
|     Roast, 3 oz | 230 |

## CANNED, CURED, PROCESSED

| | |
|---|---|
| Bacon, cooked | |
|     **Hormel Black Label** / 1 slice | 35 |
|     **Hormel Range Brand** / 1 slice | 45 |
|     **Hormel Red Label** / 1 slice | 37 |
|     **Oscar Mayer** / 1 slice | 40 |
|     **Swift Lazy Maple** / 1 slice | 40 |
|     **Swift Premium** / 1 slice | 40 |
|     **Wilson's** Certified / 1 oz | 169 |
|     Canadian: 1 slice / **Oscar Mayer** | 40 |
|     Canadian: 1 oz / **Wilson's** Certified | 42 |
| Bacon bits, canned, cooked: 1 oz / **Wilson's** | 140 |
| Banquet loaf: 1 slice / **Eckrich** 8 oz pkg | 75 |
| Banquet loaf: 1 slice / **Eckrich** Beef Smorgas Pac | 105 |
| Bar-B-Q Loaf: 1 slice / **Oscar Mayer** | 50 |
| Beef, chopped: 1 slice / **Eckrich** Slender-Sliced | 40 |
| Beef, chopped, canned: 1 oz / **Wilson's** | |
|     Certified Bif | 91 |
| Beef, corned, canned: 3 oz / **Dinty Moore** | 190 |
| Beef, corned, canned: 2.3 oz / **Libby's** | 240 |
| Beef, corned, canned: 1 oz / **Safeway** | 35 |
| Beef, corned brisket, cooked: 3½ oz / | |
|     **Swift** Premium for Oven Roasting | 270 |
| Beef, corned brisket, canned: 1 oz / | |
|     **Wilson's** Certified | 45 |
| Beef, corned, chopped: 1 slice / | |
|     **Eckrich** Slender-Sliced | 40 |
| Beef, dried, chunked and formed: | |
|     ¾ oz / **Swift** Premium | 35 |
| Beef, smoked, sliced: 1 oz / **Safeway** | 35 |
| Beef, smoked, sliced: 1 oz / **Safeway** Spicy | 40 |
| Beef roast, canned: 1 oz / **Wilson's** Certified | 33 |

CALORIES

| | |
|---|---:|
| Beef steaks, breaded, frozen: 4 oz / **Hormel** | 370 |
| Bologna | |
|     **Eckrich** 12 oz pkg / 1 slice | 95 |
|     **Eckrich** 16 oz pkg / 1 slice | 95 |
|     **Eckrich** Smorgas Pac / 1 slice | 90 |
|     **Eckrich** thick-sliced / 1 slice (12 oz pkg) | 160 |
|     **Eckrich** thick-sliced / 1 slice (16 oz pkg) | 170 |
|     **Hormel** / 1 oz | 85 |
|     **Swift** Premium / 1 oz | 95 |
|     **Wilson's** Certified / 1 oz | 87 |
|     Beef: 1 slice / **Eckrich** 8 oz pkg | 95 |
|     Beef: 1 slice / **Eckrich** 12 oz pkg | 95 |
|     Beef: 1 slice / **Eckrich** Beef Smorgas Pac | 70 |
|     Beef: 1 slice / **Oscar Mayer** | 70 |
|     Coarse ground: 1 oz / **Hormel** | 75 |
|     Fine ground: 1 oz / **Hormel** | 80 |
|     Garlic: 1 slice / **Eckrich** | 95 |
|     Ring: 2 oz / **Eckrich** | 200 |
|     Ring, garlic: 1 slice / **Eckrich** | 95 |
|     Ring, pickled: 2 oz / **Eckrich** | 190 |
| Braunschweiger: 1 oz / **Oscar Mayer** | 100 |
| Braunschweiger: 1 oz / **Wilson's** Certified | 90 |
| Breakfast strips: 1 strip / **Swift Sizzlean** | 50 |
| Frankfurters: 1 frank | |
|     **Eckrich** 12 oz pkg | 120 |
|     **Eckrich** Jumbo | 190 |
|     **Eckrich** Skinless 16 oz pkg | 150 |
|     **Hormel Range Brand Wranglers** | |
|       Smoked Franks | 180 |
|     **Hormel** Wieners 12 oz pkg | 105 |
|     **Hormel** Wieners 16 oz pkg | 140 |
|     **Oscar Mayer** Wieners | 140 |
|     **Wilson's** Certified Skinless | 139 |
|     Beef / **Eckrich** | 150 |
|     Beef / **Eckrich** Jumbo | 190 |
|     Beef / **Hormel** Wieners 12 oz pkg | 105 |
|     Beef / **Hormel** Wieners 16 oz pkg | 140 |
|     Beef / **Hormel Wranglers** Smoked Franks | 160 |

CALORIES

| | |
|---|---:|
| Beef / **Oscar Mayer** | 140 |
| Beef / **Wilson's** Certified | 136 |
| Frozen, batter-wrapped / **Hormel Corn Dogs** | 230 |
| Frozen, batter-wrapped / **Hormel Tater Dogs** | 190 |
| Gourmet Loaf: 1 slice / **Eckrich** | 40 |
| Gourmet Loaf: 1 slice / **Eckrich** Beef Smorgas Pac | 30 |
| Ham, luncheon type | |
|     Cooked: 1 slice / **Eckrich** | 40 |
|     Cooked: 1 oz / **Hormel** | 35 |
|     Cooked, sliced: 1 oz / **Safeway** | 50 |
|     Cooked, smoked: 1 slice / **Oscar Mayer** | 30 |
|     Chopped: 1 oz / **Hormel** | 70 |
|     Chopped: 2 oz / **Hormel** 8 lb can | 180 |
|     Chopped: 1 slice / **Oscar Mayer** | 65 |
|     Chopped, smoked: 1 slice / | |
|       **Eckrich** Slender-Sliced | 40 |
| Ham, whole, canned | |
|     **Oscar Mayer** Jubilee / 4 oz | 130 |
|     **Swift** Premium / 3½ oz | 220 |
|     **Swift** Premium Hostess / 3½ oz | 140 |
|     **Wilson's** Certified Boned and Rolled / 1 oz | 56 |
|     **Wilson's** Certified Fully Cooked / 1 oz | 48 |
|     **Wilson's** Certified Tender-Made / 1 oz | 44 |
| Ham, whole, plastic or other wrap | |
|     **Hormel** Bone-In / 6 oz | 310 |
|     **Hormel** Cure 81 / 6 oz | 290 |
|     **Hormel** Curemaster / 6 oz | 210 |
|     **Swift** Premium Hostess / 3½ oz | 150 |
|     Smoked, aged: | |
|       1 oz / **Wilson's** Certified Festival Ham | 48 |
| Ham slice, smoked: 4 oz / **Oscar Mayer** Jubilee | 140 |
| Ham steaks: 1 slice / **Oscar Mayer** Jubilee | 70 |
| Ham patties: 1 patty / **Hormel** | 200 |
| Ham patties: | |
|   1 patty / **Swift** Premium Brown 'n Serve | 250 |
| Ham and cheese loaf: 1 slice / **Oscar Mayer** | 75 |
| Honey loaf: 1 slice / **Eckrich** | 45 |
| Honey loaf: 1 slice / **Eckrich** Smorgas Pac | 45 |

| | |
|---|---|
| Honey loaf: 1 slice / **Oscar Mayer** | 40 |
| Liver, beef, thin sliced: | |
|   2.6 oz / **Swift's** Tru Tender | 140 |
| Liver cheese: 1 slice / **Oscar Mayer** | 110 |
| Luncheon meat: 1 slice / **Oscar Mayer** | 100 |
| Luncheon meat, spiced: 1 oz / **Hormel** | 80 |
| Old fashioned loaf: 1 slice / **Eckrich** | 75 |
| Old fashioned loaf: 1 slice / **Eckrich** Smorgas Pac | 75 |
| Old fashioned loaf: 1 slice / **Oscar Mayer** | 65 |
| Olive loaf: 1 slice / **Oscar Mayer** | 65 |
| Pastrami, chopped: 1 slice / **Eckrich** Slender-Sliced | 47 |
| Pastrami, sliced: 1 oz / **Safeway** | 40 |
| Pepperoni: 1 oz / **Swift** | 150 |
| Pepperoni, sliced: 1 oz / **Hormel** | 140 |
| Pickle loaf: 1 slice / **Eckrich** 8 oz pkg | 85 |
| Pickle loaf: 1 slice / **Eckrich** Smorgas Pac | 85 |
| Pickle loaf, beef: 1 slice / **Eckrich** Smorgas Pac | 65 |
| Pickle and pimento loaf: 1 slice / **Oscar Mayer** | 65 |
| Picnic, smoked: 1 oz / **Wilson's** Certified | 70 |
| Polish sausage: | |
|   1 link / **Eckrich** Polska Kielbasa Skinless | 190 |
| Polish sausage, ring: | |
|   2 oz / **Eckrich** Polska Kielbasa | 200 |
| Polish sausage ring: 3 oz / **Hormel** Kolbase | 240 |
| Polish sausage, smoked beef: 1 oz / **Frito-Lay** | 73 |
| Pork, chopped, canned: 1 oz / **Wilson's** Mor | 87 |
| Pork butt, cured smoked: | |
|   1 oz / **Wilson's** Certified Smoked Tasty Meat | 72 |
| Pork loin, chipped, smoked: | |
|   1 slice / **Eckrich** Slender-Sliced | 47 |
| Pork roast, canned: 1 oz / **Wilson's** Certified | 440 |
| Pork steaks, breaded, frozen: 3 oz / **Hormel** | 220 |
| Salami | |
|     **Hormel** Dairy Hard / 1 oz | 120 |
|     **Hormel** Di Lusso Genoa / 1 oz | 130 |
|     **Oscar Mayer** Beef Cotto / 1 slice | 50 |
|     **Oscar Mayer** for Beer / 1 slice | 50 |
|     **Oscar Mayer** Cotto / 1 slice | 50 |

| | |
|---|---:|
| **Oscar Mayer** Hard / 1 slice | 37 |
| **Swift** Premium Genoa / 1 oz | 120 |
| **Swift** Premium Hard / 1 oz | 110 |
| Sausage, beef, smoked: 2 oz / **Eckrich** | 190 |
| Sausage, pork bulk: 1 oz / **Wilson's** Certified | 135 |
| Sausage, pork, smoked: 3 oz / **Hormel** No-Link | 290 |

Sausage links

| | |
|---|---:|
| **Hormel** Brown 'n Serve / 1 sausage | 78 |
| **Hormel Little Sizzlers** / 1 sausage | 67 |
| **Hormel** Midget Links / 1 sausage | 112 |
| **Oscar Mayer** Little Friers / 1 link | 65 |
| **Swift's** The Original / 1 link | 75 |
| **Swift** Premium Bacon 'n Sausage / 1 link | 70 |
| **Swift** Premium Brown 'n Serve Kountry Kured / 1 link | 85 |
| Beef: 1 link / **Swift** Premium Brown 'n Serve | 85 |

Sausage links, smoked

| | |
|---|---:|
| **Eckrich** 16 oz pkg / 1 link | 190 |
| **Eckrich** Skinless / 1 link | 115 |
| **Eckrich** Smok-Y-Links / 1 link | 75 |
| **Eckrich** Skinless Smok-Y-Links / 1 link | 85 |
| **Hormel** Smokies / 1 sausage | 92 |
| **Oscar Mayer** / 1 link | 140 |
| **Wilson's** Certified Smokies / 1 oz | 84 |
| Beef: 1 link / **Eckrich** Smok-Y-Links | 75 |

Sausage sticks

| | |
|---|---:|
| Beef: 1¼ oz / **Slim Jim** Polish Sausage | 108 |
| Beef: ⅝ oz / **Cow-Boy Jo's** | 81 |
| Beef, smoked: ¼ oz / **Cow-Boy Jo's** Smok-O-Roni | 42 |
| Beef, smoked: ½ oz / **Slim Jim** | 83 |
| Pickled: 1¼ oz / **Lowrey's** Hot Sausage | 110 |
| Pickled: ⅝ oz / **Lowrey's** Polish Sausage | 50 |
| Scrapple, in tube: 1 oz / **Oscar Mayer** | 50 |
| Scrapple, Philadelphia style, canned: 1 oz / **Oscar Mayer** | 45 |
| **Spam**: 3 oz / **Hormel** | 260 |
| **Spam** w cheese chunks: 3 oz / **Hormel** | 260 |

CALORIES

| | |
|---|---|
| **Spam,** smoke-flavored: 3 oz / **Hormel** | 260 |
| Substitute, meat, BV in glass jars: | |
| 1 oz / **Wilson's** Certified | 43 |
| Summer sausage: | |
| 1 slice / **Oscar Mayer** Thuringer Cervelat | 70 |
| Summer sausage, beef: 1 slice / **Oscar Mayer** | 70 |
| Summer sausage, beef: 1 oz / **Swift** Premium | 90 |
| Thuringer: 1 oz / **Hormel Old Smokehouse** | 100 |
| Tripe, canned: 5 oz / **Libby's** | 173 |
| Veal steaks, frozen: 4 oz / **Hormel** | 130 |
| Veal steaks, breaded, frozen: 4 oz / **Hormel** | 240 |
| Vienna sausage, canned: 1 piece / **Hormel** | 52 |
| Vienna sausage, canned: 1 sausage / **Libby's** | 84 |
| Vienna sausage, canned, in barbecue sauce: | |
| 1 sausage / **Libby's** | 76 |

## MEAT ENTREES, CANNED

| | |
|---|---|
| Beef w barbecue sauce: 5 oz / **Morton House** | 240 |
| Beef, corned w cabbage: 8 oz / **Hormel** | 150 |
| Beef goulash: 7½ oz can / **Hormel Short Orders** | 240 |
| Beef, sliced w gravy: 6¼ oz can / **Morton House** | 190 |
| Beef stew | |
| **Dinty Moore** / 7½ oz | 180 |
| **Dinty Moore Short Orders** / 7½ oz | 180 |
| **Libby's** / 1 cup | 78 |
| **Morton House** / 8 oz | 240 |
| **Swanson** / 7½ oz | 190 |
| Hash, beef w potatoes: | |
| 7½ oz can / **Dinty Moore Short Orders** | 270 |
| Hash | |
| Corned beef: 7½ oz / **Ann Page** | 400 |
| Corned beef: 7½ oz / **Mary Kitchen** | 400 |
| Corned beef: 3 oz / **Libby's** | 156 |
| Corned beef: | |
| 7½ oz can / **Mary Kitchen Short Orders** | 385 |
| Roast beef: 7½ oz / **Mary Kitchen** | 390 |
| Roast beef: | |
| 7½ oz can / **Mary Kitchen Short Orders** | 355 |

| | |
|---|---:|
| Pork, sliced w gravy: 6¼ oz / **Morton House** | 190 |
| Salisbury steak w mushroom gravy: | |
|     4 1/6 oz / **Morton House** | 160 |
| Sloppy Joe: 7½ oz can / **Hormel Short Orders** | 365 |
| Sloppy Joe, beef: ⅓ cup / **Libby's** | 163 |
| Sloppy Joe, pork: ⅓ cup / **Libby's** | 139 |
| Stew, meatball: 6¼ oz / **Morton House** | 290 |
| Stew, meatball: 1 cup / **Libby's** | 121 |
| Stew, Mulligan: | |
|     7½ oz can / **Dinty Moore Short Orders** | 240 |

## MEAT ENTREES, FROZEN

| | |
|---|---:|
| Beef, chipped, creamed: | |
|     5 oz / **Banquet** Cookin' Bag | 124 |
| Beef, chipped, creamed: 1 pkg / **Stouffer's** 5½ oz | 235 |
| Beef, sirloin, chopped w green beans, cauliflower | |
|     and sauce: 9½ oz / **Weight Watchers** | 560 |
| Beef, sliced: 1 entree / **Swanson** Hungry-Man | 330 |
| Beef, sliced w barbecue sauce: | |
|     5 oz / **Banquet** Cookin' Bag | 126 |
| Beef, sliced w gravy: | |
|     32 oz / **Banquet** Buffet Supper | 782 |
| Beef, sliced w gravy: 5 oz / **Banquet** Cookin' Bag | 116 |
| Beef, sliced w gravy: | |
|     5 oz / **Green Giant** Boil-in-Bag Toast Toppers | 130 |
| Beef, sliced w gravy and whipped potatoes: | |
|     1 entree / **Swanson** "TV" | 190 |
| Beef stroganoff: 1 pkg / **Stouffer's** 9¾ oz | 390 |
| Green pepper steak: 1 pkg / **Stouffer's** 10½ oz | 350 |
| Meat loaf | |
|     **Banquet** Buffet Supper / 32 oz | 1445 |
|     **Banquet** Cookin' Bag / 5 oz | 224 |
|     **Banquet** Man Pleaser / 19 oz | 916 |
|     **Morton** Country Table / 1 entree | 430 |
|     w tomato sauce and whipped potatoes: | |
|         1 entree / **Swanson** "TV" | 330 |
| Meatballs w gravy and whipped potatoes: | |
|     1 entree / **Swanson** "TV" | 330 |

CALORIES

| | |
|---|---|
| Noodles and beef: 32 oz / **Banquet** Buffet Supper | 754 |
| Salisbury steak | |
|     **Banquet** Man Pleaser / 19 oz | 873 |
|     **Morton** Country Table / 1 entree | 490 |
|     **Stouffer's** 12 oz / ½ pkg | 250 |
|     **Swanson** Hungry-Man / 1 entree | 640 |
|     w crinkle-cut potatoes: 1 entree / | |
|        **Swanson** "TV" | 370 |
|     w gravy: 32 oz / **Banquet** Buffet Supper | 1454 |
|     w gravy: 5 oz / **Banquet** Cookin' Bag | 246 |
|     w gravy: 7 oz / **Green Giant** Oven Bake | |
|        Entrees | 290 |
|     w tomato sauce: 9 oz / **Green Giant** | |
|        Boil-in-Bag Entrees | 390 |
| Sausage, cheese and tomato pies: | |
|     7 oz / **Weight Watchers** | 390 |
| Sloppy Joe: 5 oz / **Banquet** Cookin' Bag | 199 |
| Sloppy Joe: 5 oz / **Green Giant** Boil-in-Bag | |
|     Toast Toppers | 160 |
| Steak, beef, chopped w carrots, green peppers and | |
|     mushroom sauce: 10 oz / **Weight Watchers** | 390 |
| Stew, beef: 32 oz / **Banquet** Buffet Supper | 700 |
| Stew, beef: 9 oz / **Green Giant** Boil-in-Bag | |
|     Entrees | 160 |
| Stew, beef: 1 pkg / **Stouffer's** 10 oz | 310 |
| Stew, beef w biscuits: 7 oz / **Green Giant** | |
|     Oven Bake Entrees | 190 |
| Stuffed cabbage w beef, in tomato sauce: | |
|     7 oz / **Green Giant** Oven Bake Entrees | 220 |
| Stuffed green pepper w beef: | |
|     7 oz / **Green Giant** Oven Bake Entrees | 200 |

## MEAT SUBSTITUTES

| | |
|---|---|
| Breakfast links: 1 link / **Morningstar Farms** | 62 |
| Breakfast patties: 1 pattie / **Morningstar Farms** | 111 |
| Breakfast strips: 1 strip / **Morningstar Farms** | 38 |

Grillers: 1 griller / **Morningstar Farms**          211
Luncheon slices: 1 slice / **Morningstar Farms**          25

# Mexican Foods

CALORIES

Beans
    Pinto, in chili sauce, canned:
        4 oz / **Old El Paso** Mexe Beans          124
        Refried, canned: 4 oz / **Old El Paso**          108
    Refried, canned:
        ½ cup / **Ortega** Lightly Spicy          170
        Refried, canned: ½ cup / **Ortega** True Bean          170
Burritos, beef, canned: 4 oz / **Hormel**          220
Chiles, diced, canned: 1 oz / **Ortega**          7
Chiles, in strips, canned: 1 oz / **Ortega**          7
Chiles, whole, canned: 1 oz / **Ortega**          7
Chili con carne, canned
    w beans: 8 oz / **A & P**          440
    w beans: 7½ oz / **Hormel**          320
    w beans: 7½ oz can / **Hormel Short Orders**          320
    w beans: 1 cup / **Libby's**          178
    w beans: 7½ oz / **Morton House**          340
    w beans: 7¾ oz / **Swanson**          310
    w beans, hot: 7½ oz can /
        **Hormel Short Orders**          320
    w beans, low sodium: 7¾ oz / **Campbell**          310
    wo beans: 7½ oz / **Hormel**          340
    wo beans: 7½ oz can / **Hormel Short Orders**          340
    wo beans: 1 cup / **Libby's**          130
    wo beans: 7½ oz / **Morton House**          340
Chili Mac, canned:
    7½ oz can / **Hormel Short Orders**          220

CALORIES

Enchiladas
  Canned, beef w chili gravy:
    4 oz / **Old El Paso**    200
  Frozen: 1 dinner / **El Chico**    880
  Frozen, beef w cheese and chili gravy:
    32 oz / **Banquet** Buffet Supper    1118
  Frozen, beef and cheese w gravy:
    3 enchiladas / **El Chico**    710
  Frozen, beef w gravy:
    3 enchiladas / **El Chico**    710
  Frozen, beef w sauce:
    6 oz / **Banquet** Cookin' Bag    207
Mexican dinner, frozen: 1 dinner / **El Chico**    1080
Queso dinner, frozen: 1 dinner / **El Chico**    810
Pepper, hot, diced, canned: 1 oz / **Ortega**    8
Peppers, hot, whole, canned: 1 oz / **Ortega**    8
Salsa, green chile, canned: 1 oz / **Ortega**    7
Saltillo dinner, frozen: 1 dinner / **El Chico**    930
Tacos, beef, frozen: 3 tacos / **El Chico**    410
Tacos, prepared: 1 taco / **Ortega**    220
Taco shell: 1 shell / **Lawry's**    48
Taco shell: 1 shell / **Ortega**    50
Tamales
  Canned: 4 oz / **Old El Paso**    160
  Beef, canned: 1 tamale / **Hormel**    70
  Beef, canned:
    7½ oz can / **Hormel Short Orders**    320
  Beef, in jar: 2 tamales / **Swift** Derby    240
Tomatoes and hot green chiles, canned:
  1 oz / **Ortega**    7
Tostada dinner mix:
  1 complete pkg (shells, sauce, seasonings) /
  **Lawry's** Tostada Kit    1041
Tostada shells: 1 shell / **Lawry's**    48

# Milk

CALORIES

| | |
|---|---:|
| Buttermilk: 8 fl oz (1 cup) | |
| .1% fat / **Borden** | 88 |
| .2% fat / **Sealtest** Skim milk | 71 |
| .5% fat / **Borden** | 90 |
| .5% fat / **Meadow Gold** | 105 |
| .8% fat / **Golden Nugget** | 92 |
| .8% fat / **Light n' Lively** | 95 |
| 1% fat / **Borden** | 107 |
| 1.5% fat / **Borden** | 110 |
| 1.4% fat / **Friendship** | 120 |
| 1.5% fat / **Lucerne** | 120 |
| 2% fat / **Borden** | 122 |
| 2% fat / **Sealtest** Lowfat | 114 |
| 3.5% fat / **Borden** | 158 |
| Condensed, swt: ¼ cup / **Borden** Dime Brand | 252 |
| Condensed, swt: ¼ cup / **Borden** Eagle Brand | 250 |
| Condensed, swt: | |
| ¼ cup / **Borden** Magnolia Brand | 252 |
| Dry, nonfat | |
| ¼ cup / **Carnation** | 61 |
| Reconstituted: 8 oz glass / **Borden** | 82 |
| Reconstituted: 8 oz glass / **Carnation** | 81 |
| Reconstituted: 8 oz glass / **Lucerne** | 80 |
| Reconstituted: 8 oz glass / **Sannalec** | 82 |
| Evaporated, canned: 8 fl oz (1 cup) | |
| **Carnation** | 348 |
| **Carnation** Skimmed | 192 |
| **Lucerne** | 345 |
| **Pet** / ½ cup | 170 |
| Evaporated skim: ½ cup / **Pet** | 100 |
| Imitation milk: 8 fl oz / **Lucerne** | 150 |
| Skim or low-fat: 8 fl oz | |
| 0% fat / **Lucerne** | 90 |
| .1% fat / **Borden** | 81 |

CALORIES

| | |
|---|---:|
| .1% fat / **Sealtest** | 79 |
| .4% fat / **Sealtest** Diet Skim | 103 |
| .5% fat / **Meadow Gold** | 87 |
| 1% fat / **Lucerne** 1-10 | 110 |
| 2% fat / **Lucerne** 2-10 | 130 |
| 2% fat / **Meadow Gold** Viva | 137 |
| Fortified, .1% fat / **Borden** | 81 |
| Fortified, .1% fat / **Gail Borden** | 81 |
| Fortified, 1% fat / **Light n' Lively** Lowfat | 114 |
| Fortified, 1.75% fat / **Borden** Lite Line | 117 |
| Fortified, 2% fat / **Borden** Hi-Protein | 132 |
| Fortified, 2% fat / **Sealtest** Vita-lure | 137 |

Whole: 8 fl oz

| | |
|---|---:|
| 3.25% fat / **Sealtest** | 144 |
| 3.3% fat / **Meadow Gold** | 166 |
| 3.5% fat / **Borden** | 160 |
| 3.5% fat / **Lucerne** | 160 |
| 3.5% fat / **Sealtest** | 151 |
| 3.7% fat / **Borden** Cream Line | 159 |
| 3.7% fat / **Sealtest** | 157 |
| 3.8% fat / **Lucerne** | 170 |
| Fortified / **Sealtest** Multivitamin Milk | 151 |

## FLAVORED MILK BEVERAGES

| | |
|---|---:|
| All flavors, canned: 10 fl oz / **Carnation** Slender | 225 |
| All flavors, mix: 1 env / **Lucerne** Instant Breakfast | 290 |
| Cherry-vanilla, canned: | |
| 8 fl oz / **Borden** Milk Shake | 291 |
| Chocolate, canned: 9½ fl oz / **Borden's** Dutch | 232 |
| Chocolate, dairy pack, 3.5% fat: | |
| 8 fl oz / **Borden's** Dutch Chocolate Milk | 210 |
| Chocolate fudge, canned: | |
| 8 fl oz / **Borden's** Frosted Shake | 284 |
| Chocolate mixes | |
| **Carnation** Instant Breakfast / 1 env | 130 |
| **Carnation** Slender / 1 env | 110 |
| **Ovaltine** / ¾ oz | 80 |
| **PDQ** / 3½ tsp | 65 |

CALORIES

| | |
|---|---:|
| **Pillsbury** Instant Breakfast / 1 pouch | 290 |
| **Safeway** / 2 tsp dry | 90 |
| **Safeway** (w 8 fl oz whole milk) / 2 tsp | 215 |
| Dutch, mix: 1 env / **Carnation** Slender | 110 |
| Malt, mix: 2 heaping tsp / **Borden** | 77 |
| Malt, mix: | |
|   1 env / **Carnation** Instant Breakfast | 130 |
| Malt, mix: 1 env / **Carnation** Slender | 110 |
| Malt, mix, prepared: | |
|   1 pouch / **Pillsbury** Instant Breakfast | 290 |
| Coffee | |
|   Canned: 8 fl oz / **Borden's** Frosted Shake | 286 |
|   Canned: 8 fl oz / **Borden's** Milk Shake | 291 |
|   Mix: 1 env / **Carnation** Instant Breakfast | 130 |
|   Mix: 1 env / **Carnation** Slender | 110 |
| Eggnog | |
|   Dairy case, 4.7% fat: ½ cup / **Borden** | 132 |
|   Dairy case, 6% fat: ½ cup / **Borden** | 151 |
|   Dairy case, 8% fat: ½ cup / **Borden** | 171 |
|   Mix: 1 env / **Carnation** Instant Breakfast | 130 |
|   Mix: 2 heaping tbsp / **PDQ** | 113 |
| Malt-flavored | |
|   Instant: 3 heaping tsp / **Carnation** | 90 |
|   Mix: 2 heaping tsp / **Borden** | 80 |
|   Mix: ¾ oz / **Ovaltine** | 80 |
|   Chocolate, instant: 3 heaping tsp / **Carnation** | 85 |
| Mocha, canned: 8 fl oz / **Borden's** Milk Shake | 291 |
| Strawberry | |
|   Canned: 8 fl oz / **Borden's** Frosted Shake | 283 |
|   Canned: 8 fl oz / **Borden's** Milk Shake | 291 |
|   Mix: 1 env / **Carnation** Instant Breakfast | 130 |
|   Mix: 3½ tsp / **PDQ** | 60 |
|   Mix, prepared: | |
|     1 pouch / **Pillsbury** Instant Breakfast | 290 |
|   Wild, mix: 1 env / **Carnation** Slender | 110 |
| Vanilla | |
|   Canned: 8 fl oz / **Borden's** Frosted Shake | 291 |
|   Mix: 1 env / **Carnation** Instant Breakfast | 130 |

CALORIES

| | |
|---|---|
| Mix, prepared: | |
| 1 pouch / **Pillsbury** Instant Breakfast | 290 |
| French, mix: 1 env / **Carnation** Slender | 110 |

# Muffins: English and Sweet

CALORIES

**1 muffin unless noted**

| | |
|---|---|
| Apple cinnamon, mix, prepared / **Betty Crocker** | 160 |
| Apple cinnamon, refrigerator, to bake / **Pillsbury** | 130 |
| Banana nut, mix, prepared / | |
|    **Betty Crocker** Chiquita | 180 |
| Blueberry | |
|    **Thomas'** Toast-R-Cakes | 110 |
|    Frozen / **Howard Johnson's** Toasties | 121 |
|    Frozen / **Morton** | 120 |
|    Frozen / **Morton** Rounds | 110 |
|    Frozen / **Pepperidge Farm** | 130 |
|    Mix, prepared / **Betty Crocker** | 120 |
| Bran / **Oroweat** Bran'nola | 160 |
| Bran / **Thomas'** Toast-R-Cakes | 120 |
| Corn | |
|    **Thomas'** | 190 |
|    **Thomas'** Toast-R-Cakes | 120 |
|    Frozen / **Howard Johnson's** Toasties | 112 |
|    Frozen / **Morton** | 130 |
|    Frozen / **Morton** Rounds | 130 |
|    Frozen / **Pepperidge Farm** | 140 |
|    Frozen / **Thomas'** Toast-R-Cakes | 120 |
|    Mix, prepared / **Betty Crocker** | 160 |
|    Mix, prepared / **Flako** | 140 |

| | |
|---|---|
| Refrigerator, to bake / **Pillsbury** | 130 |
| English | |
| **Arnold** | 130 |
| **Earth Grains** / 2⅓ oz | 160 |
| **Home Pride** | 140 |
| **Pepperidge Farm** | 130 |
| **Thomas'** | 130 |
| **Wonder** | 130 |
| Frozen / **Thomas'** | 130 |
| Cinnamon-raisin / **Pepperidge Farm** | 140 |
| Onion / **Thomas'** | 130 |
| Sour dough / **Oroweat** | 150 |
| Wheat / **Home Pride** | 140 |
| Honeyberry wheat / **Oroweat** | 160 |
| Honey butter / **Oroweat** | 150 |
| Orange, frozen / **Howard Johnson's** Toasties | 113 |
| Orange, mix, prepared / **Betty Crocker** Sunkist | 160 |
| Pineapple, mix, prepared / **Betty Crocker** | 120 |
| Raisin / **Oroweat** | 160 |
| Raisin / **Wonder** Rounds | 150 |
| Raisin bran, frozen / **Pepperidge Farm** | 130 |
| Sour dough / **Wonder** | 130 |
| Wild blueberry, mix, prepared / **Duncan Hines** | 110 |

# Noodles and Noodle Dishes

| | CALORIES |
|---|---|
| Plain, cooked: 1 cup | 200 |
| Almondine, mix, prepared: | |
| ¼ pkg / **Betty Crocker** | 240 |
| w beef, canned: | |
| 7½ oz can / **Hormel Short Orders** Noodles 'n Beef | 240 |
| w beef sauce, mix, prepared: | |
| ½ cup / **Pennsylvania Dutch Brand** | 130 |
| w beef-flavored sauce, mix, prepared: | |
| 1 pouch / **Betty Crocker** Mug-O-Lunch | 170 |
| w butter sauce, mix, prepared: | |
| ½ cup / **Pennsylvania Dutch Brand** | 150 |
| w cheese, mix, prepared: | |
| 1/5 pkg / **Noodle-Roni** Parmesano | 130 |
| w cheese sauce, mix, prepared: | |
| ½ cup / **Pennsylvania Dutch Brand** | 150 |
| w chicken, canned: | |
| 7½ oz can / **Dinty Moore Short Orders** | 215 |
| w chicken sauce, mix, prepared: | |
| ½ cup / **Pennsylvania Dutch Brand** | 150 |
| Romanoff, frozen: | |
| ⅓ pkg / **Stouffer's** | 170 |
| Romanoff, mix, prepared: | |
| ¼ pkg / **Betty Crocker** | 230 |
| Stroganoff, mix: | |
| 2 oz / **Pennsylvania Dutch Brand** | 210 |

Stroganoff, mix, prepared:
  ¼ pkg / **Betty Crocker** 230
w tuna, frozen:
  ½ pkg / **Stouffer's** 11½ oz 200

# Nuts

## SALTED AND FLAVORED

| | CALORIES |
|---|---|
| **1 oz unless noted** (1 oz = 1/5 cup) | |
| Almonds / **Granny Goose** | 155 |
| Almonds, dry roasted / **Planters** | 170 |
| Cashews | |
|     **Frito-Lay** | 168 |
|     **Granny Goose** | 169 |
|     **Planters** | 170 |
|     **Planters** Unsalted | 160 |
|     Dry roasted, in jar / **A & P** | 170 |
|     Dry roasted / **Planters** | 160 |
|     Dry roasted / **Skippy** | 165 |
| Mixed | |
|     **Excel** | 190 |
|     **Granny Goose** | 168 |
|     w peanuts / **Planters** | 180 |
|     wo peanuts / **A & P** Fancy | 190 |
|     wo peanuts / **Planters** | 180 |
|     Unsalted / **Planters** | 170 |
|     Dry roasted, in jar / **A & P** | 180 |
|     Dry roasted / **Planters** | 160 |
|     Dry roasted / **Skippy** | 170 |
| Peanuts | |
|     **A & P** | 180 |

| | |
|---|---|
| **Frito-Lay** | 172 |
| **Planters** Old Fashioned | 170 |
| Unsalted / **Planters** | 170 |
| Cocktail halves / **Excel** | 180 |
| Cocktail / **Planters** | 170 |
| Dry roasted, in jar / **A & P** | 180 |
| Dry roasted / **Planters** | 160 |
| Dry roasted / **Skippy** | 165 |
| In shell: 1 oz edible portion / **A & P** | 180 |
| In shell: | |
|    1 oz edible portion / **A & P** Raw Fancies | 170 |
| In shell: 1 oz edible portion / **Frito-Lay** | 163 |
| Spanish / **A & P** | 180 |
| Spanish / **Frito-Lay** | 168 |
| Spanish / **Granny Goose** | 168 |
| Spanish / **Planters** | 170 |
| Spanish, dry roasted / **Planters** | 160 |
| Virginia / **Granny Goose** | 166 |
| Virginia redskin / **Planters** | 170 |
| Pecans, pieces and chopped / **A & P** | 200 |
| Pecans / **Granny Goose** | 203 |
| Pecans, dry roasted / **Planters** | 190 |
| Pistachios: 1 oz of edible portion / **Frito-Lay** | 175 |
| Pistachios / **Granny Goose** | 172 |
| Pistachios, dry roasted / **Planters** Natural | 170 |
| Sesame Nut Mix / **Planters** | 160 |
| Soybeans, dry roasted / **Malt-O-Meal** | 130 |
| Soybeans, oil roasted / **Malt-O-Meal** | 140 |
| Soy nuts / **Planters** | 130 |
| Tavern / **Planters** | 170 |

## UNSALTED AND UNFLAVORED

Almonds

| | |
|---|---|
| Dried, in shell: 10 nuts | 60 |
| Dried, in shell: 1 cup | 187 |
| Dried, shelled, chopped: 1 tbsp | 48 |
| Dried, shelled, chopped: 1 cup | 777 |
| Dried, shelled, slivered: 1 cup | 688 |

CALORIES

| | |
|---|---|
| Dried, shelled, whole: 1 cup | 849 |
| Roasted, in oil: 1 cup | 984 |
| Beechnuts, in shell: 1 lb | 1572 |
| Beechnuts, shelled: 1 lb | 2576 |
| Brazil nuts, in shell: 1 cup | 383 |
| Brazil nuts, shelled: 1 oz or 6-8 kernels | 185 |
| Brazil nuts, shelled: 1 cup | 916 |
| Butternuts, in shell: 1 lb | 399 |
| Butternuts, shelled: 1 lb | 2853 |
| Cashew nuts, roasted in oil: 1 cup | 785 |
| Cashew nuts, roasted in oil: 1 lb | 2545 |
| Chestnuts | |
| Fresh, in shell: 1 cup | 189 |
| Fresh, in shell: 1 lb | 713 |
| Fresh, shelled: 1 cup | 310 |
| Fresh, shelled: 1 lb | 880 |
| Filberts, in shell: 1 lb | 1323 |
| Filberts, shelled, chopped: 1 cup | 729 |
| Filberts, shelled, whole: 1 cup | 856 |
| Peanuts | |
| Roasted, in shell: 10 jumbo nuts | 105 |
| Roasted, in shell: 1 lb | 1769 |
| Roasted (Spanish and Virginia): 1 lb | 2654 |
| Roasted (Spanish and Virginia), chopped: 1 cup | 842 |
| Hickory nuts, shelled: 1 oz | 201 |
| Macadamia nuts, shelled: 1 oz | 207 |
| Pecans | |
| In shell: 10 large (64-77 per lb) | 236 |
| In shell: 10 extra large (56-63 per lb) | 277 |
| In shell: 10 oversize (55 or fewer per lb) | 299 |
| Chopped or pieces: 1 tbsp | 52 |
| Chopped or pieces: 1 cup | 811 |
| Halves: 10 large (451-550 per lb) | 62 |
| Halves: 10 jumbo (301-350 per lb) | 96 |
| Halves: 10 mammoth (250 or fewer per lb) | 124 |
| Pinenuts, Pignolias, shelled: 1 oz | 156 |
| Pinenuts, Piñon, shelled: 1 oz | 180 |

CALORIES

| | |
|---|---:|
| Pistachio nuts, in shell: 1 lb | 1347 |
| Pistachio nuts, shelled: 1 lb | 2694 |
| Walnuts | |
|     Black, in shell: 1 lb | 627 |
|     Black, shelled, chopped or broken kernels:<br>      1 tbsp | 50 |
|     Black, shelled, chopped or broken kernels:<br>      1 cup | 785 |
|     Persian or English, in shell: 1 lb | 1329 |
|     Persian or English, shelled, halves: 1 cup | 651 |
|     Persian or English: 10 large nuts | 322 |
|     Persian or English, chopped: 1 tbsp | 52 |

# Oils

**1 tbsp unless noted**

| | |
|---|---|
| Corn / **Mazola** | 125 |
| Corn: 2-second spray residue / **Mazla No Stick** | 7 |
| Corn / **Mrs. Tucker's** Salad Oil | 130 |
| Corn / **Nu Made** | 120 |
| Peanut / **Planters** | 130 |
| Popcorn / **Planters** | 130 |
| Safflower / **Nu Made** | 120 |
| Soybean / **Mrs. Tucker's** Salad Oil | 130 |
| Sunflower / **Sunlight** | 120 |
| Vegetable | |
|     **Crisco** | 120 |
|     **Puritan** | 120 |
|     **Swift** Hi Lite | 120 |
|     **Swift** Pour 'n Fry | 120 |
|     **Wesson** | 120 |
| Vegetable-cottonseed / **Swift Jewel** | 120 |
| Vegetable-soybean / **Swift Jcwel** | 120 |

# Olives

|  | CALORIES |
|---|---|
| **Green** | |
| 10 small | 33 |
| 10 large | 45 |
| 10 giant | 76 |
| **Ripe, black** | |
| Ascolano: 10 extra large | 61 |
| Ascolano: 10 giant | 89 |
| Ascolano: 10 jumbo | 105 |
| Manzanillo: 10 small | 38 |
| Manzanillo: 10 medium | 44 |
| Manzanillo: 10 large | 51 |
| Manzanillo: 10 extra large | 61 |
| Mission: 10 small | 54 |
| Mission: 10 medium | 63 |
| Mission: 10 large | 73 |
| Mission: 10 extra large | 87 |
| Sevillano: 10 giant | 64 |
| Sevillano: 10 jumbo | 76 |
| Sevillano: 10 colossal | 95 |
| Sevillano: 10 supercolossal | 114 |
| Greek style: 10 medium | 65 |
| Greek style: 10 extra large | 89 |

# Pancakes, Waffles and Similar Breakfast Foods

CALORIES

Breakfast, frozen, French toast w sausages:
1 entree / Swanson "TV" — 300

Breakfast, frozen, pancakes w sausages:
1 entree / Swanson "TV" — 500

Breakfast, frozen, scrambled eggs w sausage and
coffee cake: 1 entree / Swanson "TV" — 460

Breakfast bars, chocolate chip: 1 bar / Carnation — 210

Breakfast bars, chocolate crunch:
1 bar / Carnation — 210

Breakfast bars, peanut butter crunch:
1 bar / Carnation — 200

Breakfast squares: 1 bar / General Mills — 190

Crepes, mix, prepared:
2 crepes 6-inch diam / Aunt Jemima — 110

French toast, frozen: 1 slice / Aunt Jemima — 85

French toast, frozen: 1 slice / Downyflake — 135

French toast w cinnamon, frozen:
1 slice / Aunt Jemima Cinnamon Swirl — 105

Fritters, apple, frozen: 1 fritter / Mrs. Paul's — 120

Fritters, corn, frozen: 1 fritter / Mrs. Paul's — 130

Pancakes, frozen: 1 pancake / Downyflake — 80

Pancake batter, frozen:
3 cakes 4-in diam / Aunt Jemima — 210

Pancake batter, frozen:
3 cakes 4-in diam / Aunt Jemima Blueberry — 210

CALORIES

Pancake batter, frozen:
   3 cakes 4-in diam / **Aunt Jemima** Buttermilk   210
Pancake, mix, prepared
      **Hungry Jack** Complete / 3 cakes 4-in diam   220
      **Hungry Jack Extra Lights** / 3 cakes 4-in diam   180
      **Tillie Lewis** / 3 cakes 4-in diam   140
      Blueberry: 3 cakes 4-in diam / **Hungry Jack**   340
      Buttermilk: 3 cakes 4-in diam /
        **Betty Crocker**   270
      Buttermilk: 3 cakes 4-in diam /
        **Betty Crocker** Complete   210
      Buttermilk: 3 cakes 4-in diam / **Hungry Jack**   240
      Buttermilk: 3 cakes 4-in diam /
        **Hungry Jack** Complete   180
Pancake-waffle, mix, prepared
      **Aunt Jemima** Complete / 3 cakes 4-in diam   200
      **Aunt Jemima** Original / 3 cakes 4-in diam   220
      **Log Cabin** Complete / 3 cakes 4-in diam   180
      **Log Cabin** Regular / 3 cakes 4-in diam   180
      Buckwheat: 3 cakes 4-in diam /
        **Aunt Jemima**   200
      Buttermilk: 3 cakes 4-in diam /
        **Aunt Jemima**   300
      Buttermilk: 3 cakes 4-in diam /
        **Aunt Jemima** Complete   240
      Buttermilk: 3 cakes 4-in diam / **Log Cabin**   230
      Whole wheat: 3 cakes 4-in diam /
        **Aunt Jemima**   250
Waffles, frozen: 1 waffle
      **Aunt Jemima** Jumbo Original   90
      **Downyflake**   60
      **Downyflake** Hot 'n Buttery   65
      **Downyflake** Jumbo   85
      **Eggo**   120
      Blueberry / **Aunt Jemima** Jumbo   90
      Blueberry / **Downyflake**   90
      Blueberry / **Eggo**   130
      Bran / **Downyflake**   50

|  | CALORIES |
|---|---|
| Bran / **Eggo** | 170 |
| Buttermilk / **Aunt Jemima** Jumbo | 90 |
| Buttermilk / **Downyflake** | 85 |
| Buttermilk / **Downyflake** Round | 100 |
| Strawberry / **Eggo** | 130 |

# Pastry

## FROZEN

|  | CALORIES |
|---|---|
| Donuts: 1 donut | |
|     **Morton** Mini | 120 |
|     Bavarian creme / **Morton** | 180 |
|     Boston creme / **Morton** | 210 |
|     Chocolate iced / **Morton** | 150 |
|     Glazed / **Morton** | 150 |
|     Jelly / **Morton** | 180 |
| Dumplings, apple: 1 dumpling / **Pepperidge Farm** | 280 |
| Pie tarts, frozen: 1 tart | |
|     Apple / **Pepperidge Farm** | 280 |
|     Blueberry / **Pepperidge Farm** | 280 |
|     Cherry / **Pepperidge Farm** | 280 |
|     Lemon / **Pepperidge Farm** | 320 |
|     Raspberry / **Pepperidge Farm** | 320 |
| Strudel, apple: 3 oz / **Pepperidge Farm** | 250 |
| Turnovers: 1 turnover | |
|     Apple, frozen / **Pepperidge Farm** | 310 |
|     Apple, refrigerator / **Pillsbury** | 180 |
|     Blueberry, frozen / **Pepperidge Farm** | 320 |
|     Blueberry, refrigerator / **Pillsbury** | 180 |
|     Cherry, frozen / **Pepperidge Farm** | 340 |
|     Cherry, refrigerator / **Pillsbury** | 190 |

CALORIES

| | |
|---|---|
| Peach, frozen / **Pepperidge Farm** | 320 |
| Raspberry, frozen / **Pepperidge Farm** | 340 |

## TOASTER PASTRIES

**1 portion**

| | |
|---|---|
| Cinnamon brown sugar, frosted / **Town House** | 210 |
| **Pop-Tarts,** all flavors / Kellogg's | 210 |

# Pickles and Relishes

CALORIES

| | |
|---|---|
| Capers: 1 tbsp / **Crosse & Blackwell** | 6 |
| Cauliflower, sweet: 2 buds / **Smucker's** | 47 |
| Chow-Chow: 1 tbsp / **Crosse & Blackwell** | 21 |
| Onions, cocktail: 1 tbsp / **Crosse & Blackwell** | 1 |
| Peppers | |
|     Chile: ¼ cup / **Del Monte** | 11 |
|     Chile: 1 oz / **Ortega** Jalapenos | 8 |
|     Chile, green: 1 oz / **Ortega** | 5 |
|     Hot: 1 4-in / **Smucker's** | 10 |
|     Mild, sweet, wax: ¼ cup / **Del Monte** | 10 |
|     Pickled, hot: 1 oz / **Old El Paso** | |
|       Chilies Jalapenos | 9 |
|     Red, bell: 1 oz / **Ortega** | 9 |
| Pickles, dill | |
|     Slices: 3 / **Heinz** Hamburger Dill Slices | 1 |
|     Slices: 3 / **Smucker's** Hamburger Dill Slices | 2 |
|     Spears: 1 piece / **Bond's** Fresh-Pack | 2 |
|     Spears: 1 piece / **Bond's** Fresh-Pack Kosher | 2 |
|     Sticks, candied: 1 4-in / **Smucker's** | 40 |
|     Whole: 1 / **Bond's** Flavor Pack | 1 |
|     Whole: 1 / **Bond's** Fresh-Pack Kosher | 2 |

CALORIES

Whole: 1 large / **Del Monte** 7
Whole: 1 4-in / **Heinz** Genuine Dill 7
Whole: 1 3-in / **Heinz** Processed Dill 1
Whole: 1 large / **L & S** 15
Whole: 1 large / **L & S** Fresh-Pack Kosher 15
Whole: 1 3½-in / **Smucker's** 8
Whole: 2 2¾-in / **Smucker's**
  Fresh Pack Baby 7
Whole: 1 3½-in / **Smucker's** Kosher 8
Whole: 1 3½-in / **Smucker's**
  Kosher Fresh Pack 8
Pickles, mixed, hot: 4 pieces / **Smucker's** 5
Pickles, sour, whole: 1 large / **Del Monte** 10
Pickles, sweet
  Chips: 3 / **Smucker's** Fresh Pack 31
  Chips: 3 / **Smucker's** Sweet Pickle Chips 31
  Mixed: 3 pieces / **Heinz** 23
  Pieces, mixed: 4 / **Smucker's** 48
  Slices: 3 / **Bond's**
    Fresh-Pack Cucumber Slices 23
  Slices: 3 / **Heinz** Cucumber Slices 20
  Slices: 6 / **Lutz & Schramm**
    Fresh Cucumber Slices 29
  Sticks: 1 4-in / **Smucker's** Fresh Pack 30
  Whole: 1 pickle / **Bond's** Sweet Gherkins 19
  Whole: 1 2-in / **Heinz** Sweet Gherkin 16
  Whole: 1 med / **L & S** Sweet Pickles 11
  Whole: 2 2½-in / **Smucker's** 35
  Whole, candied: 2 2-in / **Smucker's** Midgets 29
Pimientos: 4 oz / **Dromedary** 32
Pimientos, canned: 4 oz / **Ortega** 28
Pimientos: ½ cup / **Stokely-Van Camp** 31
Relishes: 1 tbsp
  Barbecue / **Crosse & Blackwell** 22
  Barbecue / **Heinz** 35
  Corn / **Crosse & Blackwell** 15
  Hamburger / **Crosse & Blackwell** 20
  Hamburger / **Del Monte** 33

CALORIES

| | |
|---|---|
| Hamburger / Heinz | 15 |
| Hot Dog / Crosse & Blackwell | 22 |
| Hot Dog / Del Monte | 28 |
| Hot Dog / Heinz | 17 |
| Hot Pepper / Crosse & Blackwell | 22 |
| India / Crosse & Blackwell | 26 |
| India / Heinz | 17 |
| Piccalilli / Crosse & Blackwell | 26 |
| Piccalilli / Heinz Green Tomato | 23 |
| Sweet / Crosse & Blackwell | 26 |
| Sweet / Del Monte | 36 |
| Sweet / Heinz | 28 |
| Sweet / Lutz & Schramm | 14 |
| Sweet / Smucker's | 23 |
| Watermelon rind / Crosse & Blackwell | 38 |

# Pies

## FROZEN

CALORIES

**1 whole pie**

Apple
| | |
|---|---|
| Banquet 20 oz | 1440 |
| Morton 24 oz | 1740 |
| Morton Mini 8 oz | 590 |
| Mrs. Smith's 8 in | 1770 |
| Mrs. Smith's (natural juice) 8 in | 2880 |
| Dutch / Mrs. Smith's 8 in | 1860 |
| Tart / Mrs. Smith's 8 in | 1500 |

Banana cream
| | |
|---|---|
| Banquet 14 oz | 1032 |
| Morton 16 oz | 1020 |

| | |
|---|---:|
| Morton Mini 3½ oz | 230 |
| Mrs. Smith's 8 in | 1290 |
| Mrs. Smith's Light 13.8 oz | 1320 |
| Blueberry | |
| Banquet 20 oz | 1520 |
| Morton 24 oz | 1680 |
| Morton Mini 8 oz | 580 |
| Mrs. Smith's 8 in | 1740 |
| Mrs. Smith's (natural juice) 8 in | 2040 |
| Mrs. Smith's (natural juice) 9 in | 2880 |
| Boston cream / Mrs. Smith's 8 in | 1980 |
| Cherry | |
| Banquet 20 oz | 1366 |
| Morton 24 oz | 1800 |
| Morton Mini 8 oz | 590 |
| Mrs. Smith's 8 in | 1860 |
| Mrs. Smith's (natural juice) 8 in | 2040 |
| Mrs. Smith's (natural juice) 9 in | 2880 |
| Chocolate / Mrs. Smith's Light 13.8 oz | 1500 |
| Chocolate cream | |
| Banquet 14 oz | 1064 |
| Morton 16 oz | 1200 |
| Morton Mini 3½ oz | 260 |
| Mrs. Smith's 8 in | 1470 |
| Coconut / Mrs. Smith's Light 13.8 oz | 1380 |
| Coconut cream | |
| Banquet 14 oz | 1044 |
| Morton 16 oz | 1140 |
| Morton Mini 3½ oz | 260 |
| Mrs. Smith's 8 in | 1380 |
| Coconut custard / Banquet 20 oz | 1219 |
| Coconut custard / Morton Mini 6½ oz | 370 |
| Coconut custard / Mrs. Smith's 8 in | 1590 |
| Custard / Banquet 20 oz | 1236 |
| Egg custard / Mrs. Smith's 8 in | 1470 |
| Lemon / Mrs. Smith's 8 in | 2040 |
| Lemon cream | |
| Banquet 14 oz | 1008 |

CALORIES

| | |
|---|---:|
| **Morton** 16 oz | 1080 |
| **Morton** Mini 3½ oz | 240 |
| **Mrs. Smith's** 8 in | 1350 |
| Lemon Krunch / **Mrs. Smith's** 8 in | 2480 |
| Lemon meringue / **Mrs. Smith's** 8 in | 1560 |
| Lemon yogurt / **Mrs. Smith's** 15.6 oz | 1200 |
| Mince / **Morton** 24 oz | 1860 |
| Mince / **Morton** Mini 8 oz | 600 |
| Mince / **Mrs. Smith's** 8 in | 2010 |
| Mincemeat / **Banquet** 20 oz | 1514 |
| Neopolitan cream / **Morton** 16 oz | 1140 |
| Neapolitan cream / **Mrs. Smith's** 8 in | 1440 |
| Peach | |
|     **Banquet** 20 oz | 1315 |
|     **Morton** 24 oz | 1680 |
|     **Morton** Mini 8 oz | 560 |
|     **Mrs. Smith's** 8 in | 1800 |
|     **Mrs. Smith's** (natural juice) 8 in | 1980 |
|     **Mrs. Smith's** (natural juice) 9 in | 2760 |
| Pecan / **Morton** Mini 6½ oz | 580 |
| Pecan / **Mrs. Smith's** 8 in | 2580 |
| Pineapple / **Mrs. Smith's** 8 in | 1800 |
| Pineapple-cheese / **Mrs. Smith's** 8 in | 1590 |
| Pumpkin | |
|     **Banquet** 20 oz | 1236 |
|     **Morton** 24 oz | 1380 |
|     **Morton** Mini 8 oz | 440 |
|     **Mrs. Smith's** 8 in | 1440 |
| Raisin / **Mrs. Smith's** 8 in | 1890 |
| Strawberry cream / **Banquet** 14 oz | 1016 |
| Strawberry cream / **Morton** 16 oz | 1080 |
| Strawberry cream / **Mrs. Smith's** 8 in | 1320 |
| Strawberry-rhubarb / **Mrs. Smith's** 8 in | 1890 |
| Strawberry-rhubarb / **Mrs. Smith's** (natural juice) 8 in | 1920 |
| Strawberry-rhubarb / **Mrs. Smith's** (natural juice) 9 in | 2700 |
| Strawberry yogurt / **Mrs. Smith's** 15.6 oz | 1200 |

## PIE MIXES

CALORIES

**Prepared: 1 whole pie**

| | |
|---|---:|
| Boston cream / Betty Crocker | 2080 |
| Chocolate creme / Pillsbury No Bake | 2460 |
| Lemon chiffon / Pillsbury No Bake | 1980 |
| Vanilla marble / Pillsbury No Bake | 2340 |

## PIE CRUSTS AND PASTRY SHELLS

| | |
|---|---:|
| Pastry sheets, frozen: 1 sheet / Pepperidge Farm | 570 |
| Pastry shells: 1 piece / Stella D'Oro | 140 |
| Patty shells, frozen: 1 shell / Pepperidge Farm | 240 |
| Pie crust, prepared | |
|     Mix: double crust / Betty Crocker | 1920 |
|     Mix: 1 whole crust / Flako | 1560 |
|     Mix: double crust / Pillsbury | 1740 |
|     Stick: 1 stick / Betty Crocker | 960 |
| Pie shells, deep, frozen: 1 shell / Pepperidge Farm | 520 |
| Pie shells, shallow bottom, frozen: 1 bottom / Pepperidge Farm | 440 |
| Pie shells, top, frozen: 1 top / Pepperidge Farm | 760 |
| Pot shells: 1 piece / Stella D'Oro | 238 |
| Tart shells, frozen: 1 shell / Pepperidge Farm | 90 |

## PIE FILLING

| | |
|---|---:|
| Apple: 21 oz can / Wilderness | 660 |
| Apple, French: 21 oz can / Wilderness | 660 |
| Apricot: 21 oz can / Wilderness | 720 |
| Banana cream, mix, prepared: whole 8-in pie / Jell-O | 660 |
| Blueberry: 21 oz can / Wilderness | 660 |
| Cherry: 21 oz can / Wilderness | 660 |

CALORIES

| | |
|---|---:|
| Key Lime, mix, prepared: ½ cup / **Royal** Cooked | 160 |
| Lemon: 22 oz can / **Wilderness** | 840 |
| Lemon, mix, prepared: whole 8-in pie / **Jell-O** | 1080 |
| Lemon, mix, prepared: ½ cup / **Royal** Cooked | 160 |
| Mince: 22 oz can / **Wilderness** | 840 |
| Mincemeat: ⅓ cup / **None Such** | 220 |
| Peach: 21 oz can / **Wilderness** | 660 |
| Pumpkin, canned: 1 cup / **Stokely-Van Camp** | 370 |
| Pumpkin mix, canned: 1 cup / **Libby's** | 210 |
| Raisin: 22 oz can / **Wilderness** | 720 |
| Strawberry: 21 oz can / **Wilderness** | 720 |

## PIE AND PASTRY SNACKS

**1 piece**

| | |
|---|---:|
| Apple pastry / **Stella D'Oro** Dietetic | 90 |
| Apple pie / **Hostess** | 400 |
| Apple pie / **Tastykake** 4 oz | 348 |
| Apple pie, French / **Tastykake** 4 oz | 405 |
| Berry pie / **Hostess** | 400 |
| Blueberry pie / **Hostess** | 390 |
| Blueberry pie / **Tastykake** 4 oz | 366 |
| Cherry pie / **Hostess** | 420 |
| Cherry pie / **Tastykake** 4 oz | 381 |
| Fig pastry / **Stella D'Oro** Dietetic | 95 |
| Guava pastry / **Stella D'Oro** | 127 |
| Lemon pie / **Hostess** | 420 |
| Lemon pie / **Tastykake** 4 oz | 370 |
| Peach pie / **Hostess** | 400 |
| Peach pie / **Tastykake** 4 oz | 349 |
| Peach-apricot pastry / **Stella D'Oro** | 97 |
| Peach-apricot pastry / **Stella D'Oro** Dietetic | 95 |
| Pecan pie: 3 oz / **Frito-Lay** | 353 |
| Prune pastry / **Stella D'Oro** Dietetic | 95 |

# Pizza

CALORIES

**1 whole pizza unless noted**

| | |
|---|---|
| Beef and cheese w enchilada seasoning, frozen / El Chico Mexican | 1030 |
| Beef and cheese w taco seasoning, frozen / El Chico Mexican | 1000 |
| Canadian bacon, frozen / Totino's Party | 700 |
| Cheese | |
|    Frozen: 4 oz / Buitoni | 276 |
|    Frozen / Celeste 7 oz | 480 |
|    Frozen / Celeste 19 oz | 1280 |
|    Frozen / Celeste Sicilian Style 20 oz | 1400 |
|    Frozen / Jeno's 13 oz | 840 |
|    Frozen / Jeno's Deluxe 20 oz | 1470 |
|    Frozen / La Pizzeria 20 oz | 1160 |
|    Frozen, thick crust / La Pizzeria 18.5 oz | 1230 |
|    Frozen: ½ pkg / Stouffer's | 330 |
|    Frozen / Totino's Crisp Party | 880 |
|    Frozen / Totino's Party | 880 |
|    Mix, prepared / Jeno's | 840 |
|    w mushroom, frozen / Celeste 8 oz | 460 |
|    w mushroom, frozen / Celeste 21 oz | 1200 |
| Chili and cheese, frozen / El Chico Mexican | 1040 |
| Combination | |
|    Frozen / Celeste Deluxe 9 oz | 600 |
|    Frozen / Celeste Deluxe 23½ oz | 1480 |
|    Frozen / Jeno's Deluxe 23 oz | 1680 |
|    Frozen / La Pizzeria 13.5 oz | 840 |
|    Frozen / La Pizzeria 24½ oz | 1520 |
|    Frozen: ½ pkg / Stouffer's Deluxe | 400 |
|    Frozen / Totino's Classic | 1680 |
|    Frozen, deep crust / Totino's Classic | 1860 |
| Hamburger, frozen / Jeno's | 880 |

| | |
|---|---|
| Hamburger, frozen / **Totino's** Crisp Party | 960 |
| Hamburger, frozen / **Totino's** Party | 920 |
| Open face, frozen: 4 oz / **Buitoni** | 256 |

Pepperoni

| | |
|---|---|
| Frozen / **Celeste** 7½ oz | 540 |
| Frozen / **Celeste** 20 oz | 1440 |
| Frozen / **Jeno's** 13 oz | 900 |
| Frozen / **La Pizzeria** 21 oz | 1320 |
| Frozen: ½ pkg / **Stouffer's** | 400 |
| Frozen, deep crust / **Totino's** Classic | 1800 |
| Frozen / **Totino's** Crisp Party | 960 |
| Frozen / **Totino's** Party | 920 |
| Mix, prepared / **Jeno's** | 1020 |
| w mushroom, frozen / **Totino's** Classic | 1500 |

Pizza rolls, frozen

| | |
|---|---|
| Cheeseburger: 3 oz / **Jeno's** | 270 |
| Pepperoni and cheese: 3 oz / **Jeno's** | 260 |
| Sausage and cheese: 3 oz / **Jeno's** | 260 |
| Shrimp and cheese: 3 oz / **Jeno's** | 220 |

| | |
|---|---|
| Refried bean and cheese, frozen / **El Chico** Mexican | 900 |
| Regular, mix, prepared / **Jeno's** | 840 |

Sausage

| | |
|---|---|
| Frozen / **Celeste** 8 oz | 560 |
| Frozen / **Celeste** 22 oz | 1520 |
| Frozen / **Jeno's** 13 oz | 900 |
| Frozen / **Jeno's** Deluxe 21 oz | 1500 |
| Frozen / **La Pizzeria** 13 oz | 860 |
| Frozen / **La Pizzeria** 23 oz | 1520 |
| Frozen, deep crust / **Totino's** Classic | 1800 |
| Frozen / **Totino's** Crisp Party | 980 |
| Frozen / **Totino's** Party | 940 |
| Mix, prepared / **Jeno's** | 1060 |
| w mushrooms, frozen / **Celeste** 9 oz | 580 |
| w mushrooms, frozen / **Celeste** 21 oz | 1520 |
| w mushrooms, frozen / **Totino's** Classic | 1680 |

# Popcorn

CALORIES

Note: 1 oz candy-coated popcorn =
a little over ¾ cup

|  |  |
|---|---|
| Plain, popped: 1 cup / Pops-Rite | 40 |
| Plain, popped: 1 cup / Jolly Time | 54 |
| Plain, popped: 1 cup / TNT | 52 |
| Butter flavor, read to eat: 1 cup / Wise | 42 |
| Caramel-coated: 1 oz / Old London | 117 |
| Caramel-coated: ½ cup / Wise | 53 |
| Caramel-coated w peanuts: 1 oz / Wise Pixies | 103 |
| Caramel Corn: 1 oz / Granny Goose | 110 |
| Cheese flavor, ready to eat: ½ cup / Wise | 25 |
| Cheese flavor, ready to eat: 1 oz / Old London | 114 |
| **Cracker Jack:** 1⅜ oz pkg | 193 |
| **Cracker Jack:** 6 oz pkg | 750 |
| **Fiddle Faddle,** almond: 1 oz | 119 |
| **Fiddle Faddle,** coconut: 1 oz | 128 |
| **Fiddle Faddle,** peanut: 1 oz | 125 |
| **Krazy Korn:** 1 oz | 128 |
| **Poppycock:** 1 oz | 150 |
| **Screaming Yellow Zonkers:** 1 oz | 121 |

# Pot Pies

CALORIES

**Frozen: 1 whole pie**

Beef

|  |  |
|---|---|
| Banquet 8 oz | 409 |
| Morton 8 oz | 320 |

|  | CALORIES |
|---|---|
| Stouffer's 10 oz | 550 |
| Swanson 8 oz | 430 |
| Swanson Hungry-Man 16 oz | 770 |
| Chicken | |
| Banquet 8 oz | 427 |
| Morton 8 oz | 380 |
| Stouffer's 10 oz | 500 |
| Swanson 8 oz | 450 |
| Swanson Hungry-Man 16 oz | 780 |
| Sirloin Burger / Swanson Hungry-Man 16 oz | 800 |
| Tuna | |
| Banquet 8 oz | 434 |
| Morton 8 oz | 370 |
| Turkey | |
| Banquet 8 oz | 415 |
| Morton 8 oz | 390 |
| Stouffer's 10 oz | 460 |
| Swanson 8 oz | 450 |
| Swanson Hungry-Man 16 oz | 790 |

# Poultry and Poultry Entrees

### FRESH

|  | CALORIES |
|---|---|
| Chicken, cooked | |
| 3 oz flesh only, broiled | 115 |
| 3.3 oz breast (½), fried w bone | 155 |
| 2.7 oz breast (½), fried, flesh and skin only | 155 |
| 2.1 oz fried drumstick w bone | 90 |
| 1.3 oz fried drumstick, flesh and skin only | 90 |
| Chicken, dark meat wo skin, roasted: 3½ oz | 178 |
| Chicken, light meat wo skin, roasted: 3½ oz | 153 |

CALORIES

| | |
|---|---|
| Duck, roasted wo skin: 3½ oz | 201 |
| Goose, domesticated, meat and skin, roasted: 3½ oz | 441 |
| Goose, domesticated, meat wo skin, roasted: 3½ oz | 233 |
| Turkey, dark meat, roasted: 3½ oz | 203 |
| Turkey, dark meat, roasted w skin: 3½ oz | 221 |
| Turkey, dark meat, roasted wo skin: 3½ oz | 187 |
| Turkey, light meat, roasted w skin: 3½ oz | 197 |
| Turkey, light meat, roasted wo skin: 3½ oz | 157 |
| Gizzard, chicken, cooked: 4 oz | 167 |
| Gizzard, goose, cooked: 4 oz | 157 |
| Heart, chicken, cooked: 4 oz | 195 |
| Heart, turkey, cooked: 4 oz | 244 |
| Liver, chicken, cooked: 4 oz | 186 |
| Liver, goose, raw: 4 oz | 206 |
| Liver, turkey, cooked: 4 oz | 197 |

## CANNED, FROZEN AND PROCESSED

| | |
|---|---|
| Chicken a la King, canned: 5¼ oz / Swanson | 190 |
| Chicken a la King, frozen | |
|     Banquet Cookin' Bag / 5 oz | 138 |
|     Green Giant Boil-in-Bag Toast Toppers / 5 oz | 170 |
|     Stouffer's 9½ oz / 1 pkg | 330 |
| Chicken, boned, canned: 3 oz / Hormel Tender Chunk | 110 |
| Chicken, boned, canned, white chunk: 2½ oz / Swanson | 110 |
| Chicken, boned, canned w broth: 2½ oz / Swanson | 110 |
| Chicken, chopped, pressed: 1 slice / Eckrich Slender Sliced | 47 |
| Chicken and biscuits, frozen: 7 oz / Green Giant Oven Bake Entrees | 200 |
| Chicken breast Parmigiana and spinach, frozen: 9 oz / Weight Watchers | 200 |

Chicken, creamed, frozen: 1 pkg / **Stouffer's**
  6½ oz    300
Chicken creole, frozen: 13 oz / **Weight Watchers**    250
Chicken croquette w sauce, frozen: 12 oz /
  **Howard Johnson's**    505
Chicken divan, frozen: 1 pkg / **Stouffer's**
  8½ oz    335
Chicken w dumplings, canned: 7½ oz / **Swanson**    230
Chicken w dumplings, frozen: 32 oz /
  **Banquet** Buffet Supper    1209
Chicken, escalloped, frozen: ½ pkg / **Stouffer's**
  11½ oz    250
Chicken, fried
  Frozen: 2 lb / **Banquet**    259
  Frozen: 6.4 oz / **Morton** 32 oz    440
  Frozen: 1 cntree / **Morton** Country
    Table 12 oz    600
  Frozen, assorted pieces: 3.2 edible oz /
    **Swanson**    260
  Frozen, breast portions: 3.2 edible oz /
    **Swanson**    250
  Frozen, thighs and drumsticks: 3.2
    edible oz / **Swanson**    260
  Frozen, wing sections: 3.2 edible oz /
    **Swanson** Nibbles    290
Chicken livers w broccoli, frozen: 10½ oz /
  **Weight Watchers**    220
Chicken Nibbles w french fries: 1 entree /
  **Swanson** "TV" 6 oz    370
Chicken and noodles, frozen: 32 oz /
  **Banquet** Buffet Supper    764
Chicken and noodles, frozen: 9 oz / **Green**
  **Giant** Boil-in-Bag Entrees    250
Chicken, smoked, sliced: 1 oz / **Safeway**    50
Chicken stew, canned: 7½ oz / **Swanson**    180
Chicken stew w dumplings, canned: 1 cup /
  **Libby's**    88

| | |
|---|---|
| Chicken, white meat w peas, onions, frozen: | |
| 9 oz / **Weight Watchers** | 270 |
| Turkey, boned, canned: 3 oz / **Hormel** | |
| Tender Chunk | 90 |
| Turkey, boned, canned w broth: 2½ oz / | |
| **Swanson** | 110 |
| Turkey slices | |
|     Canned w gravy: 6¼ oz / **Morton House** | 140 |
|     Frozen entree / **Morton** Country Table | |
|     12¼ oz | 390 |
|     Frozen entree / **Swanson** Hungry-Man | |
|     13¼ oz | 380 |
|     Frozen entree / **Swanson** "TV" 8¾ oz | 260 |
|     Frozen w giblet gravy: 32 oz / | |
|     **Banquet** Buffet Supper | 564 |
|     Frozen w giblet gravy: 5 oz / **Banquet** | |
|     Cookin' Bag | 98 |
|     Frozen w gravy: 5 oz / **Green Giant** | |
|     Boil-in-Bag Toast Toppers | 100 |
| Turkey tetrazzini, frozen: ½ pkg / **Stouffer's** | |
| 12 oz | 240 |
| Turkey tetrazzini w mushrooms, red peppers, | |
| frozen: 13 oz / **Weight Watchers** | 380 |
| Turkey, roast, frozen, cooked | |
|     Dark meat: 3½ oz / **Swift** Butterball | 210 |
|     White meat: 3½ oz / **Swift** Butterball | 170 |
|     White and dark meat w skin: 3½ oz / | |
|     **Swift** Butterball | 220 |
|     Roll, boneless white and dark meat: 3½ | |
|     oz / **Swift** Park Lane | 140 |
|     Roll, boneless white and dark meat: 3½ | |
|     oz / **Swift** Premium Perfect Slice | 120 |
|     Roll, white meat: 3½ oz / **Swift** | |
|     Park Lane | 140 |
|     Roll, white meat: 3½ oz / **Swift** Premium | |
|     Perfect Slice | 120 |

Turkey, smoked, chopped: 1 slice / **Eckrich**
   Slender Sliced     47
Turkey, smoked, sliced: 1 oz / **Safeway**     50

# Pretzels

CALORIES

**1 oz**

Bavarian / **Granny Goose**     112
Mini / **Granny Goose**     110
Ring / **Granny Goose**     112
Stick
     **Granny Goose**     108
     **Pepperidge Farm Thin**     100
     **Planters**     110
Twists
     **Granny Goose**     109
     **Pepperidge Farm Tiny**     100
     **Planters**     110
     **Rold Gold**     111

# Pudding

CALORIES

**½ cup unless noted**

All flavors, mix, prepared / **Estee Low Calorie**     85
Banana
     Canned, ready to serve: 5 oz can /
     **Del Monte**     180

| | |
|---|---|
| Canned: 8 oz can / **Sego** | 250 |
| Mix, prepared / **Ann Page** | 170 |
| Mix, prepared / **Jell-O** Instant | 180 |
| Mix, prepared / **Royal** | 160 |
| Mix, prepared / **Royal** Instant | 180 |
| Butter pecan, mix, prepared / **Jell-O** Instant | 180 |

**Butterscotch**

| | |
|---|---|
| Canned, ready to serve: 5 oz can / **Del Monte** | 180 |
| Canned: 8 oz can / **Sego** | 250 |
| Mix, prepared / **Ann Page** | 190 |
| Mix, prepared / **Ann Page** Instant | 170 |
| Mix, prepared / **Jell-O** | 180 |
| Mix, prepared / **Jell-O** Instant | 180 |
| Mix, prepared / **My-T-Fine** | 143 |
| Mix, prepared / **Royal** | 160 |
| Mix, prepared / **Royal** Instant | 180 |
| Mix, prepared w nonfat milk / **D-Zerta** | 70 |
| Mix, as packaged / **De-Zerta** | 25 |

**Chocolate**

| | |
|---|---|
| Canned, ready to serve / **Betty Crocker** | 180 |
| Canned, ready to serve: 5 oz can / **Del Monte** | 190 |
| Canned: 8 oz can / **Sego** | 250 |
| Mix, prepared / **Ann Page** | 180 |
| Mix, prepared / **Ann Page** Instant | 190 |
| Mix, prepared / **Jell-O** | 170 |
| Mix, prepared / **Jell-O** Instant | 190 |
| Mix, prepared / **My-T-Fine** | 133 |
| Mix, prepared / **Royal** | 180 |
| Mix, prepared / **Royal** Instant | 190 |
| Mix, prepared w nonfat milk / **De-Zerta** | 70 |
| Mix, as packaged / **D-Zerta** | 20 |
| Almond, mix, prepared / **My-T-Fine** | 169 |
| Fudge, canned, ready to serve / **Betty Crocker** | 180 |
| Fudge, canned, ready to serve: 5 oz can / **Del Monte** | 190 |

CALORIES

| | |
|---|---|
| Fudge, mix, prepared / Jell-O | 170 |
| Fudge, mix, prepared / Jell-O Instant | 190 |
| Fudge, mix, prepared / My-T-Fine | 151 |
| Milk, mix, prepared / Jell-O | 170 |
| Chocolate fudge: 8 oz can / Sego | 250 |
| Chocolate marshmellow: 8 oz can / Sego | 250 |
| Coconut | |
|    Mix, prepared / Royal Instant | 170 |
|    Cream, mix, prepared / Ann Page | 190 |
|    Cream, mix, prepared / Jell-O | 110 |
|    Cream, mix, prepared / Jell-O Instant | 190 |
|    Toasted, mix, prepared / Ann Page | 170 |
| Coffee, mix, prepared / Royal Instant | 180 |
| Custard, mix, prepared / Royal | 150 |
| Custard, egg, mix, prepared / Ann Page | 150 |
| Custard, egg, mix, prepared / Jell-O Americana | 170 |
| Custard, rennet, all flavors, mix, prepared / | |
|    Junket | 120 |
| Dark 'N Sweet, mix, prepared / Royal | 180 |
| Dark 'N Sweet, mix, prepared / Royal Instant | 190 |
| Flan, mix, prepared / Royal | 150 |
| Lemon | |
|    Mix, prepared / Ann Page | 150 |
|    Mix, prepared / Ann Page Instant | 180 |
|    Mix, prepared / Jell-O Instant | 180 |
|    Mix, prepared / My-T-Fine | 164 |
|    Mix, prepared / Royal Instant | 180 |
| Pineapple cream, mix, prepared / Jell-O | |
|    Instant | 180 |
| Pistachio, mix, prepared / Ann Page Instant | 180 |
| Pistachio, mix, prepared / Jell-O Instant | 180 |
| Pistachio nut, mix, prepared / Royal Instant | 170 |
| Plum pudding, canned, ready to serve / R & R | 300 |
| Rice, canned, ready to serve / Betty Crocker | 150 |
| Rice, mix, prepared / Jell-O Americana | 180 |
| Tapioca | |
|    Minute Tapioca: 1 tbsp | 40 |
|    Minute (Fluffy Pudding recipe) | 150 |

CALORIES

| | |
|---|---|
| Canned, ready to serve / **Betty Crocker** | 150 |
| Chocolate, mix, prepared / **Ann Page** | 180 |
| Chocolate. mix, prepared / **Jell-O** Americana | 170 |
| Chocolate, mix, prepared / **Royal** | 180 |
| Vanilla, mix, prepared / **Ann Page** | 170 |
| Vanilla. mix, prepared / **Jell-O** Americana | 170 |
| Vanilla, mix, prepared / **My-T-Fine** | 130 |
| Vanilla, mix, prepared / **Royal** | 160 |

Vanilla

| | |
|---|---|
| Canned, ready to serve / **Betty Crocker** | 190 |
| Canned, ready to serve: 5 oz can / **Del Monte** | 190 |
| Canned: 8 oz can / **Sego** | 250 |
| Mix, prepared / **Ann Page** | 170 |
| Mix, prepared / **Jell-O** | 170 |
| Mix, prepared / **Jell-O** Instant | 180 |
| Mix, prepared / **My-T-Fine** | 133 |
| Mix, prepared / **Royal** | 160 |
| Mix, prepared / **Royal** Instant | 180 |
| Mix, prepared w nonfat milk / **D-Zerta** | 70 |
| Mix, as packaged / **D-Zerta** | 30 |
| French, mix, prepared / **Jell-O** | 180 |
| French, mix, prepared / **Jell-O** Instant | 180 |

# Rice and Rice Dishes

|  | CALORIES |
|---|---|
| Brown, long grain, parboiled: ⅔ cup cooked | 200 |
| Brown and wild, seasoned, mix, prepared: | |
| ½ cup / **Uncle Ben's** | 126 |
| White, instant: 1 cup | 180 |
| White, long grain: ⅔ cup cooked | 225 |
| White, parboiled: 1 cup, cooked | 185 |
| White and wild, frozen: 1 cup / **Green Giant** | |
| Boil-in-Bag | 220 |
| White and wild, w bean sprouts, pea pods | |
| and water chestnuts, frozen: 1 cup / | |
| **Green Giant** Boil-in-Bag Oriental | 230 |
| White and wild, w peas, celery, mushrooms | |
| and almonds, frozen: 1 cup / | |
| **Green Giant** Boil-in-Bag Medley | 320 |
| White, long grain and wild, mix, prepared: | |
| ½ cup / **Uncle Ben's** | 97 |
| White, long grain and wild, mix, prepared: | |
| ½ cup / **Uncle Ben's** Fast Cooking | 95 |
| Beef-flavored, mix, prepared | |
| 1/6 pkg / **Ann Page** Rice 'n Easy | 170 |
| ½ cup / **Minute** Rice Rib Roast | 150 |
| 1/6 pkg / **Rice-A-Roni** | 130 |
| ½ cup / **Uncle Ben's** | 98 |
| w bell peppers and parsley, frozen: | |
| 1 cup / **Green Giant** Boil-in-Bag Verdi | 270 |
| w broccoli, in cheese sauce, frozen: 1 cup / | |
| **Green Giant** Boil-in-Bag | 250 |
| Chicken-flavored, mix, prepared | |
| 1/6 pkg / **Ann Page** Rice 'n Easy | 180 |

CALORIES

| | |
|---|---|
| 1/5 pkg / **Rice-A-Roni** | 160 |
| ½ cup / **Uncle Ben's** | 103 |
| Curried, mix, prepared: ½ cup / **Uncle Ben's** | 99 |
| Fried, mix, prepared: ½ cup / **Minute** | 160 |
| w green beans and almonds, frozen: 1 cup / **Green Giant** Boil-in-Bag Continental | 230 |
| w peas, mushrooms, frozen: 2.3 oz / **Bird's Eye** Combinations | 100 |
| w peas, mushrooms, frozen: 1 cup / **Green Giant** Boil-in-Bag Medley | 200 |
| Pilaf, mix, prepared: ½ cup / **Uncle Ben's** | 101 |
| Pilaf, w mushrooms and onions, frozen: 1 cup / **Green Giant** Boil-in-Bag | 230 |
| Poultry-flavored, mix, prepared: ½ cup / **Minute** Drumstick | 170 |
| Spanish | |
| Canned: 1 cup / **Libby's** | 57 |
| Mix, prepared: ½ cup / **Minute** | 150 |
| Mix, prepared: 1/6 pkg / **Rice-A-Roni** | 120 |
| Mix, prepared: ½ cup / **Uncle Ben's** | 106 |

# Rolls and Buns

CALORIES

**1 roll or bun unless noted**

| | |
|---|---|
| Bagel, egg, 3-in diam | 165 |
| Bagel, water, 3-in diam | 165 |
| Buns for sandwiches | |
| **Arnold** Dutch Egg Buns | 130 |
| **Arnold** Francisco Sandwich Rolls | 180 |
| **Arnold** Soft Sandwich | 110 |
| w poppy seeds / **Arnold** Soft Sandwich | 110 |

CALORIES

| | |
|---|---:|
| w sesame seeds / **Arnold** Soft Sandwich | 110 |
| w sesame seeds / **Pepperidge Farm** | 120 |
| Hamburger / **Arnold** 8's | 110 |
| Hamburger: 2 oz / **Colonial** | 160 |
| Hamburger: 2 oz / **Kilpatrick's** | 160 |
| Hamburger: 2 oz / **Manor** | 160 |
| Hamburger / **Mrs. Wright's** 12 oz pkg | 130 |
| Hamburger / **Mrs. Wright's** 16 oz pkg | 110 |
| Hamburger / **Pepperidge Farm** | 110 |
| Hamburger: 2 oz / **Rainbo** | 160 |
| Hamburger / **Wonder** | 160 |
| Hamburger w sesame seeds / **Mrs. Wright's** | 140 |
| Hot dog / **Arnold** | 110 |
| Hot dog: 2 oz / **Colonial** | 160 |
| Hot dog: 2 oz / **Kilpatrick's** | 160 |
| Hot dog / **Mrs. Wright's** 11 oz pkg | 110 |
| Hot dog / **Mrs. Wright's** 13½ oz pkg | 110 |
| Hot dog: 2 oz / **Manor** | 160 |
| Hot dog / **Pepperidge Farm** | 120 |
| Hot dog: 2 oz / **Rainbo** | 160 |
| Hot dog / **Wonder** | 160 |
| Dinner and soft rolls | |
|    **Arnold** Deli-Twist | 110 |
|    **Arnold** Finger 24's | 55 |
|    **Arnold** Francisco Variety | 100 |
|    **Arnold** Party Finger 12's | 55 |
|    **Arnold** Party Parkerhouse 12's | 55 |
|    **Arnold** Party Rounds 12's | 55 |
|    **Arnold** Party Tea 20's | 35 |
|    **Arnold** 12's | 60 |
|    **Arnold** 24's | 60 |
|    **Colonial** | 80 |
|    **Home Pride** | 90 |
|    **Kilpatrick's** | 80 |
|    **Mrs. Wright's** Buttermilk | 100 |
|    **Mrs. Wright's** Cloverleaf | 90 |
|    **Mrs. Wright's** Flaky Gem | 90 |
|    **Mrs. Wright's** Twin | 90 |

CALORIES

| | |
|---|---|
| Manor | 80 |
| Pepperidge Farm Butter Crescent | 130 |
| Pepperidge Farm Dinner | 65 |
| Pepperidge Farm Finger | 60 |
| Pepperidge Farm Finger w poppy seeds | 60 |
| Pepperidge Farm Finger w sesame seeds | 60 |
| Pepperidge Farm Golden Twist | 120 |
| Pepperidge Farm Old-Fashioned | 37 |
| Pepperidge Farm Parkerhouse | 60 |
| Pepperidge Farm Party | 35 |
| Pepperidge Farm Party Pan | 35 |
| Rainbo Dinner | 80 |
| Wonder Buttermilk | 85 |
| Wonder Gem Style Dinner | 85 |
| Wonder Half & Half Dinner | 85 |
| Wonder Home Bake Dinner | 85 |
| Wonder Pan | 105 |
| Mix, prepared / Pillsbury Hot Roll Mix | 95 |
| Refrigerator / Ballard Crescent | 95 |
| Refrigerator / Pillsbury Butterflake | 110 |
| Refrigerator / Pillsbury Crescent | 95 |

Hard rolls

| | |
|---|---|
| Club / Pepperidge Farm | 120 |
| Deli / Pepperidge Farm | 180 |
| French / Wonder | 85 |
| French, four / Pepperidge Farm | 230 |
| French, large: ½ roll / Pepperidge Farm | 190 |
| French, nine / Pepperidge Farm | 110 |
| French, small: ½ roll / Pepperidge Farm | 130 |
| French sourdough / Arnold Francisco | 100 |
| French sourdough / Arnold Francisco Brown and Serve | 90 |
| Hearth / Pepperidge Farm | 60 |
| Italian: 2 oz / Pepperidge Farm | 150 |
| Kaiser: 2 oz / Earth Grains | 140 |
| Kaiser & Hoagie Rolls: 6 oz / Wonder | 460 |
| Onion: 2 oz / Earth Grains | 170 |
| Sandwich / Pepperidge Farm | 140 |

| | |
|---|---:|
| Sesame Crisp / **Pepperidge Farm** | 70 |
| Popovers, mix, prepared: 1 popover / **Flako** | 170 |

## SWEET ROLLS

**1 roll unless noted**

| | |
|---|---:|
| Caramel, refrigerated / **Pillsbury** Danish | 160 |
| Cinnamon, refrigerated / **Ballard** | 100 |
| Cinnamon w icing, refrigerated / **Hungry Jack Butter Tastin** | 145 |
| Cinnamon w icing, refrigerated / **Pillsbury** | 115 |
| Cinnamon-nut: 3 oz / **Rainbo** | 330 |
| Cinnamon-raisin, refrigerated / **Merico** | 180 |
| Cinnamon-raisin, refrigerated / **Pillsbury** Danish | 150 |
| Danish, apple: 2 oz / **Earth Grains** | 230 |
| Danish Bear Claws: 2 oz / **Earth Grains** | 250 |
| Danish, cinnamon: 2 oz / **Earth Grains** Pastry | 220 |
| Danish, cherry: 2 oz / **Earth Grains** Pastry | 170 |
| Danish, fruit, refrigerated / **Merico** | 180 |
| Danish Horns: 2 oz / **Earth Grains** | 260 |
| Honey Buns / **Hostess** | 580 |
| Honey Buns: 3 oz / **Rainbo** | 380 |
| Honey Buns, frozen / **Morton** | 230 |
| Honey Buns, frozen / **Morton** Mini | 100 |
| Orange, refrigerated / **Pillsbury** Danish | 130 |

# Salad Dressings

**Bottled unless noted: 1 tbsp unless noted**

| | CALORIES |
|---|---|
| **Ann Page** Salad Dressing | 70 |
| **Mrs. Filbert's** Salad Dressing | 65 |
| **Nu Made** Salad Dressing | 80 |
| **Piedmont** Salad Dressing | 70 |
| **Sultana** Salad Dressing | 50 |
| Avocado / **Kraft** | 70 |
| Bacon, mix: ¾ oz pkg / **Lawry's** | 69 |
| Blue cheese | |
|     **Ann Page** Low Calorie | 18 |
|     **Kraft** Chunky | 70 |
|     **Kraft** Low Calorie | 14 |
|     **Kraft** Low Calorie Chunky | 30 |
|     **Lawry's** | 57 |
|     **Nu Made** | 75 |
|     **Roka** | 60 |
|     **Seven Seas** Real | 70 |
|     **Tillie Lewis** / 1 tsp | 4 |
|     **Wish-Bone** Chunky | 80 |
|     Mix: ¾ oz pkg / **Lawry's** | 79 |
|     Mix, prepared / **Weight Watchers** | 10 |
| Caesar | |
|     **Kraft** Golden | 70 |
|     **Lawry's** | 70 |
|     **Nu Made** | 75 |
|     **Pfeiffer** | 70 |
|     **Pfeiffer** Low-Cal | 10 |
|     **Seven Seas** | 70 |
|     **Wish-Bone** | 80 |
|     Mix: ¾ oz pkg / **Lawry's** | 71 |

CALORIES

| | |
|---|---|
| Canadian bacon-flavored / **Lawry's** | 72 |
| Chef Style / **Ann Page** Low Calorie | 20 |
| Chef Style / **Kraft** Low Calorie | 18 |
| Coleslaw dressing / **Kraft** | 70 |
| Coleslaw dressing / **Kraft** Low Calorie | 30 |
| Cucumber, creamy / **Kraft** | 80 |
| Cucumber, creamy / **Kraft** Low Calorie | 30 |
| French | |
|     **Casino** | 70 |
|     **Kraft** | 60 |
|     **Kraft** Casino Garlic | 70 |
|     **Kraft** Catalina | 60 |
|     **Kraft** Herb and Garlic | 90 |
|     **Kraft** Low Calorie | 25 |
|     **Kraft** Miracle | 70 |
|     **Lawry's** | 54 |
|     **Lawry's** San Francisco French | 53 |
|     **Lawry's** Sherry French | 55 |
|     **Nu Made** Low Calorie | 20 |
|     **Nu Made** Savory | 65 |
|     **Nu Made** Zesty | 65 |
|     **Pfeiffer** | 55 |
|     **Pfeiffer** Low-Cal | 18 |
|     **Seven Seas** Creamy | 60 |
|     **Seven Seas** Family Style | 60 |
|     **Seven Seas** Low Calorie | 30 |
|     **Wish-Bone** Deluxe | 50 |
|     **Wish-Bone** Garlic French | 70 |
|     **Wish-Bone** Low Calorie | 25 |
|     **Wish-Bone** Sweet 'n Spicy | 70 |
|     Mix: 4/5 oz pkg / **Lawry's** Old Fashioned | 72 |
|     Mix, prepared / **Weight Watchers** | 4 |
| French Style / **Ann Page** Low Calorie | 25 |
| French Style / **Kraft** Low Calorie | 25 |
| French Style: 1 tsp / **Tillie Lewis** | 4 |
| Garlic, creamy / **Kraft** | 50 |
| Garlic, creamy / **Wish-Bone** | 80 |

| | |
|---|---:|
| Green Goddess | |
| **Kraft** | 80 |
| **Lawry's** | 59 |
| **Nu Made** | 80 |
| **Seven Seas** | 60 |
| **Wish-Bone** | 70 |
| Mix: ¾ oz pkg / **Lawry's** | 69 |
| Green onion / **Kraft** | 80 |
| Hawaiian / **Lawry's** | 77 |
| Herbs and spices / **Seven Seas** | 60 |
| Italian | |
| **Ann Page** Low Calorie | 14 |
| **Kraft** | 80 |
| **Kraft** Golden Blend | 70 |
| **Kraft** Low Calorie | 6 |
| **Lawry's** | 79 |
| **Nu Made** | 90 |
| **Nu Made** Low Calorie | 16 |
| **Pfeiffer** Chef | 60 |
| **Pfeiffer** Low-Cal | 10 |
| **Seven Seas** | 70 |
| **Seven Seas** Family Style | 60 |
| **Seven Seas** Low Calorie | 35 |
| **Seven Seas** Viva | 70 |
| **Tillie Lewis** / 1 tsp | 2 |
| **Wish-Bone** | 80 |
| **Wish-Bone** Low Calorie | 20 |
| Cheese / **Lawry's** | 60 |
| Creamy / **Kraft** | 50 |
| Creamy / **Seven Seas** Creamy | 70 |
| Creamy / **Weight Watchers** | 50 |
| Mix, prepared / **Good Seasons** Low Calorie | 8 |
| Mix: 3/5 oz pkg / **Lawry's** | 44 |
| Mix, prepared / **Weight Watchers** | 2 |
| Mix, cheese: ¾ oz pkg / **Lawry's** | 69 |
| Mix, creamy, prepared / **Weight Watchers** | 4 |
| Lemon garlic, mix: ⅞ oz pkg / **Lawry's** | 64 |

CALORIES

| | |
|---|---|
| May Lo Naise / **Tillie Lewis** | 25 |
| Oil and vinegar | |
|     **Kraft** | 70 |
|     **Lawry's** | 55 |
|     **Nu Made** | 60 |
|     Red wine / **Seven Seas Viva** | 70 |
| Onion / **Wish-Bone** California | 80 |
| Red wine: 1 oz / **Pfeiffer** Low-Cal | 20 |
| Russian | |
|     **Kraft** Low Calorie | 30 |
|     **Nu Made** | 55 |
|     **Pfeiffer** | 65 |
|     **Pfeiffer** Low-Cal | 15 |
|     **Seven Seas** Creamy | 80 |
|     **Tillie Lewis** / 1 tsp | 4 |
|     **Weight Watchers** | 50 |
|     **Wish-Bone** | 60 |
|     **Wish-Bone** Low Calorie | 25 |
|     Creamy / **Kraft** | 60 |
|     w honey / **Kraft** | 60 |
|     Mix, prepared / **Weight Watchers** | 4 |
| Salad Secret / **Kraft** | 60 |
| Sour Treat: 1 oz / **Friendship** | 49 |
| Spin Blend / **Hellmann's** | 55 |
| Thousand Island | |
|     **Ann Page** Low Calorie | 25 |
|     **Kraft** | 60 |
|     **Kraft** Low Calorie | 30 |
|     **Lawry's** | 69 |
|     **Nu Made** | 30 |
|     **Nu Made** Low Calorie | 30 |
|     **Pfeiffer** | 65 |
|     **Pfeiffer** Low-Cal | 15 |
|     **Seven Seas** | 50 |
|     **Tillie Lewis** / 1 tsp | 6 |
|     **Weight Watchers** | 50 |
|     **Wish-Bone** | 70 |
|     **Wish-Bone** Low Calorie | 25 |

CALORIES

| | |
|---|---:|
| Mix: ⅞ oz pkg / **Lawry's** | 78 |
| Mix, prepared / **Weight Watchers** | 12 |
| Whipped / **Tillie Lewis** | 25 |
| Yogonaise / **Henri's** | 60 |
| Yogowhip / **Henri's** | 60 |
| Yogurt | |
|   Blue cheese / **Henri's** | 35 |
|   Creamy garlic / **Henri's** | 35 |
|   Cucumber and onion / **Henri's** | 35 |
|   French / **Henri's** | 40 |
|   Italian / **Henri's** | 35 |
|   Thousand Island / **Henri's** | 30 |

# Sauces

CALORIES

| | |
|---|---:|
| A la King, mix, prepared: ½ cup / **Durkee** | 66 |
| Barbecue, bottled or canned: 1 tbsp | |
|   **Chris' and Pitt's** | 15 |
|   **French's** | 14 |
|   **Open Pit** | 26 |
|   Hickory smoke flavor / **French's** Smoky | 14 |
|   Hickory smoke flavor / **Open Pit** | 27 |
|   Hot / **French's** | 14 |
|   Hot / **Open Pit** Hot 'n Spicy | 27 |
|   w onions / **Open Pit** | 27 |
| Cheese, mix, prepared: ½ cup / **Durkee** | 169 |
| Cheese, mix, prepared: ¼ cup / **French's** | 80 |
| Cheese, mix, prepared: ¼ cup / **McCormick** | 78 |
| Cheese, mix, prepared: ¼ cup / **Schilling** | 78 |
| Enchilada | |
|   Canned: 4 oz / **Old El Paso** Hot | 36 |
|   Canned: 4 oz / **Old El Paso** Mild | 40 |

| | |
|---|---:|
| Mix: 1⅝ oz pkg / **Lawry's** | 144 |
| Mix: 1½ oz pkg / **McCormick** | 115 |
| Mix: 1½ oz pkg / **Schilling** | 115 |
| Hollandaise, mix, prepared: ¾ cup / **Durkee** | 173 |
| Hollandaise, mix, prepared: 3 tbsp / **French's** | 45 |
| Hollandaise, mix, prepared: ½ cup / **McCormick** | 170 |
| Hollandaise, mix, prepared: ½ cup / **Schilling** | 170 |
| Horseradish sauce: 1 tbsp / **Kraft** | 50 |
| Italian, canned: 2 fl oz / **Contadina** Cookbook | 43 |
| Italian, red, in jar: 5 oz / **Ragu** | 45 |
| Lasagna, mix: 1⅝ oz pkg / **Lawry's** | 86 |
| Lemon-butter-flavored, mix, prepared: | |
| 1 tbsp / **Weight Watchers** | 8 |
| Mushroom steak, canned: 1 oz / **Dawn Fresh** | 9 |
| Pizza, canned: 4 oz / **Buitoni** | 92 |
| Pizza, in jar: 5 oz / **Ragu** | 120 |
| Sour cream, mix, prepared: ⅔ cup / **Durkee** | 214 |
| Sour cream, mix, prepared: 2½ tbsp / **French's** | 40 |
| Sour cream, mix, prepared: ¼ cup / **McCormick** | 73 |
| Sour cream, mix, prepared: ¼ cup / **Schilling** | 73 |
| Spaghetti | |
| Canned: 4 oz / **Ann Page** | 70 |
| Canned: 4 oz / **Buitoni** | 92 |
| Canned: ½ cup / **Town House** | 80 |
| In jar: 5 oz / **Ragu** Extra Thick | 120 |
| In jar: 5 oz / **Ragu** Plain | 105 |
| Mix, prepared: 1 env / **Ann Page** | 120 |
| Mix, prepared: ½ cup / **Durkee** | 45 |
| Mix, prepared: ⅝ cup / **French's** | |
| Italian Style | 100 |
| Mix: 1½ oz pkg / **Lawry's** | 147 |
| Mix, prepared: ½ cup / **McCormick** | 53 |
| Mix, prepared: ½ cup / **Schilling** | 53 |
| Mix, prepared: 4 fl oz / **Spatini** | 160 |
| Clam, canned: 5 oz / **Ragu** | 110 |
| Clam, red, canned: 4 oz / **Buitoni** | 108 |
| Clam, white, canned: 4 oz / **Buitoni** | 144 |
| Marinara, canned: 4 oz / **Ann Page** | 70 |

CALORIES

| | |
|---|---:|
| Marinara, canned: 4 oz / **Buitoni** | 88 |
| Marinara, in jar: 5 oz / **Ragu** | 120 |
| Meat flavor, canned: 4 oz / **Ann Page** | 80 |
| Meat flavor, canned: 4 oz / **Buitoni** | 120 |
| Meat flavor, canned: ½ cup / **Town House** | 80 |
| Meat flavor, in jar: 5 oz / **Ragu** | 115 |
| Meat flavor, in jar: 5 oz / **Ragu** Extra Thick | 130 |
| w meatball seasonings, mix: | |
|   3¼ oz pkg / **Lawry's** | 316 |
| w mushrooms, canned: 4 oz / **Ann Page** | 70 |
| w mushrooms, canned: 4 oz / **Buitoni** | 88 |
| w mushrooms, canned: ½ cup / | |
|   **Town House** | 90 |
| w mushrooms, in jar: 5 oz / **Ragu** | 105 |
| w mushrooms, in jar: 5 oz / **Ragu** | |
|   Extra Thick | 110 |
| w mushrooms, mix, prepared: | |
|   1 env / **Ann Page** | 120 |
| w mushrooms, mix, prepared: ⅔ | |
|   cup / **Durkee** | 52 |
| w mushrooms, mix, prepared: ⅝ | |
|   cup / **French's** | 100 |
| Pepperoni flavor, in jar: 5 oz / **Ragu** | 120 |
| Stroganoff | |
|   Mix, prepared: 1 cup / **Durkee** | 820 |
|   Mix, prepared: ⅓ cup / **French's** | 110 |
|   Mix: 1½ oz pkg / **Lawry's** | 118 |
|   Mix, prepared: ½ cup / **McCormick** | 115 |
|   Mix, prepared: ½ cup / **Schilling** | 115 |
| Sweet and sour, canned: 2 fl oz / | |
|   **Contadina** Cookbook | 79 |
| Sweet and sour, canned: 1 cup / **La Choy** | 524 |
| Sweet and sour, mix, prepared: 1 cup / **Durkee** | 230 |
| Sweet and sour, mix, prepared: ½ cup / **French's** | 55 |
| Swiss steak, canned: 2 fl oz / **Contadina** Cookbook | 24 |
| Teriyaki, mix, prepared: 2 tbsp / **French's** | 35 |
| Tomato, canned | |
|   **Contadina** / 1 cup | 90 |

CALORIES

| | |
|---|---|
| **Del Monte** / 1 cup | 80 |
| **Hunt's** / 4 oz | 35 |
| **Hunt's** Prima Salsa Regular / 4 oz | 110 |
| **Hunt's** Special / 4 oz | 40 |
| **Stokely-Van Camp** / 1 cup | 70 |
| **Town House** Spanish Style / 8 oz | 80 |
| w bits: 4 oz / **Hunt's** | 35 |
| w cheese: 4 oz / **Hunt's** | 70 |
| w herbs: 4 oz / **Hunt's** | 80 |
| Meat-flavored: 4 oz / **Hunt's** Prima Salsa | 120 |
| w mushrooms: 1 cup / **Del Monte** | 100 |
| w mushrooms: 4 oz / **Hunt's** | 40 |
| w mushrooms: 4 oz / **Hunt's** Prima Salsa | 110 |
| w onion: 1 cup / **Del Monte** | 100 |
| w onions: 4 oz / **Hunt's** | 45 |
| w tidbits: 1 cup / **Del Monte** | 80 |
| Tuna casserole, mix, prepared: ½ cup / **McCormick** | 128 |
| Tuna casserole, mix, prepared: ½ cup / **Schilling** | 128 |
| White, mix, prepared: ½ cup / **Durkee** | 119 |
| Wine, burgundy, mix: 1 oz / **Lawry's** | 98 |
| Wine, sherry, mix: 1 oz / **Lawry's** | 94 |
| Wine, white, mix: 1 oz / **Lawry's** | 113 |

# Seasonings

CALORIES

**1 tsp unless noted**

| | |
|---|---|
| **Accent** | 9 |
| Bacon, imitation, crumbled: 1 tbsp | |
|      **Ann Page** | 25 |
|      **Baco's** | 40 |

   CALORIES

| | |
|---|---|
| **Durkee** Bacon Bits | 8 |
| **French's** Bacon Crumbles | 6 |
| **Lawry's** Baconion | 40 |
| **McCormick** Bacon Bits | 30 |
| **McCormick** Bacon Chips | 35 |
| **Schilling** Bacon Bits | 30 |
| **Schilling** Bacon Chips | 35 |
| Barbecue / **French's** | 6 |
| Chili powder / **Lawry's** | 9 |
| Garlic concentrate: 1 tbsp / **Lawry's** | 88 |
| Herb blend / **Lawry's** | 9 |
| Lemon pepper marinade / **Lawry's** | 7 |
| Meat tenderizer / **French's** | 2 |
| Meat tenderizer, seasoned / **French's** | 2 |
| Pepper, lemon-flavored / **French's** Lemon and Pepper Seasoning | 6 |
| Pepper, seasoned / **French's** | 8 |
| Pepper, seasoned / **Lawry's** | 8 |
| Pizza / **French's** | 4 |
| Salad / **Durkee** | 4 |
| Salad / **French's** Salad Lift | 6 |
| Salad w cheese / **Durkee** | 10 |
| Salt | |
|     Butter flavor, imitation / **French's** | 8 |
|     Celery / **French's** | 2 |
|     Garlic / **French's** | 4 |
|     Garlic-flavored / **Lawry's** | 5 |
|     Garlic, parslied / **French's** | 6 |
|     Hickory smoke / **French's** | 2 |
|     Onion / **French's** | 6 |
|     Onion-flavored / **Lawry's** | 4 |
|     Seasoned / **French's** | 2 |
|     Seasoned / **Lawry's** | 1 |
| Seafood / **French's** | 2 |
| Stock base, chicken-flavored / **French's** | 8 |
| Stock base, beef-flavored / **French's** | 8 |
| Sugar, cinnamon-flavored / **French's** | 16 |

## SEASONING MIXES

CALORIES

Beef
| | |
|---|---|
| **Lawry's** Beef Olé / 1¼ oz pkg | 126 |
| **Lawry's** Marinade / 1 1/16 oz pkg | 69 |
| Stew, mix, prepared: 1 cup / **Durkee** | 379 |
| Stew, dry mix: 1 pkg / **Durkee** | 99 |
| Stew: 1 env / **French's** | 150 |
| Stew:1⅔ oz pkg / **Lawry's** | 131 |
| Stew: 1½ oz pkg / **McCormick** | 90 |
| Stew: 1½ oz pkg / **Schilling** | 90 |
| Burger: ⅓ oz / **Lipton** Make-A-Better-Burger | 30 |
| Burger, onion: ⅓ oz / **Lipton** Make-A-Better-Burger | 30 |
| Chili: 1 env / **Ann Page** | 120 |
| Chili: 1 env / **French's** Chili-O | 150 |

Chili con carne
| | |
|---|---|
| Mix, prepared: 1 cup / **Durkee** | 465 |
| Mix dry: 1 pkg / **Durkee** | 148 |
| **Lawry's** / 1⅝ oz pkg | 137 |
| **McCormick** / 1¼ oz pkg | 225 |
| **Schilling** / 1¼ oz pkg | 225 |
| Chop suey, prepared: 1 cup / **Durkee** | 318 |
| Chop suey, dry mix: 1 pkg / **Durkee** | 128 |
| Enchilada, prepared: 1 cup / **Durkee** | 57 |
| Enchilada, dry mix: 1 pkg / **Durkee** | 89 |
| Enchilada: 1 env / **French's** | 120 |
| Fried rice, prepared: 1 cup / **Durkee** | 215 |
| Fried rice, dry mix: 1 pkg / **Durkee** | 62 |
| Goulash: 1⅝ pkg / **Lawry's** | 127 |

Ground beef
| | |
|---|---|
| Mix, prepared: 1 cup / **Durkee** | 653 |
| Mix, dry: 1 pkg / **Durkee** | 91 |
| **French's** Hamburger Seasoning / 1 env | 100 |
| w onions: 1 env / **Ann Page** | 100 |
| w onions, prepared: 1 cup / **Durkee** | 659 |
| w onions, dry mix: 1 pkg / **Durkee** | 102 |
| w onions: 1 env / **French's** | 100 |

| | |
|---|---|
| Hamburger, prepared: 1 cup / **Durkee** | 603 |
| Hamburger, dry mix: 1 pkg / **Durkee** | 110 |
| Meatball: 1 env / **French's** | 140 |
| Meatball, Italian, prepared: 1 cup / **Durkee** | 619 |
| Meatball, Italian, dry mix: 1 pkg / **Durkee** | 22 |
| Meatball, Italian w cheese, prepared: 1 cup / **Durkee** | 650 |
| Meatball, Italian w cheese, dry mix: 1 pkg / **Durkee** | 85 |
| Meatloaf | |
|  **Contadina** / 1 env | 363 |
|  **French's** / 1 env | 160 |
|  **Lawry's** / 3½ oz pkg | 333 |
|  **McCormick** / 1½ oz pkg | 120 |
|  **Schilling** / 1½ oz pkg | 120 |
| Meat marinade, prepared: ½ cup / **Durkee** | 47 |
| Meat marinade: 1 env / **French's** | 80 |
| Sloppy Joe | |
|  **Ann Page** / 1 env | 128 |
|  **Durkee** / 1 cup prepared | 581 |
|  **Durkee** / dry mix: 1 pkg | 118 |
|  **French's** / 1 env | 128 |
|  **Lawry's** / 1½ oz pkg | 139 |
|  **McCormick** / 1 5/16 oz pkg | 170 |
|  **Schilling** / 1 5/16 oz pkg | 170 |
|  Pizza flavor, prepared: 1 cup / **Durkee** | 597 |
|  Pizza flavor, dry mix: 1 pkg / **Durkee** | 99 |
| Spanish rice, prepared: 1 cup / **Durkee** | 274 |
| Spanish rice, dry mix: 1 pkg / **Durkee** | 129 |
| Spanish rice: 1½ oz pkg / **Lawry's** | 125 |
| Swiss steak: 1 oz pkg / **McCormick** | 45 |
| Swiss steak: 1 oz pkg / **Schilling** | 45 |
| Taco | |
|  Mix, prepared: 1 cup / **Durkee** | 642 |
|  Mix, dry: 1 pkg / **Durkee** | 67 |
|  **French's** / 1 env | 150 |
|  **McCormick** / 1¼ oz pkg | 65 |
|  **Schilling** / 1¼ oz pkg | 65 |

# Shortening

| | CALORIES |
|---|---|
| **Solid** | |
| Lard: 1 cup | 1850 |
| 1 tbsp | 115 |
| Vegetable: 1 tbsp / **Crisco** | 110 |
| Vegetable: 1 tbsp / **Fluffo** | 110 |
| Vegetable: 1 tbsp / **Mrs. Tucker's** | 120 |
| Vegetable: 1 tbsp / **Snowdrift** | 110 |

# Soft Drinks

| | CALORIES |
|---|---|
| **8 fl oz unless noted** | |
| All flavors: 6 fl oz / **Weight Watchers** Dietary Carbonated Beverages | 1 |
| Birch beer / **Canada Dry** | 110 |
| Bitter Lemon / **Canada Dry** | 100 |
| Bitter lemon / **Schweppes** | 112 |
| Black cherry | |
|     **Canada Dry** Low Calorie | 2 |
|     **No-Cal** | 0 |
|     **Shasta** | 104 |
|     **Shasta** Diet | 0 |
|     **Tab** | 2 |
| Black raspberry / **No-Cal** | 2 |
| **Bubble Up** | 97 |
| **Bubble Up** Sugar Free | 1 |
| Cactus Cooler / **Canada Dry** | 120 |

CALORIES

| | |
|---|---|
| Chocolate / **Canada Dry Low Calorie** | 2 |
| Chocolate / **No-Cal** | 2 |
| Chocolate / **Shasta** Diet | 0 |
| Chocolate mint / **No-Cal** | 2 |
| Club soda / **Canada Dry** | 0 |
| Club soda / **Schweppes** | 0 |
| Club soda / **Shasta** | 0 |
| Coffee / **No-Cal** | 2 |
| Cola | |
|     **Canada Dry** Low Calorie | 2 |
|     **Coca-Cola** | 96 |
|     **Diet-Rite** | 1 |
|     Jamaica cola / **Canada Dry** | 110 |
|     **No-Cal** | 0 |
|     **Pepsi-Cola** | 104 |
|     **Pepsi-Cola,** Diet | 1 |
|     **Pepsi** Light | 47 |
|     **Royal Crown** | 104 |
|     **Shasta** | 90 |
|     **Shasta** Diet | 0 |
|     **Tab** | 1 |
| Collins mixer / **Shasta** | 78 |
| Cream / **No-Cal** | 0 |
| Cream / **Shasta** | 100 |
| Cream / **Shasta** Diet | 0 |
| **Dr. Nehi** | 98 |
| **Dr. Pepper** | 98 |
| **Dr. Pepper** Sugar Free | 1 |
| **Fresca** | 2 |
| Ginger ale | |
|     **Canada Dry** | 90 |
|     **Canada Dry** Golden | 100 |
|     **Canada Dry** Low Calorie | 2 |
|     **Fanta** | 84 |
|     **Nehi** | 91 |
|     **No-Cal** | 0 |
|     **Schweppes** | 88 |
|     **Shasta** | 78 |

  CALORIES

| | |
|---|---|
| **Shasta** Diet | 0 |
| **Tab** | 3 |
| Ginger beer / **Schweppes** | 96 |
| Grape | |
| **Canada Dry** | 130 |
| **Canada Dry** Low Calorie | 2 |
| **Crush** | 120 |
| **Fanta** | 114 |
| **Nehi** | 116 |
| **No-Cal** | 0 |
| **Patio** | 128 |
| **Schweppes** | 129 |
| **Shasta** | 114 |
| **Shasta** Diet | 0 |
| **Tab** | 2 |
| Grapefruit / **Shasta** | 103 |
| Grapefruit / **Shasta** Diet | 2 |
| Half and Half / **Canada Dry** | 110 |
| Hi Spot / **Canada Dry** | 100 |
| **Kick** | 118 |
| Lemon / **Canada Dry** Low Calorie | 2 |
| Lemon-lime / **Shasta** | 93 |
| Lemon-lime / **Shasta** Diet | 0 |
| Lemon-lime / **TAB** | 3 |
| Lime / **Canada Dry** | 130 |
| **Mello Yello** | 115 |
| **Mr. PiBB** | 93 |
| **Mr. PiBB** wo sugar | 1 |
| **Mountain Dew** | 118 |
| Orange | |
| **Canada Dry** Low Calorie | 2 |
| **Canada Dry** Sunripe | 130 |
| **Crush** | 114 |
| **Fanta** | 117 |
| **Nehi** | 124 |
| **No-Cal** | 0 |
| **Patio** | 128 |

| | CALORIES |
|---|---|
| Schweppes Sparkling | 118 |
| Shasta | 114 |
| Shasta Diet | 0 |
| Tab | 1 |
| Pineapple / Canada Dry | 110 |
| Purple Passion / Canada Dry | 120 |
| Raspberry / Canada Dry Low Calorie | 2 |
| Red creme / Schweppes | 115 |
| Red Pop / No-Cal | 0 |
| Root beer | |
|    A & W | 114 |
|    A & W Sugar Free | 11 |
|    Berks County | 116 |
|    Canada Dry Barrelhead | 110 |
|    Canada Dry Barrelhead Low Calorie | 2 |
|    Canada Dry Low Calorie | 2 |
|    Canada Dry Rooti | 110 |
|    Dad's | 105 |
|    Diet Dad's | 1 |
|    Fanta | 103 |
|    Hires | 100 |
|    Hires Sugar Free | 1 |
|    No-Cal | 0 |
|    Patio | 110 |
|    Schweppes | 105 |
|    Shasta | 100 |
|    Shasta Diet | 0 |
|    Tab | 1 |
| 7 Up | 97 |
| 7 Up Diet | 2 |
| Shape-Up / No Cal | 0 |
| Sprite | 95 |
| Sprite wo sugar | 3 |
| Strawberry | |
|    Canada Dry California | 120 |
|    Canada Dry Low Calorie | 2 |
|    Crush | 114 |

CALORIES

| | |
|---|---|
| **Nehi** | 116 |
| **Shasta** | 94 |
| **Shasta** Diet | 0 |
| **Tab** | 2 |
| **Sun-Drop** | 118 |
| **Sun-Drop** Sugar Free | 1 |
| **Teem** | 93 |
| TNT / **No-Cal** | 0 |
| Tahitian Treat / **Canada Dry** | 130 |
| **Tiki** | 100 |
| **Tiki** Diet | 0 |
| Tonic water | |
| **Canada Dry** | 90 |
| **Canada Dry** Low Calorie | 2 |
| **No-Cal** | 0 |
| **Schweppes** | 88 |
| **Shasta** | 66 |
| **Upper 10** | 101 |
| Vanilla cream / **Canada Dry** | 130 |
| Vanilla Cream / **Canada Dry** Low Calorie | 2 |
| Wild cherry / **Canada Dry** | 130 |
| Wink / **Canada Dry** | 120 |
| Wink / **Canada Dry** Low Calorie | 2 |

# Soups

CALORIES

| | |
|---|---|
| Alphabet vegetable, mix, prepared: 6 fl oz / **Lipton** Cup-A-Soup | 40 |
| Asparagus, cream of, condensed, prepared: 10 oz / **Campbell** | 100 |
| Bean, canned | |
| Condensed, prepared: 8 oz / **Manischewitz** | 111 |

| | |
|---|---:|
| Condensed, prepared: 1 cup / **Wyler's** | 96 |
| Semi-condensed, prepared: 1 can / | |
|   **Campbell** Soup for One | 210 |
| w bacon, condensed, prepared: 1 cup / | |
|   **Ann Page** | 140 |
| w bacon, condensed, prepared: 10 oz / | |
|   **Campbell** | 190 |
| w bacon, condensed, prepared: 1 cup / | |
|   **Town House** | 157 |
| Black, condensed, prepared: 10 oz / | |
|   **Campbell** | 130 |
| Black, ready to serve: ½ can / | |
|   **Crosse & Blackwell** | 80 |
| w ham, ready to serve: ½ can / **Campbell** | |
|   Chunky 9½ oz | 260 |
| w ham, ready to serve, individual service | |
|   size: 1 can / **Campbell** Chunky 10¾ oz | 300 |
| w hot dogs, condensed, prepared: 10 oz / | |
|   **Campbell** | 210 |
| Lima, condensed, prepared: 8 oz / | |
|   **Manischewitz** | 93 |
| **Beef** | |
| Condensed, prepared: 10 oz / **Campbell** | 100 |
| Ready to serve: ½ can / **Campbell** | |
|   Chunky 9½ oz | 190 |
| Ready to serve, individual service size: | |
|   1 can / **Campbell** Chunky 10¾ oz | 220 |
| Flavor, mix, prepared: 8 oz / **Lipton** | |
|   Lite-Lunch | 200 |
| Barley, mix, prepared: 6 oz serving / **Wyler's** | 54 |
| Cabbage, condensed, prepared: 8 oz / | |
|   **Manischewitz** | 62 |
| Low sodium, ready to serve, individual service | |
|   size: 1 can / **Campbell** Chunky 7¼ oz | 170 |
| Mushroom, mix, prepared: 8 fl oz / **Lipton** | 45 |
| Noodle, condensed, prepared: 10 oz / | |
|   **Campbell** | 90 |

|  |  |
|---|---|
| Noodle, condensed, prepared: 8 oz / **Manischewitz** | 83 |
| Noodle, condensed, prepared: 1 cup / **Town House** | 74 |
| Noodle, mix, prepared: 1 env / **Souptime** | 30 |
| Noodle, mix, prepared: 6 oz serving / **Wyler's** | 37 |
| Vegetable, condensed, prepared: 8 oz / **Manischewitz** | 59 |

Bouillon

|  |  |
|---|---|
| Beef: 1 cube / **Herb-Ox** | 6 |
| Beef: 1 cube / **Maggi** | 6 |
| Beef: 1 cube / **Wyler's** | 7 |
| Beef-flavored: 1 cube / **Wyler's** | 6 |
| Beef-flavored, powder: 1 tsp / **Wyler's Instant** | 10 |
| Beef, powder: 1 tsp / **Wyler's Instant** | 7 |
| Chicken: 1 cube / **Herb-Ox** | 6 |
| Chicken: 1 cube / **Maggi** | 7 |
| Chicken-flavored: 1 cube / **Wyler's** | 8 |
| Chicken-flavored, powder: 1 tps / **Wyler's Instant** | 8 |
| Chicken, powder: 1 tsp / **Wyler's Instant** | 6 |
| Onion: 1 cube / **Herb-Ox** | 10 |
| Onion: 1 cube / **Wyler's** | 5 |
| Vegetable: 1 cube / **Herb-Ox** | 6 |
| Vegetable: 1 cube / **Wyler's** | 6 |
| Vegetable-flavored, powder: 1 tsp /**Wyler's Instant** | 6 |

Broth

|  |  |
|---|---|
| Beef: 1 packet / **Herb-Ox** | 8 |
| Beef: 1 tsp / **Herb-Ox Instant** | 7 |
| Beef, canned: 6¾ oz / **Swanson** | 20 |
| Beef, condensed, prepared: 10 oz / **Campbell** | 35 |
| Beef, mix: 1 packet / **Weight Watchers** | 10 |
| Chicken: 1 packet / **Herb-Ox** | 12 |
| Chicken: 1 tsp / **Herb-Ox Instant** | 6 |
| Chicken, canned: 6¾ oz / **Swanson** | 25 |
| Chicken, condensed, prepared: 10 oz / **Campbell** | 50 |

CALORIES

| | |
|---|---:|
| Chicken, mix, prepared: 6 fl oz / **Lipton** Cup-A-Broth | 25 |
| Chicken, mix: 1 packet / **Weight Watchers** | 10 |
| Onion: 1 packet / **Herb-Ox** | 14 |
| Onion, mix: 1 packet / **Weight Watchers** | 10 |
| Vegetable: 1 packet / **Herb-Ox** | 12 |
| Vegetable: 1 tsp / **Herb-Ox** Instant | 6 |
| Celery, cream of, condensed, prepared: 1 cup / **Ann Page** | 60 |
| Celery, cream of, condensed, prepared: 10 oz / **Campbell** | 110 |
| Celery, cream of, condensed, prepared: 1 cup / **Town House** | 101 |
| Cheddar cheese, condensed, prepared: 10 oz / **Campbell** | 180 |
| Chickarina, canned, ready to serve: 8 fl oz / **Progresso** | 100 |
| Chicken | |
|   Canned, ready to serve: ½ can / **Campbell** Chunky 9½ oz | 200 |
|   Canned, ready to serve, individual service size: 1 can / **Campbell** Chunky 10¾ oz | 230 |
|   Flavor, mix, prepared: 8 oz / **Lipton** Lite-Lunch | 220 |
|   Alphabet, condensed, prepared: 10 oz / **Campbell** | 110 |
|   Barley, condensed, prepared: 8 oz / **Manischewitz** | 83 |
|   Cream of, condensed, prepared: 1 cup / **Ann Page** | 90 |
|   Cream of, condensed, prepared: 10 oz / **Campbell** | 140 |
|   Cream of, condensed, prepared: 1 cup / **Town House** | 93 |
|   Cream of, mix, prepared: 6 fl oz / **Lipton** Cup-A-Soup | 80 |
|   Cream of, mix, prepared: 1 env / **Souptime** | 100 |

w dumplings, condensed, prepared: 10 oz /
   **Campbell**                                           120
Gumbo, condensed, prepared: 10 oz /
   **Campbell**                                            70
Kasha, condensed, prepared: 8 oz /
   **Manischewitz**                                        41
Low sodium, ready to serve: 1 can /
   **Campbell** Chunky 7½ oz                              170
Noodle, condensed, prepared: 1 cup /
   **Ann Page**                                            70
Noodle, condensed, prepared: 1 cup /
   **A & P** "O" Style                                     67
Noodle, condensed, prepared: 10 oz /
   **Campbell**                                            90
Noodle, condensed, prepared: 10 oz /
   **Campbell** Noodle-O's                                 90
Noodle, condensed, prepared: 8 oz /
   **Manischewitz**                                        46
Noodle, condensed, prepared: 1 cup /
   **Town House**                                          75
Noodle, condensed, prepared: 1 cup /
   **Town House** Star Noodle                              66
Noodle, semi-condensed, prepared: 1 cup /
   **Campbell** Soup for One 11⅝ oz                       120
Noodle, mix, prepared: 6 fl oz /
   **Lipton** Cup-A-Soup                                   45
Noodle, mix, prepared: 8 fl oz /
   **Lipton** Noodle                                       70
Noodle, mix, prepared: 8 fl oz /
   **Lipton** Ripple Noodle                                80
Noodle, mix, prepared: 1 env / **Souptime**               30
Noodle, mix, prepared: 6 oz serving /
   **Wyler's**                                             33
Rice, canned, ready to serve: ½ can /
   **Campbell** Chunky 9½ oz                              160
Rice, condensed, prepared: 1 cup /
   **Ann Page**                                            50

CALORIES

Rice, condensed, prepared: 10 oz /
  **Campbell**                                              80
Rice, condensed, prepared: 8 oz /
  **Manischewitz**                                         47
Rice, condensed, prepared: 1 cup /
  **Town House**                                          61
Rice, mix, prepared: 8 fl oz / **Lipton**           60
Rice, mix, prepared: 6 fl oz / **Lipton**
  Cup-A-Soup                                            50
Rice, mix, prepared: 6 oz serving / **Wyler's**     37
w stars, condensed, prepared: 1 cup /
  **Ann Page**                                            60
w stars, condensed, prepared: 10 oz /
  **Campbell**                                            80
Vegetable, canned, ready to serve: ½ can /
  **Campbell Chunky** 9½ oz                             190
Vegetable, condensed, prepared: 1 cup /
  **Ann Page**                                            80
Vegetable, condensed, prepared: 10 oz /
  **Campbell**                                            90
Vegetable, condensed, prepared: 8 oz /
  **Manischewitz**                                        55
Vegetable, condensed, prepared: 1 cup /
  **Town House**                                          85
Vegetable, mix, prepared: 6 fl oz /
  **Lipton Cup-A-Soup**                                  40
Vegetable, mix, prepared: 6 oz serving /
  **Wyler's**                                             28
Chili beef
  Condensed, prepared: 10 oz / **Campbell**           190
  Condensed, prepared: 1 cup / **Town House**         161
  Ready to serve: ½ can / **Campbell**
    **Chunky** 9¾ oz                                 260
  Ready to serve, individual service size:
    1 can / **Campbell Chunky** 11 oz               300
Chowder
  Clam, prepared: 1 cup / **Howard**
    **Johnson's**                                    176

CALORIES

| | |
|---|---:|
| Clam, ready to serve: 8 fl oz / **Progresso** | 100 |
| Clam, Manhattan, ready to serve: ½ can / **Campbell** Chunky 9½ oz | 160 |
| Clam, Manhattan, condensed, prepared: 10 oz / **Campbell** | 100 |
| Clam, Manhattan, condensed, prepared: 1 cup / **Snow's** | 58 |
| Clam, Manhattan, condensed, prepared: 7 oz / **Snow's** | 130 |
| Clam, Manhattan, ready to serve: ½ can / **Crosse & Blackwell** | 50 |
| Clam, New England, condensed prepared: 10 oz / **Campbell** | 100 |
| Clam, New England, condensed, made w milk: 10 oz / **Campbell** | 200 |
| Clam, New England, condensed, prepared: 7 oz / **Snow's** | 130 |
| Clam, New England, condensed, prepared: 1 cup / **Snow's** | 147 |
| Clam, New England, semi-condensed, prepared: 1 can / **Campbell** Soup for One 11⅝ oz | 125 |
| Clam, New England, ready to serve: ½ can / **Crosse & Blackwell** | 90 |
| Corn, condensed, prepared: 1 cup / **Snow's** | 154 |
| Fish, condensed, prepared: 1 cup / **Snow's** | 134 |
| Seafood, New England, condensed, prepared: 1 cup / **Snow's** | 147 |
| Consommé, beef, condensed, prepared: 10 oz / **Campbell** | 45 |
| Consommé Madrilene, clear, ready to serve: ½ can / **Crosse & Blackwell** | 25 |
| Consommé Madrilene, red, ready to serve: ½ can / **Crosse & Blackwell** | 25 |
| Crab, ready to serve: ½ can / **Crosse & Blackwell** | 50 |
| Escarole, in chicken broth, ready to serve: 1 cup / **Progresso** | 25 |

CALORIES

Gazpacho, ready to serve: ½ can / **Crosse & Blackwell**          30
Lentil, condensed, prepared: 8 oz / **Manischewitz**          166
Lentil, ready to serve: 1 cup / **Progresso**          150
Lentil w ham, ready to serve: ½ can / **Crosse & Blackwell**          80
Meatball Alphabet, condensed, prepared: 10 oz / **Campbell**          140
Minestrone
   Condensed, prepared: 1 cup / **Ann Page**          80
   Condensed, prepared: 10 oz / **Campbell**          110
   Condensed, prepared: 1 can / **Town House**          200
   Ready to serve: ½ can / **Campbell** Chunky 9½ oz          160
   Ready to serve: ½ can / **Crosse & Blackwell**          90
Mushroom
   Condensed, prepared: 10 oz / **Campbell**          110
   Mix, prepared: 1 env / **Souptime**          80
   Mix, prepared: 6 oz serving / **Wyler's**          113
   Barley, condensed, prepared: 8 oz / **Manischewitz**          72
   Bisque, ready to serve: ½ can / **Crosse & Blackwell**          90
   Cream of, condensed, prepared: 1 cup / **Ann Page**          120
   Cream of, condensed, prepared: 10 oz / **Campbell**          150
   Cream of, condensed, prepared: 1 cup / **Town House**          124
   Cream of, semi-condensed, prepared: 1 can / **Campbell** Soup for One 11¼ oz          160
   Cream of, mix, prepared: 6 fl oz / **Lipton** Cup-A-Soup          80
   Cream of, low sodium, ready to serve, individual service size: 1 can / **Campbell** 7¼ oz          140

Noodle
    Mix, prepared: 6 fl oz / **Lipton**
      Cup-A-Soup Giggle        40
    Mix, prepared: 6 fl oz / **Lipton**
      Cup-A-Soup Ring        50
    Mix, prepared: 8 fl oz / **Lipton**
      Giggle Noodle        80
    Mix, prepared: 8 fl oz / **Lipton**
      Ring-O-Noodle        50
    w beef flavor, mix, prepared: 6 fl oz /
      **Lipton** Cup-A-Soup        35
    w chicken, condensed, prepared: 10 oz /
      **Campbell** Curley        100
    w chicken broth, mix: 1/5 env / **Ann Page**   45
    w chicken broth, mix, prepared: 8 fl oz /
      **Lipton** Noodle        60
    w ground beef, condensed, prepared: 10 oz /
      **Campbell**        110
Onion
    Condensed, prepared: 10 oz / **Campbell**   80
    Mix: 1/5 env / **Ann Page**        25
    Mix, prepared: 8 fl oz / **Lipton**        40
    Mix, prepared: 8 fl oz / **Lipton** Beefy   30
    Mix, prepared: 6 fl oz / **Lipton** Cup-A-Soup   30
    Mix, prepared: 6 oz serving / **Wyler's**   28
    Cream of, condensed, prepared: 10 oz /
      **Campbell**        180
    French, condensed, prepared: 1 can /
      **Town House**        180
    French, mix, prepared: 1 env / **Souptime**   20
    Mushroom, mix, prepared: 8 fl oz / **Lipton**   35
Oriental style, mix, prepared: 8 oz / **Lipton**
    Lite-Lunch        210
Oyster stew, condensed, prepared: 10 oz /
    **Campbell**        70
Oyster stew, condensed, prepared w milk:
    10 oz / **Campbell**        170

Pea, green
    Condensed, prepared: 10 oz / **Campbell**     180
    Mix, prepared: 8 fl oz / **Lipton**     130
    Mix, prepared: 6 fl oz / **Lipton** Cup-A-Soup     120
    Mix, prepared: 1 env / **Souptime**     70
    Low sodium, ready to serve, individual
       service size: 1 can / **Campbell** 7½ oz     150
Pea, split
    Condensed, prepared: 8 oz / **Manischewitz**     133
    w ham, condensed, prepared: 1 cup /
      **Ann Page**     180
    w ham, condensed, prepared: 1 cup /
      **Town House**     153
    w ham, ready to serve: ½ can / **Campbell**
      Chunky 9½ oz     220
    w ham and bacon, condensed, prepared:
      10 oz / **Campbell**     210
Pepper Pot, condensed, prepared: 10 oz /
    **Campbell**     130
Potato, cream of, condensed, prepared: 10 oz /
    **Campbell**     90
Potato, cream of, condensed, prepared w
    milk: 10 oz / **Campbell**     140
Potato, cream of, condensed, prepared:
    1 can / **Town House**     220
Potato w leeks, mix, prepared: 6 oz serving /
    **Wyler's**     116
Scotch broth, condensed, prepared: 10 oz /
    **Campbell**     100
Shrimp, cream of, condensed, prepared: 10 oz /
    **Campbell**     110
Shrimp, cream of, condensed, prepared w milk:
    10 oz / **Campbell**     210
Shrimp, cream, ready to serve: ½ can /
    **Crosse & Blackwell**     90
Sirloin burger, ready to serve: ½ can /
    **Campbell** Chunky 9½ oz     210

Sirloin burger, ready to serve, individual service
   size: 1 can / **Campbell** Chunky 10¾ oz    230
Steak & potato, ready to serve: ½ can /
   **Campbell** Chunky 9½ oz    190
Stockpot, vegetable, mix, prepared: 8 oz /**Lipton**
   Lite-Lunch    220
Stockpot, vegetable-beef, condensed, prepared:
   10 oz / **Campbell**    120
Tomato
   Condensed, prepared: 1 cup / **Ann Page**    80
   Condensed, prepared: 10 oz / **Campbell**    110
   Condensed, prepared w milk: 10 oz /
     **Campbell**    210
   Condensed, prepared: 8 oz / **Manischewitz**    60
   Condensed, prepared: 1 cup / **Town House**    87
   Mix, prepared: 6 fl oz / **Lipton** Cup-A-Soup    70
   Mix, prepared: 1 env / **Souptime**    70
   Ready to serve: 8 fl oz / **Progresso**    110
   Beef, condensed, prepared: 10 oz /
     **Campbell** Noodle-O's    160
   Bisque, condensed, prepared: 10 oz /
     **Campbell**    140
   Low sodium, ready to serve, individual
     service size: 1 can / **Campbell** 7¼ oz    130
   Rice, condensed, prepared: 1 cup /
     **Ann Page**    90
   Rice, condensed, prepared: 10 oz /
     **Campbell** Old Fashioned    130
   Rice, condensed, prepared: 8 oz /
     **Manischewitz**    78
   Rice, condensed, prepared: 1 can /
     **Town House**    280
   Royale, semi-condensed, prepared: 1 can /
     **Campbell** Soup for One    180
Turkey
   Ready to serve: ½ can / **Campbell**
     Chunky 9¼ oz    160

| | |
|---|---|
| Noodle, condensed, prepared: 1 cup / **Ann Page** | 70 |
| Noodle, condensed, prepared: 10 oz / **Campbell** | 80 |
| Noodle, condensed, prepared: 1 cup / **Town House** | 83 |
| Noodle, low sodium, ready to serve, individual service size: 1 can / **Campbell** 7¼ oz | 60 |
| Vegetable, condensed, prepared: 1 cup / **Ann Page** | 60 |
| Vegetable, condensed, prepared: 10 oz / **Campbell** | 90 |

Vegetable

| | |
|---|---|
| Canned, ready to serve: ½ can / **Campbell** Chunky 9½ oz | 140 |
| Canned, ready to serve, individual service size: 1 can / **Campbell** Chunky 10¾ oz | 150 |
| Condensed, prepared: 1 cup / **Ann Page** Vegetarian | 70 |
| Condensed, prepared: 10 oz / **Campbell** | 100 |
| Condensed, prepared: 10 oz / **Campbell** Old Fashioned | 90 |
| Condensed, prepared: 10 oz / **Campbell** Vegetarian | 90 |
| Condensed, prepared: 8 oz / **Manischewitz** | 63 |
| Condensed, prepared: 1 cup / **Town House** Vegetarian | 83 |
| Semi-condensed, prepared: 1 can / **Campbell** Old World Soup for One | 125 |
| Mix, prepared: 8 fl oz / **Lipton** Country | 70 |
| Mix, prepared: 8 fl oz / **Lipton** Italian | 100 |
| Mix, prepared: 6 oz serving / **Wyler's** | 56 |
| Beef, condensed, prepared: 1 cup / **Ann Page** | 80 |
| Beef, condensed, prepared: 10 oz / **Campbell** | 90 |
| Beef, condensed, prepared: 1 cup / **Town House** | 66 |
| Beef, mix, prepared: 8 fl oz / **Lipton** | 60 |

CALORIES

| | |
|---|---|
| Beef, mix, prepared: 6 fl oz / **Lipton** Cup-A-Soup | 60 |
| Beef, ready to serve: ½ can / **Campbell** Chunky 9½ oz | 160 |
| Beef, low sodium, ready to serve: 1 can / **Campbell** 7¼ oz | 80 |
| Beef w shells, mix, prepared: 8 fl oz / **Lipton** | 100 |
| w beef stock, condensed, prepared: 1 cup / **Ann Page** | 70 |
| w beef stock, condensed, prepared: 1 cup / **Town House** | 83 |
| Cream of, mix, prepared: 1 env / **Souptime** | 80 |
| Low sodium, ready to serve, individual service size: 1 can / **Campbell** 7¼ oz | 90 |
| w noodles, condensed, prepared: 10 oz / **Campbell** Noodle-O's | 90 |
| Spring, mix, prepared: 6 fl oz / **Lipton** Cup-A-Soup | 45 |
| Vichyssoise, ready to serve: ½ can / **Crosse & Blackwell** | 70 |

# Spaghetti and Spaghetti Dishes

CALORIES

| | |
|---|---|
| Spaghetti, plain, enriched, cooked firm, "al dente": 1 cup | 192 |
| Spaghetti, plain, enriched, cooked, tender stage: 1 cup | 155 |
| Spaghetti, in tomato sauce, canned **Buitoni** Twists / ½ can | 160 |

CALORIES

w beef: 7½ oz can / **Hormel Short Orders** 280
w cheese: 7⅜ oz / **Franco-American** 170
w cheese sauce: 7⅜ oz / **Franco-American**
 **"SpaghettiOs"** 160
w frankfurters: 7⅜ oz / **Franco-American**
 **"SpaghettiOs"** 210
w meat sauce: 7¾ oz / **Franco-American** 220
w meatballs: ½ can / **Buitoni** 228
w meatballs: ½ can / **Buitoni** Twists 228
w meatballs: 7¼ oz / **Franco-American** 210
w little meatballs: 7⅜ oz / **Franco-American**
 **"SpaghettiOs"** 210
 w meatballs: 7½ oz can /
 **Hormel Short Orders** 205
w meatballs: 1 cup / **Libby's** 84
Spaghetti w sauce, frozen
 **Banquet** / 3 oz 311
 **Morton** Casserole / 1 pkg 220
 **Stouffer's** / 1 pkg (14 oz) 445
 w meatballs: 32 oz / **Banquet** Buffet Supper 1127
 w meatballs: 9 oz / **Green Giant** Boil-in-Bag
 Entrees 280
Spaghetti and sauce, mixes
 Prepared: 1 pouch / **Betty Crocker**
 Mug-O-Lunch 170
 Prepared: 1 cup / **Kraft** American Style 260
 Prepared: 1 cup / **Kraft** Tangy Italian Style 260

# Spreads

CALORIES

**1 oz = about ¼ cup**

Anchovy paste: 1tbsp / **Crosse & Blackwell** 20
Chicken, canned: 1 oz / **Swanson** 70
Chicken: 1 oz / **Underwood** 63

CALORIES

| | |
|---|---|
| Chicken salad: 1½ oz / **Carnation** Spreadables | 94 |
| Corned beef: 1 oz / **Underwood** | 55 |
| Ham | |
|     Deviled: 1 oz / **Hormel** | 70 |
|     Deviled, canned: 1½ tbsp / **Libby's** | 300 |
|     Deviled: 1 oz / **Underwood** | 97 |
|     Salad: 1½ oz / **Carnation** Spreadables | 78 |
| Liverwurst: 1 oz / **Underwood** | 92 |
| Peanut butter: 1 tbsp unless noted | |
|     **Ann Page** Krunchy | 105 |
|     **Ann Page** Smooth | 105 |
|     **Ann Page** Regular Grand | 105 |
|     **Home Brands** Natural | 100 |
|     **Home Brands** Real | 100 |
|     **Kitchen King** Crunchy | 95 |
|     **Kitchen King** Smooth | 95 |
|     **Peter Pan** Crunchy | 95 |
|     **Peter Pan,** low sodium | 95 |
|     **Peter Pan** Smooth | 95 |
|     **Planters** Creamy | 95 |
|     **Planters** Crunchy | 95 |
|     **Skippy** Creamy Smooth | 95 |
|     **Skippy** Old Fashioned Super Chunk | 95 |
|     **Skippy** Super Chunk | 95 |
|     **Smucker's** Crunchy | 95 |
|     **Smucker's** Natural | 100 |
|     **Smucker's** Smooth | 90 |
|     Sultana Krunchy | 105 |
|     and jelly: 1 oz / **Smucker's** Goober Grape | 125 |
| Potted meat: 1½ tbsp / **Libby's** | 208 |
| Roast Beef: 1 oz / **Underwood** | 58 |
| Sandwich spread: 1 tbsp unless noted | |
|     **Best Foods** Spred | 60 |
|     **Hellmann's** | 60 |
|     **Kraft** | 50 |
|     **Mrs. Filbert's** | 50 |
|     **Nu Made** | 60 |
|     **Oscar Mayer** / 1 oz | 65 |

CALORIES

**Spam,** deviled: 1 oz / **Hormel**                      80
Tuna salad: 1½ oz / **Carnation** Spreadables    81
Turkey salad: 1½ oz / **Carnation** Spreadables   86

# Sugar and Sweeteners

CALORIES

Honey, strained or extracted: 1 tbsp              64
Honey, strained or extracted: 1 cup             1031
Sugar
    Brown, not packed: 1 cup                  541
    Brown, packed: 1 cup                      821
    Maple: 1 oz                                99
    Powdered, unsifted: 1 cup                 462
    Powdered, unsifted: 1 tbsp                 31
    Powdered, sifted: 1 cup                   385
    White, granulated: 1 cup                  770
    White, granulated: 1 tbsp                  46
    White, granulated: 1 tsp                   15
Sugar substitute, granulated: 1 packet /
  **Weight Watchers** Sweet'ner                   4
Sweetener, artificial: 1 tsp / **Sprinkle Sweet**    2
Sweetener, artificial: ⅛ tsp / **Sweet 10**         0

# Syrups

**1 tbsp**

Pancake, waffle

|  |  |
|---|---|
| Aunt Jemima | 53 |
| Cary's Diet | 10 |
| Diet Delight | 15 |
| Golden Griddle | 50 |
| Karo | 60 |
| Karo Imitation Maple | 55 |
| Log Cabin Buttered | 52 |
| Log Cabin Country Kitchen | 51 |
| Log Cabin Maple-Honey | 54 |
| Mrs. Butterworth's | 53 |
| S & W Nutradiet | 12 |
| Tillie Lewis | 14 |
| Corn, dark / Karo | 60 |
| Corn, light / Karo | 60 |
| Maple, pure / Cary's | 60 |
| Maple blend / Log Cabin | 46 |
| Molasses, cane, dark (third extraction) | 45 |
| Molasses, cane, light (first extraction) | 50 |
| Sorghum | 55 |

# Tea

Bags, or loose tea prepared: 1 cup                                       1
Iced tea
    Canned: 8 fl oz / **No-Cal**                    0
    Instant: 1 level tsp / **Nestea**      less than 1
    Instant, lemon-flavored: 8 fl oz / **Nestea**   2
    Instant lemon flavored: 1 tsp dry mix /
      **A & P** Our Own Low Calorie       4
    Instant, lemon-flavored, w sugar: 1 env
      **A & P** Our Own                 480
    Instant, w sugar and lemon: 6 fl oz / **Nestea**  70

# Toppings

CALORIES

**1 tbsp unless noted**

Black cherry: 1 tsp / **No-Cal**                                        0
Black raspberry: 1 tsp / **No-Cal**                                     0
Butterscotch / **Kraft**                                              60
Butterscotch / **Smucker's**                                         70
Caramel / **Smucker's**                                              70
Caramel, chocolate-flavored / **Kraft**                              50
Cherry / **Smucker's**                                               65

CALORIES

| | |
|---|---|
| Chocolate | |
| **Bosco** | 50 |
| **Hershey's** | 45 |
| **Kraft** | 50 |
| **No-Cal** / 1 tsp | 2 |
| **Smucker's** | 65 |
| **Tillie Lewis** | 16 |
| Fudge / **Hershey's** | 45 |
| Fudge / **Kraft** | 70 |
| Fudge / **Smucker's** | 65 |
| Fudge, chocolate-mint / **Smucker's** | 70 |
| Fudge, Swiss milk chocolate / **Smucker's** | 70 |
| Coffee: 1 tsp / **No-Cal** | 2 |
| Cola: 1 tsp / **No-Cal** | 0 |
| Grape: 1 tsp / **No-Cal** | ¼ |
| Marshmallow / **Kraft** | 35 |
| Peanut butter caramel / **Smucker's** | 75 |
| Pecans in syrup / **Smucker's** | 65 |
| Pineapple / **Kraft** | 50 |
| Pineapple / **Smucker's** | 65 |
| Strawberry / **Kraft** | 45 |
| Strawberry: 1 tsp / **No-Cal** | 0 |
| Strawberry / **Smucker's** | 60 |
| Walnut / **Kraft** | 90 |
| Walnuts in syrup / **Smucker's** | 65 |
| Whipped, non-dairy, frozen / **Cool Whip** | 14 |
| Whipped, mix, prepared / **D-Zerta** | 8 |
| Whipped, mix, prepared / **Dream Whip** | 10 |

# Vegetables

## FRESH

| | CALORIES |
|---|---|
| Amaranth, raw, leaves: 1 lb | 163 |
| Artichokes (calorie range from 8 for freshly harvested artichokes to 44 for stored artichokes), cooked, bud or globe: 1 small | |
| Artichokes (calorie range from 10 for freshly harvested artichokes to 53 for stored artichokes), cooked, bud or globe: 1 medium | |
| Artichokes (calorie range from 12 for freshly harvested artichokes to 67 for stored artichokes), cooked, bud or globe: 1 large | |
| Asparagus | |
|     Raw: 1 lb | 118 |
|     Raw, cut (1½–2 in): 1 cup | 35 |
|     Cooked, cut (1½–2 in), drained: 1 cup | 29 |
|     Spears, cooked, drained: 1 small | 8 |
|     Spears, cooked, drained: 1 medium | 12 |
|     Spears, cooked, drained: 1 large | 20 |
| Bamboo shoots, raw, 1-in pieces: 1 lb | 122 |
| Barley, pearled, light: 1 cup | 698 |
| Barley, pearled, Pot or Scotch: 1 cup | 696 |
| Beans | |
|     Great Northern, cooked, drained: 1 cup | 212 |
|     Lima, immature (green), raw: 1 cup | 191 |
|     Lima, immature (green), cooked, drained: 1 cup | 189 |

CALORIES

| | |
|---|---|
| Lima, mature, cooked, drained: 1 cup | 262 |
| Mung, mature, dry, raw: 1 cup | 714 |
| Mung, mature, dry, raw: 1 lb | 1542 |
| Mung, sprouted seeds, raw: 1 cup | 37 |
| Mung, sprouted seeds, cooked, drained: 1 cup | 35 |
| Pea (navy), cooked, drained: 1 cup | 224 |
| Pinto, dry, raw: 1 cup | 663 |
| Pinto or calico or red Mexican, dry, raw: 1 lb | 1583 |
| Red, dry, cooked: ½ cup | 118 |
| Red, dry, raw: ½ cup | 343 |
| Red, kidney, cooked, drained: 1 cup | 218 |
| Snap, green, raw, cut: 1 cup | 35 |
| Snap, green, cooked, drained: 1 cup | 31 |
| Snap, yellow or wax, raw, cut: 1 cup | 30 |
| Snap, yellow or wax, cooked, drained: 1 cup | 28 |
| White, dry, raw: 1 lb | 1542 |
| Beets, common, red, raw, peeled, diced: 1 cup | 58 |
| Beets, common, red, peeled, cooked, drained, whole (2-in diam): 2 beets | 32 |
| Beets, common, red, peeled, cooked, drained, diced or sliced: 1 cup | 54 |
| Beets greens, common, edible leaves and stems, raw: 1 lb | 109 |
| Beet greens, common, edible leaves and stems, cooked, drained: 1 cup | 26 |
| Broadbeans, raw, immature seeds: 1 lb | 476 |
| Broadbeans, raw, mature seeds, dry: 1 lb | 1533 |
| Broccoli | |
| Stalks, raw: 1 lb | 145 |
| Cooked, drained: 1 small stalk | 36 |
| Cooked, drained: 1 medium stalk | 47 |
| Cooked, drained: 1 large stalk | 73 |
| Cooked, drained, ½-in pieces: 1 cup | 40 |
| Cooked, drained, whole or cut: 1 lb | 118 |

CALORIES

| | |
|---|---|
| Brussels sprouts, cooked: ½ cup | 28 |
| Brussels sprouts, raw: 9 med | 45 |

Cabbage

| | |
|---|---|
| Raw: 1 lb | 109 |
| Raw, ground: 1 cup | 36 |
| Raw, shredded coarsely or sliced: 1 cup | 17 |
| Raw, shredded finely or chopped: 1 cup | 22 |
| Chinese, raw: 1 lb | 109 |
| Chinese, raw, 1-in pieces: 1 cup | 11 |
| Red, raw: 1 lb | 141 |
| Red, raw, shredded coarsely or sliced: 1 cup | 22 |
| Red, raw, shredded finely or chopped: 1 cup | 28 |
| Savoy, raw: 1 lb | 109 |
| Savoy, raw, shredded coarsely or sliced: 1 cup | 17 |
| Spoon, raw, 1-in pieces: 1 cup | 11 |
| Spoon, cooked, drained, 1-in pieces: 1 cup | 24 |

Carrots

| | |
|---|---|
| Raw: 1 carrot( 2⅞ oz) | 30 |
| Raw: 1 lb | 191 |
| Raw, grated or shredded: 1 cup | 46 |
| Raw, strips: 1 oz or 6-8 strips | 12 |
| Cooked, drained, diced: 1 cup | 45 |
| Cooked, drained, sliced crosswise: 1 cup | 48 |

Cauliflower

| | |
|---|---|
| Raw: 1 head (1.9 lb) | 232 |
| Raw, flowerbuds, whole: 1 cup | 27 |
| Raw, flowerbuds, sliced: 1 cup | 23 |
| Raw, flowerbuds, chopped: 1 cup | 31 |
| Cooked, drained: 1 cup | 28 |

| | |
|---|---|
| Celeriac, raw: 4 to 6 roots | 40 |

Celery

| | |
|---|---|
| Raw: 1 lb | 77 |
| Raw, large outer stalk (8-in long, 1½-in wide): 1 stalk | 7 |
| Raw, small inner stalk (5-in long, ¾-in wide): 3 stalks | 9 |

CALORIES

| | |
|---|---:|
| Raw, chopped or diced: 1 cup | 20 |
| Cooked, diced: 1 cup | 21 |
| Chard, Swiss, raw: 1 lb | 113 |
| Chard, Swiss, cooked, drained, leaves: 1 cup | 32 |
| Chayote, raw: ½ med squash | 28 |
| Chickpeas or garbanzos, mature seeds, dry, raw: 1 cup | 720 |
| Chickpeas or garbanzos, mature seeds, dry, raw: 1 lb | 1633 |
| Chicory, Witloof, raw: 1 head (5-7 in long) | 8 |
| Chicory, Witloof, raw: 1 lb | 68 |
| Chicory, Witloof, raw, chopped, ½-in pieces: 1 cup | 14 |
| Chives, raw, chopped: 1 tbsp | 1 |
| Collards | |
|    Raw, leaves w stems: 1 lb | 181 |
|    Raw, leaves wo stems: 1 lb | 204 |
|    Cooked, drained, leaves w stems: 1 cup | 42 |
|    Cooked, drained, leaves wo stems: 1 cup | 63 |
| Corn, sweet, raw, white and yellow, husked: 1 lb | 240 |
| Corn, sweet, white and yellow, cooked, drained, kernels only: 1 cup | 137 |
| Corn, sweet, white and yellow, cooked, drained, on cob: 1 ear (5 x 1¾ in) | 70 |
| Cowpeas (including blackeye peas) | |
|    Immature, raw: 1 cup blackeye peas | 184 |
|    Immature, cooked, drained: 1 cup blackeye peas | 178 |
|    Mature seeds, dry, cooked, drained: 1 cup | 190 |
|    Young pods w seeds, raw: 1 lb | 200 |
|    Young pods w seeds, cooked, drained: 1 lb | 154 |
| Cress, garden, raw, trimmed: 5 to 8 sprigs | 3 |
| Cress, garden, raw, trimmed: ½ lb | 72 |
| Cucumbers | |
|    Raw, unpeeled, whole: 1 small | 25 |
|    Raw, unpeeled, whole: 1 large | 45 |
|    Raw, unpeeled, sliced: 1 cup | 16 |

CALORIES

| | |
|---|---|
| Raw, peeled, whole: 1 small | 22 |
| Raw, peeled, whole: 1 large | 39 |
| Dandelion greens, raw: 1 lb | 204 |
| Dandelion greens, cooked, drained: 1 cup | 35 |
| Dock or sorrel, raw: ½ lb | 45 |
| Eggplant, cooked, drained, diced: 1 cup | 38 |
| Endive, raw: 1 lb | 91 |
| Endive, raw, small pieces: 1 cup | 10 |
| Fennel leaves, raw, trimmed: ½ lb | 59 |
| Garlic, cloves, raw: 1 clove | 4 |
| Hyacinth-beans, raw, young pods, ½-in pieces: 1 cup | 32 |
| Hyacinth-beans, raw, mature, dry: 1 lb | 1533 |
| Kale, leaves wo stems, raw: 1 lb | 240 |
| Kale, cooked, drained: 1 cup | 43 |
| Kohlrabi, raw, diced: 1 cup | 41 |
| Kohlrabi, cooked, drained: 1 cup | 40 |
| Leeks, raw: 3 (5-in long) | 52 |
| Lentils, mature seeds, dry, whole, raw: 1 cup | 646 |
| Lentils, mature seeds, cooked, drained: 1 cup | 212 |
| Lettuce | |
| Butternut (Boston types and Bibb): 1 head | 23 |
| Butternut (Boston types and Bibb), chopped or shredded: 1 cup | 8 |
| Cos or romaine: 1 lb | 82 |
| Cos or romaine, chopped or shredded: 1 cup | 10 |
| Crisphead (including Iceberg): 1 wedge (¼ head) | 18 |
| Crisphead (including Iceberg): 1 head | 70 |
| Crisphead (including Iceberg), chopped or shredded: 1 cup | 7 |
| Looseleaf varieties, chopped or shredded: 1 cup | 10 |
| Mushrooms: 1 lb | 127 |
| Mushrooms, sliced, chopped or diced: 1 cup | 20 |
| Mustard greens, raw: 1 lb | 141 |
| Mustard greens, cooked, drained: 1 cup | 32 |

CALORIES

| | |
|---|---:|
| Mustard spinach, raw: 1 lb | 100 |
| Mustard spinach, cooked, drained: 1 cup | 29 |
| New Zealand spinach, raw: 1 lb | 86 |
| New Zealand spinach, cooked, drained: 1 cup | 23 |
| Okra, crosscut slices, cooked, drained: 1 cup | 46 |
| Onions | |
|     Raw: 1 lb | 172 |
|     Raw, chopped: 1 cup | 65 |
|     Raw, chopped or minced: 1 tbsp | 4 |
|     Raw, sliced: 1 cup | 44 |
|     Cooked, drained, whole or sliced: 1 cup | 61 |
|     Young green: 2 medium or 6 small | 14 |
|     Young green, chopped: 1 tbsp | 2 |
|     Young green, chopped or sliced: 1 cup | 36 |
| Parsley, raw: 10 sprigs (2½-in long) | 4 |
| Parsley, raw, chopped: 1 tbsp | 2 |
| Parsnips, raw: 1 lb | 293 |
| Parsnips, cooked, drained: 1 large parsnip | 106 |
| Parsnips, cooked, drained, diced: 1 cup | 102 |
| Peas | |
|     Green, immature, raw: 1 cup | 122 |
|     Green, immature, raw: 1 lb | 381 |
|     Cooked, drained: 1 cup | 114 |
|     Mature, dry, split, cooked: 1 cup | 230 |
| Peppers, chili, green, raw: ½ lb | 62 |
| Peppers, chili, red w seeds: ½ lb | 203 |
| Peppers, chili, red wo seeds: ½ lb | 108 |
| Peppers, hot, red, wo seeds, dried: 1 tbsp | 50 |
| Peppers, sweet | |
|     Green, raw, whole: 1 small (about 5 per lb) | 16 |
|     Green, raw, whole: 1 large | |
|       (about 2¼ per lb) | 36 |
|     Green, chopped or diced: 1 cup | 33 |
|     Green, cooked, drained: 1 large | 29 |
|     Red, raw, whole: 1 small (about 5 per lb) | 23 |
|     Red, raw, whole: 1 large | |
|       (about 2¼ per lb) | 51 |

CALORIES

Red, chopped or diced: 1 cup                                    47
Pokeberry (poke), shoots, cooked, drained:
  1 cup                                                         33
Potatoes
  Baked in skin: 1 potato (2⅓ x 4¾ in)                         145
  Boiled in skin: 1 potato (2⅓ x 4¾ in)                        173
  Boiled in skin: 1 potato, round, 2½-in diam                  104
  Boiled in skin, diced or sliced: 1 cup                       101
  Peeled, boiled: 1 potato (2⅓ x 4¾ in)                        146
  Peeled, boiled: 1 potato, round, 2½-in diam                   88
  Peeled, boiled, diced or sliced: 1 cup                       101
  French fried: 10 strips, 2–3½-in long                        137
  Fried from raw: 1 cup                                        456
  Mashed w milk and butter or margarine:
    1 cup                                                      197
Pumpkin, pulp: 8 oz                                            42
Purslane leaves and stems, raw: ½ lb                           48
Radishes, raw, whole: 10 medium                                8
Radishes, raw, whole: 10 large                                 14
Radishes, raw, sliced: 1 cup                                   20
Rutabagas, raw, cubed: 1 cup                                   64
Rutabagas, cooked, drained, cubed or sliced:
  1 cup                                                        60
Shallot bulbs, raw, chopped: 1 tbsp                            7
Soybeans
  Mature seeds, dry, cooked: 1 cup                             234
  Sprouted seeds, raw: 1 cup                                   48
  Sprouted seeds, cooked, drained: 1 cup                       48
  Curd (tofu): 1 piece (2½ x 2¾ x 1 in)                        86
Spinach, raw: 1 lb                                             118
Spinach, raw, chopped: 1 cup                                   14
Spinach, leaves, cooked, drained: 1 cup                        41
Squash
  Acorn, baked: ½ squash                                       97
  Acorn, baked, mashed: 1 cup                                  113
  Butternut, baked, mashed: 1 cup                              139
  Butternut, boiled, mashed: 1 cup                             100

CALORIES

| | |
|---|---|
| Crookneck and straightneck, yellow, raw, sliced: 1 cup | 26 |
| Crookneck and straightneck, yellow, raw: 1 lb | 91 |
| Crookneck and straightneck, yellow, cooked, sliced: 1 cup | 27 |
| Crookneck and straightneck, yellow, cooked, mashed: 1 cup | 36 |
| Hubbard, baked, mashed: 1 cup | 103 |
| Hubbard, boiled, mashed: 1 cup | 74 |
| Hubbard, boiled, diced: 1 cup | 71 |
| Scallop varieties, white and pale green, raw, sliced: 1 cup | 27 |
| Scallop varieties, white and pale green, raw: 1 lb | 95 |
| Summer, all varieties, cooked, sliced: 1 cup | 25 |
| Summer, all varieties, cooked, cubed or diced: 1 cup | 29 |
| Summer, all varieties, cooked, mashed: 1 cup | 34 |
| Winter, all varieties, cooked, baked, mashed: 1 cup | 129 |
| Winter, all varieties, cooked, boiled, mashed: 1 cup | 93 |
| Zucchini and Cocozelle, green, raw, sliced: 1 cup | 22 |
| Zucchini and Cocozelle, green, raw: 1 lb | 77 |
| Zucchini and Cocozelle, green, cooked, sliced: 1 cup | 22 |
| Zucchini and Cocozelle, green, cooked, mashed: 1 cup | 29 |
| Sweet potatoes, baked in skin: 1 potato (5 x 2 in) | 161 |
| Sweet potatoes, boiled in skin: 1 potato (5 x 2 in) | 172 |
| Sweet potatoes, mashed: 1 cup | 291 |
| Tomatoes, raw: 1 small (3½ oz) | 20 |
| Tomatoes, raw: 1 large (4¾ oz) | 27 |
| Tomatoes, boiled: 1 cup | 63 |

|  | CALORIES |
|---|---|
| Turnips, raw: 1 cup | 39 |
| Turnips, cooked, drained, cubed: 1 cup | 36 |
| Turnips, mashed: 1 cup | 53 |
| Turnip greens, raw: 1 lb | 127 |
| Turnip greens, cooked, drained: 1 cup | 29 |
| Water chestnut, peeled: 4 chestnuts | 20 |
| Watercress, raw, whole: 1 cup | 7 |
| Watercress, raw, finely chopped: 1 cup | 24 |

## CANNED AND FROZEN

| | |
|---|---|
| Artichoke hearts, frozen: 3 oz (5 or 6 hearts) / Birds Eye | 20 |
| Asparagus, canned: 1 cup unless noted | |
|     Cut / Green Giant | 40 |
|     Cut / Kounty Kist | 40 |
|     Cut / Lindy | 40 |
|     Cut / Stokely-Van Camp | 45 |
|     Spears / Green Giant | 40 |
|     Spears / Le Sueur | 40 |
|     Spears: 5 whole / S and W Nutradiet | 16 |
|     Spears / Town House | 35 |
|     Spears and tips / Del Monte | 35 |
|     Spears, tipped / Del Monte | 35 |
|     Whole / Stokely-Van Camp | 50 |
|     White / Del Monte | 35 |
| Asparagus, frozen | |
|     Cut: 3.3 oz (about ½ cup / Birds Eye | 25 |
|     Cut, in butter sauce: 1 cup / Green Giant | 90 |
|     Cuts and tips: ½ cup / Seabrook Farms | 23 |
|     Cuts and tips, in Hollandaise sauce: ½ cup / Seabrook Farms | 84 |
|     Spears: 3.3 oz (about ½ cup) / Birds Eye | 25 |
|     Spears: 5 spears / Seabrook Farms | 19 |

CALORIES

| | |
|---|---:|
| Spears, jumbo: 3.3 oz (about ½ cup) / **Birds Eye** | 25 |
| Beans, baked: 1 cup | |
| **Howard Johnson's** | 340 |
| Pea / **B & M** | 336 |
| Red kidney / **B & M** | 336 |
| Yellow eye / **B & M** | 360 |
| Beans, baked style | |
| w bacon: 7½ oz can / **Hormel Short Orders** | 340 |
| In barbecue sauce: 8 oz / **Campbell** | 280 |
| In chili gravy: 8 oz / **Ann Page** | 230 |
| w frankfurters: 7½ oz can / **Hormel Short Orders** Beans 'n Wieners | 310 |
| w frankfurters, in tomato and molasses sauce: 8 oz / **Campbell** Beans & Franks | 370 |
| w ham: 7½ oz can / **Hormel Short Orders** | 385 |
| In molasses and brown sugar sauce: 8 oz / **Campbell Old Fashioned** | 290 |
| w pork and molasses: 8 oz / **Ann Page** Boston Style | 290 |
| w pork, in molasses sauce: 1 cup / **Libby's** | 270 |
| w pork and tomato sauce: 8 oz / **Ann Page** | 240 |
| w pork, in tomato sauce: 8 oz / **Campbell** | 260 |
| w pork, in tomato sauce: 1 cup / **Libby's** | 280 |
| In tomato sauce: 8 oz / **Ann Page** Vegetarian | 230 |
| In tomato sauce: 1 cup / **Libby's** Vegetarian | 260 |
| In tomato sauce: 8 oz / **Morton House** | 270 |
| Beans, black turtle, canned: 1 cup / **Progresso** | 205 |
| Beans, fava, canned: 1 cup / **Progresso** | 180 |
| Beans, garbanzo, canned: 8 oz / **Old El Paso** | 184 |
| Beans, green, canned: 1 cup unless noted | |
| Cut / **Del Monte** | 40 |
| Cut / **Green Giant** | 30 |
| Cut / **Kounty Kist** | 40 |
| Cut / **Libby's** Blue Lake | 40 |
| Cut / **Lindy** | 40 |

CALORIES

| | |
|---|---|
| Cut: ½ cup / S and W Nutradiet | 16 |
| Cut / Stokely-Van Camp | 40 |
| French / Del Monte | 40 |
| French / Green Giant | 30 |
| French / Kounty Kist | 40 |
| French / Libby's Blue Lake | 35 |
| French / Lindy | 40 |
| Italian / Del Monte | 60 |
| Seasoned / Del Monte | 40 |
| Sliced / Stokely-Van Camp | 40 |
| Whole / Del Monte | 35 |
| Whole / Green Giant | 30 |
| Whole / Kounty Kist | 40 |
| Whole / Libby's Blue Lake | 35 |
| Whole / Lindy | 40 |
| Whole / Stokely-Van Camp | 40 |
| Whole, tiny / Del Monte | 40 |

Beans, green, frozen

| | |
|---|---|
| Cut: 3 oz (about ½ cup) / Birds Eye | 25 |
| Cut: 1 cup / Kounty Kist Poly Bag | 30 |
| Cut: ½ cup / Seabrook Farms | 21 |
| Cut, in butter sauce: 1 cup / Green Giant | 70 |
| Cut, in mushroom sauce: ½ cup / Seabrook Farms | 100 |
| French: 3 oz (about ½ cup) / Birds Eye | 30 |
| French: ½ cup / Seabrook Farms | 23 |
| French, in butter sauce: 1 cup / Green Giant | 70 |
| French w sliced mushrooms: 3 oz (about ½ cup) / Birds Eye Combinations | 30 |
| French w toasted almonds: 3 oz (about ½ cup) / Birds Eye Combinations | 50 |
| Italian: 3 oz (about ½ cup) / Birds Eye | 30 |
| w onions and bacon bits: 1 cup / Green Giant | 80 |
| and pearl onions: 3 oz (about ½ cup) / Birds Eye Combinations | 30 |
| and spaetzle w sauce: 3.3 oz (about ½ cup) / Birds Eye International | 50 |
| Whole: 3 oz (about ½ cup) / Birds Eye | 25 |

CALORIES

| | |
|---|---|
| Beans, kidney, red: 8 oz / **Ann Page** | 220 |
| Beans, kidney, red, canned: 1 cup / **Progresso** | 185 |
| Beans, kidney, white, canned: 1 cup / **Progresso** Cannellini | 190 |
| Beans, lima | |
|     Baby, canned: 8oz / **Sultana** | 200 |
|     Baby, frozen: 3.3 oz (about ½ cup) / **Birds Eye** | 120 |
|     Baby, frozen: 1 cup / **Green Giant** Poly Bag | 150 |
|     Baby, frozen: 1 cup / **Kounty Kist** Poly Bag | 190 |
|     Baby, frozen: ½ cup / **Seabrook Farms** | 95 |
|     Baby, in butter sauce, frozen: 1 cup / **Green Giant** | 220 |
|     Canned: 1 cup / **Del Monte** | 150 |
|     Canned: 1 cup / **Libby's** | 160 |
|     Canned: 1 cup / **Stokely-Van Camp** | 180 |
|     Canned, seasoned: 1 cup / **Del Monte** | 160 |
|     Fordhook, frozen: 3.3 oz (about ½ cup) / **Birds Eye** | 100 |
|     Fordhook, frozen: ½ cup / **Seabrook Farms** | 85 |
|     Tiny, frozen: 3.3 oz (about ½ cup) / **Birds Eye** | 120 |
| Beans, pinto, canned: 1 cup / **Progresso** | 165 |
| Beans, red, canned: 8 oz / **Ann Page** | 220 |
| Beans, Roman, canned: 1 cup / **Progresso** | 210 |
| Bean, salad, canned: 1 cup / **Green Giant** 3 Bean | 190 |
| Beans, Shellie, canned, 1 cup / **Stokely-Van Camp** | 80 |
| Beans, wax or yellow: 1 cup unless noted | |
|     Cut, canned / **Del Monte** | 35 |
|     Cut, canned / **Libby's** | 40 |
|     Cut, canned / **Stokely-Van Camp** | 45 |
|     Cut, frozen: 3 oz (about ½ cup) / **Birds Eye** | 30 |
|     Cut, frozen: ½ cup / **Seabrook Farms** | 20 |
|     French cut, canned / **Del Monte** | 35 |
|     Sliced, canned / **Stokely-Van Camp** | 40 |
| Beets, canned: 1 cup unless noted | |
|     Cut / **Del Monte** | 70 |

| | |
|---|---:|
| Cut / Libby's | 70 |
| Cut / Stokely-Van Camp | 90 |
| Diced / Libby's | 70 |
| Diced / Stokely-Van Camp | 70 |
| Harvard / Stokely-Van Camp | 160 |
| Harvard, diced / Libby's | 160 |
| Pickled, crinkle cut / Del Monte | 150 |
| Pickled, sliced / Libby's | 150 |
| Pickled, sliced / Stokely-Van Camp | 190 |
| Pickled, sliced / Town House | 140 |
| Pickled, whole / Libby's | 150 |
| Pickled, whole / Stokely-Van Camp | 200 |
| Shoestring / Libby's | 50 |
| Sliced / Del Monte | 70 |
| Sliced / Libby's | 70 |
| Sliced: ½ cup / S and W Nutradiet | 28 |
| Sliced / Stokely-Van Camp | 80 |
| Whole / Del Monte | 70 |
| Whole / Libby's | 70 |
| Whole / Stokely-Van Camp | 90 |
| Broccoli, frozen | |
| Au gratin: ½ pkg / Stouffer's | 170 |
| w cauliflower and carrots, in cheese sauce: 1 cup / Green Giant | 140 |
| w cheese sauce: 3.3 oz (about ½ cup)/ Birds Eye Combinations | 110 |
| In cheese sauce: 1 cup / Green Giant | 130 |
| In cheese sauce: 1 cup / Green Giant Bake n' Serve | 260 |
| Chopped: 3.3 oz (about ½ cup) / Birds Eye | 25 |
| Chopped: ½ cup / Seabrook Farms | 23 |
| Cut: 1 cup / Green Giant Poly Bag | 30 |
| Cut: 1 cup / Kounty Kist Poly Bag | 30 |
| Spears: 3.3 oz (about ½ cup) / Birds Eye | 25 |
| Spears: ⅓ pkg / Seabrook Farms | 21 |
| Spears, baby: 3.3 oz (about ½ cup) / Birds Eye | 25 |
| Spears, in butter sauce: 1 cup / Green Giant | 90 |

CALORIES

Brussels sprouts, frozen
    **Birds Eye** / 3.3 oz (about ½ cup)    30
    **Green Giant** Poly Bag / 1 cup    50
    **Kounty Kist** Poly Bag / 1 cup    50
    **Seabrook Farms** / ½ cup    38
    Baby: 3.3 oz (about ½ cup) / **Birds Eye**    35
    In butter sauce: 1 cup / **Green Giant**    110
    Halves, in cheese sauce: 1 cup / **Green Giant**    170
Butterbeans, canned: 8 oz / **Sultana**    170
Butterbeans, frozen: ½ cup / **Seabrook Farms**    102
Butterbeans, baby, frozen: 3.3 oz (about ½
    cup) / **Birds Eye**    130
Butterbeans, speckled, frozen: 1 cup / **Green Giant**
    Boil-in-Bag Southern Recipe    280
Butterbeans w ham, canned: 1 cup / **Libby's**    100
Carrots: 1 cup unless noted
    Cut, canned: ½ cup / **S & W Nutradiet**    22
    Diced, canned / **Del Monte**    60
    Diced, canned / **Libby's**    40
    Diced, canned / **Stokely-Van Camp**    60
    Sliced, canned / **Del Monte**    60
    Sliced, canned / **Libby's**    40
    Sliced, canned / **Stokely-Van Camp**    50
    w brown sugar glaze, frozen: 3.3 oz (about
    ½ cup) / **Birds Eye** Combinations    80
    In butter sauce, frozen / **Green Giant**
    Nuggets    100
Cauliflower, frozen
    **Birds Eye** / 3.3 oz (about ½ cup)    25
    **Green Giant** Poly Bag / 1 cup    25
    **Kounty Kist** Poly Bag / 1 cup    25
    **Seabrook Farms** / ½ cup    17
    w cheese sauce: 3.3 oz (about ½ cup) /
    **Birds Eye** Combinations    110
    In cheese sauce: 1 cup / **Green Giant**    130
    In cheese sauce: 1 cup / **Green Giant**
    Bake n' Serve    220

CALORIES

| | |
|---|---:|
| Chick-peas, canned: 1 cup / **Progresso** | 195 |
| Collard greens, chopped, frozen: 3.3 oz (about ½ cup) / **Birds Eye** | 30 |
| Collard greens, frozen: ½ cup / **Seabrook Farms** | 22 |
| Corn, golden, canned: 1 cup unless noted | |
|     Cream style / **Del Monte** | 210 |
|     Cream style / **Green Giant** | 210 |
|     Cream style / **Kounty Kist** | 230 |
|     Cream style / **Libby's** | 170 |
|     Cream style / **Lindy** | 230 |
|     Cream style: ½ cup / **S and W Nutradiet** | 84 |
|     Cream style / **Stokely-Van Camp** | 210 |
|     Liquid pack / **Del Monte** Family Style | 170 |
|     Liquid pack / **Green Giant** | 160 |
|     Liquid pack / **Kounty Kist** | 180 |
|     Liquid pack / **Le Sueur** | 170 |
|     Liquid pack / **Libby's** | 160 |
|     Liquid pack / **Lindy** | 180 |
|     Liquid pack: ½ cup / **S and W Nutradiet** | 52 |
|     Liquid pack / **Stokely-Van Camp** | 180 |
|     Vacuum pack / **Del Monte** | 200 |
|     Vacuum pack / **Green Giant** Niblets | 150 |
|     Vacuum pack / **Kounty Kist** | 160 |
|     Vacuum pack / **Lindy** | 160 |
|     Vacuum pack / **Stokely-Van Camp** | 240 |
|     w peppers / **Del Monte Corn 'n Peppers** | 190 |
|     w peppers / **Green Giant Mexicorn** | 150 |
| Corn, golden, frozen | |
|     In butter sauce: 1 cup / **Green Giant** Niblets | 190 |
|     On cob: 1 ear / **Birds Eye** | 130 |
|     On cob: 1 ear / **Birds Eye Little Ears** | 70 |
|     On cob: 1 ear / **Green Giant** | 160 |
|     On cob: 1 ear / **Green Giant** Nibbler | 90 |
|     Cream style: 1 cup / **Green Giant** | 180 |
|     w peppers, in butter sauce: 1 cup / **Green Giant** Mexican | 190 |
|     Souffle: ⅓ pkg / **Stouffer's** | 155 |

Whole kernel: 3.3 oz (about ½ cup) /
   **Birds Eye** — 70
Whole kernel: 1 cup / **Green Giant** Poly Bag — 130
Whole kernel: 1 cup / **Kounty Kist** Poly Bag — 140
Whole kernel: 3 oz / **Ore-Ida** — 100
Whole kernel: ½ cup / **Seabrook Farms** — 70
Corn, white: 1 cup
  Canned / **Stokely-Van Camp** — 240
  Cream style, canned / **Del Monte** — 190
  Cream style, canned / **Stokely-Van Camp** — 220
  Whole kernel, canned / **Del Monte** — 150
  Whole kernel, vacuum pack, canned /
    **Green Giant** — 150
  Whole kernel, frozen / **Green Giant** Poly Bag — 130
  Whole kernel, frozen / **Kounty Kist** Poly Bag — 140
  Whole kernel, in butter sauce, frozen /
    **Green Giant** — 190
Eggplant Parmesan, frozen: 5½ oz / **Mrs. Paul's** — 250
Eggplant slices, fried, frozen: 3 oz / **Mrs. Paul's** — 230
Eggplant sticks, fried, frozen: 3½ oz /
  **Mrs. Paul's** — 260
Green peppers, stuffed, frozen: 1 pkg / **Stouffer's** — 225
Green peppers stuffed, frozen: 13 oz /
  **Weight Watchers** — 320
Kale, chopped, frozen: 3.3 oz (about ½ cup) /
  **Birds Eye** — 30
Kale, chopped, frozen: ½ cup / **Seabrook Farms** — 30
Kale, leaf, frozen: ½ cup / **Seabrook Farms** — 30
Mixed, canned: 1 cup
  **Del Monte** — 80
  **Libby's** Garden Vegetables — 80
  **Stokely-Van Camp** — 80
  **Town House** — 90
Mixed, frozen
  **Birds Eye** / 3.3 oz (about ½ cup) — 60
  **Green Giant** Poly Bag / 1 cup — 90
  **Kounty Kist** Poly Bag / 1 cup — 90

CALORIES

**Seabrook Farms** / ½ cup                                    50
California blend: 1 cup / **Kounty Kist**
  Poly Bag                                          30
Cantonese style: 3.3 oz (about ½ cup) /
  **Birds Eye** Stir-Fry                            50
Chinese: 1 pkg / **La Choy**                                 72
Chinese style: 1 cup / **Green Giant**
  Boil-in-Bag Oriental Combination                 130
Chinese style w sauce: 3.3 oz (about ½ cup) /
  **Birds Eye** International                       20
Chinese style w seasonings: 3.3 oz (about
  ½ cup) / **Birds Eye** Stir-Fry                   35
Danish style w sauce: 3.3 oz (about ½ cup) /
  **Birds Eye** International                       30
Hawaiian style: 1 cup / **Green Giant**
  Boil-in-Bag Oriental Combination                 200
Hawaiian style w sauce: 3.3 oz (about ½
  cup) / **Birds Eye** International                40
Italian style w sauce: 3.3 oz (about ½ cup) /
  **Birds Eye** International                       45
Japanese: 1 pkg / **La Choy**                                72
Japanese style: 1 cup / **Green Giant**
  Boil-in-Bag Oriental Combination                 130
Japanese style w sauce: 3.3 oz (about ½ cup) /
  **Birds Eye** International                       40
Japanese style w seasonings: 3.3 oz (about ½
  cup) / **Birds Eye** Stir-Fry                     30
Jubilee: 3.3 oz (about ½ cup) / **Birds Eye**
  Combinations                                     120
Mandarin style w seasonings: 3.3 oz (about ½
  cup) / **Birds Eye** Stir-Fry                     30
New England style: 3.3 oz (about ½ cup) /
  **Birds Eye** Americana Recipe                    60
New Orleans creole style: 3.3 oz (about ½
  cup) / **Birds Eye** Americana Recipe             70
Parisian style w sauce: 3.3 oz (about ½
  cup) / **Birds Eye** International                30

Pennsylvania Dutch style: 3.3 oz (about ½
cup) / **Birds Eye** Americana Recipe    40
San Francisco style: 3.3 oz (about ½
cup) / **Birds Eye** Americana Recipe    45
Wisconsin country style: 3.3 oz (about ½
cup) / **Birds Eye** Americana Recipe    40
In butter sauce: 1 cup / **Green Giant**    130
In onion sauce: 2.6 oz / **Birds Eye**    100
Mushrooms
   Canned: 4 oz / **Dole**    19
   Pieces and stems, canned: 1 oz /
     **Green Giant**    7
   Sliced, canned: 1 oz / **Green Giant**    7
   Whole, canned: 1 oz / **Green Giant**    7
   In butter sauce, frozen: 2 oz / **Green Giant**    30
Mustard greens, chopped, frozen: 3.3 oz
(about ½ cup) / **Birds Eye**    18
Mustard greens, chopped, frozen: ½ cup /
**Seabrook Farms**    21
Mustard greens, leaf, frozen: ½ cup /
**Seabrook Farms**    21
Okra
   Cut, frozen: 3.3 oz (about ½ cup) /
     **Birds Eye**    25
   Cut, frozen: ½ cup / **Seabrook Farms**    26
   Gumbo, frozen: 1 cup / **Green Giant**
     Boil-in-Bag Southern Recipe    220
   Whole, frozen: 3.3 oz (about ½ cup) /
     **Birds Eye**    35
   Whole, frozen: ½ cup / **Seabrook Farms**    26
Onions, boiled, canned: 4 oz / **O & C**    32
Onions, in cream sauce, canned: ½ cup / **O & C**    90
Onions, frozen
   Chopped: 1 oz / **Birds Eye**    8
   Chopped: 2 oz / **Ore-Ida**    20
   Small, whole: 3.3 oz (about ½ cup) /
     **Birds Eye**    40

| | |
|---|---:|
| In cheese flavor sauce: 1 cup / **Green Giant** | 140 |
| In cream sauce: 3 oz (about ½ cup) / **Birds Eye** | 100 |
| In cream sauce: ½ cup / **Seabrook Farms** | 116 |
| Onion rings, fried, canned: 1 oz / **O & C** | 178 |
| Onion rings, fried, frozen: 2½ oz / **Mrs. Paul's** | 150 |
| Onion rings, fried, frozen: 2 oz / **Ore-Ida Onion Ringers** | 160 |
| **Peas, black-eye** | |
| Canned: 1 cup / **Progresso** | 165 |
| Canned w pork: 8 oz / **Sultana** | 220 |
| Frozen: 3.3 oz (about ½ cup) / **Birds Eye** | 120 |
| Frozen: 1 cup / **Green Giant** Boil-in-Bag Southern Recipe | 280 |
| Frozen: ½ cup / **Seabrook Farms** | 100 |
| **Peas, green, canned: 1 cup unless noted** | |
| Early / **April Showers** | 120 |
| Early / **Del Monte** | 110 |
| Early / **Kounty Kist** | 140 |
| Early / **Lindy** | 140 |
| Early / **Minnesota Valley** | 110 |
| Early / **Stokely-Van Camp** | 130 |
| Early, small / **Le Sueur** | 110 |
| Early w onions / **Green Giant** | 120 |
| Seasoned / **Del Monte** | 120 |
| Sweet / **Green Giant** | 110 |
| Sweet / **Kounty Kist** | 130 |
| Sweet / **Le Sueur** | 100 |
| Sweet / **Libby's** | 120 |
| Sweet / **Lindy** | 130 |
| Sweet: ½ cup / **S and W Nutradiet** | 35 |
| Sweet / **Stokely-Van Camp** | 130 |
| Sweet, small / **Green Giant** Sweetlets | 100 |
| Sweet, tiny / **Del Monte** | 100 |
| Sweet w onions / **Green Giant** | 110 |

CALORIES

| | |
|---|---|
| and carrots / **Del Monte** | 100 |
| and carrots / **Libby's** | 100 |
| and carrots: ½ cup / **S and W Nutradiet** | 32 |
| and carrots / **Stokely-Van Camp** | 120 |

Peas, green, frozen

| | |
|---|---|
| Early: 3.3 oz (about ½ cup) / **Birds Eye** | 70 |
| Early: 1 cup / **Kounty Kist** Poly Bag | 120 |
| Early: 1 cup / **Green Giant** Poly Bag | 100 |
| Early: ½ cup / **Seabrook Farms** | 74 |
| Early, in butter sauce: 1 cup / **Le Sueur** | 150 |
| Sweet: 1 cup / **Green Giant** Poly Bag | 100 |
| Sweet: ½ cup / **Seabrook Farms** | 52 |
| Sweet, in butter sauce: 1 cup / **Green Giant** | 150 |
| Tiny: 3.3 oz (about ½ cup) / **Birds Eye** | 60 |
| and carrots: 3.3 oz (about ½ cup) / **Birds Eye** | 50 |
| and carrots: 1 cup / **Kounty Kist** Poly Bag | 90 |
| and carrots: ½ cup / **Seabrook Farms** | 41 |
| and cauliflower w cream sauce: 3.3 oz (about ½ cup) / **Birds Eye Combinations** | 100 |
| w cream sauce: 2.6 oz / **Birds Eye Combinations** | 120 |
| Creamed w bread crumb topping: 1 cup / **Green Giant** Bake n' Serve | 300 |
| In onion sauce: ½ cup / **Seabrook Farms** | 96 |
| w onions and carrots, in butter sauce: 1 cup / **Le Sueur** | 160 |
| w pea pods and water chestnuts, in sauce: 1 cup / **Le Sueur** | 180 |
| and pearl onions: 3.3 oz (about ½ cup) / **Birds Eye Combinations** | 60 |
| and potatoes w cream sauce: 2.6 oz / **Birds Eye Combinations** | 140 |
| w sliced mushrooms: 3.3 oz (about ½ cup) / **Birds Eye Combinations** | 70 |

Potatoes, canned

| | |
|---|---|
| Au gratin w bacon: 7½ oz can / **Hormel Short Orders** | 270 |

CALORIES

| | |
|---|---|
| New: 1 cup / **Del Monte** | 90 |
| Scalloped w ham: 7½ oz can / **Hormel** Short Orders | 255 |
| Whole: 1 cup / **Stokely-Van Camp** | 100 |
| Potatoes, frozen | |
| Au gratin: 1 cup / **Green Giant** Bake n' Serve | 390 |
| Au gratin: ⅓ pkg / **Stouffer's** | 135 |
| Diced, in sour cream sauce: 1 cup / **Green Giant** Boil-in-Bag | 270 |
| French-fried: 2.8 oz / **Birds Eye** Cottage Fries | 120 |
| French-fried: 3 oz / **Birds Eye** Crinkle Cuts | 110 |
| French-fried: 3 oz / **Birds Eye** Deep Gold Crinkle Cuts | 140 |
| French-fried: 3 oz / **Birds Eye** French Fries | 110 |
| French-fried: 3.3 oz / **Birds Eye** Shoestrings | 140 |
| French-fried: 3 oz / **Birds Eye** Steak Fries | 110 |
| French-fried: 3 oz / **Ore-Ida** Cottage Fries | 140 |
| French-fried: 3 oz / **Ore-Ida** Country Style Dinner Fries | 120 |
| French-fried: 3 oz / **Ore-Ida** Crispers | 230 |
| French-fried: 3 oz / **Ore-Ida** Golden Crinkles | 130 |
| French-fried: 3 oz / **Ore-Ida** Golden Fries | 130 |
| French-fried: 3 oz / **Ore-Ida** Pixie Crinkles | 170 |
| French-fried: 3 oz / **Ore-Ida** Self Sizzling Crinkles | 160 |
| French-fried: 3 oz / **Ore-Ida** Self Sizzling Fries | 160 |
| French-fried: 3 oz / **Ore-Ida** Self Sizzling Shoestrings | 220 |
| French-fried: 3 oz / **Ore-Ida** Shoestrings | 170 |
| Fried: 3 oz (about ½ cup) / **Birds Eye** Deep Gold | 160 |
| Fried: 2.5 oz / **Birds Eye** Tasti Fries | 140 |
| Fried: 2.5 oz / **Birds Eye** Tasti Puffs | 190 |

CALORIES

| | |
|---|---|
| Fried: 3.2 oz / **Birds Eye** Tiny Taters | 200 |
| Hash browns: 4 oz / **Birds Eye** | 70 |
| Hash browns: 4 oz / **Birds Eye** O'Brien | 60 |
| Hash browns: 3 oz / **Ore-Ida** Southern Style | 70 |
| Hash browns w butter sauce: 3 oz / **Ore-Ida** Southern Style | 120 |
| Hash browns w butter sauce and onions: 3 oz / **Ore-Ida** Southern Style | 130 |
| Hash browns, shredded: 3 oz (about ½ cup) / **Birds Eye** | 60 |
| Hash browns, shredded: 3 oz / **Ore-Ida** | 60 |
| O'Brien: 3 oz / **Ore-Ida** | 60 |
| Parsley: ½ cup / **Seabrook Farms** | 104 |
| Scalloped: ⅓ pkg / **Stouffer's** | 126 |
| Shoestring, in butter sauce: 1 cup / **Green Giant** Boil-in-Bag | 310 |
| Slices, in butter sauce: 1 cup / **Green Giant** Boil-in-Bag | 210 |
| Stuffed w cheese-flavored topping: 5 oz / **Green Giant** Oven Bake | 240 |
| Stuffed w sour cream and chives: 5 oz/ **Green Giant** Oven Bake | 230 |
| and sweet peas, in bacon cream sauce: 1 cup / **Green Giant** Boil-in-Bag | 240 |
| Tater Tots: 3 oz / **Ore-Ida** | 160 |
| Tater Tots w bacon flavor: 3 oz / **Ore-Ida** | 150 |
| Tater Tots w onions: 3 oz / **Ore-Ida** | 160 |
| Vermicelli: 1 cup / **Green Giant** Bake n' Serve | 390 |
| Whole, boiled: ½ cup / **Seabrook Farms** | 76 |
| Whole, peeled: 3.2 oz (about ½ cup) / **Birds Eye** | 60 |
| Whole, small, peeled: 3 oz / **Ore-Ida** | 70 |
| Potatoes, mix, prepared: ½ cup unless noted | |
| Au gratin / **Betty Crocker** | 150 |
| Au gratin / **French's Big Tate** | 190 |
| Creamed / **Betty Crocker** | 160 |

CALORIES

| | |
|---|---|
| Hash browns / **French's** Big Tate | 165 |
| Hash browns w onions / **Betty Crocker** | 150 |
| Julienne / **Betty Crocker** | 130 |
| Mashed / **French's** | 120 |
| Mashed / **French's** Big Tate | 140 |
| Mashed / **Hungry Jack** (4 serving container) | 170 |
| Mashed / **Hungry Jack** (12, 24, 40 serving container) | 140 |
| Mashed / **Magic Valley** | 110 |
| Pancakes: three 3-in cakes / **French's** Big Tate | 130 |
| Potato Buds / **Betty Crocker** | 130 |
| Scalloped / **Betty Crocker** | 150 |
| Scalloped / **French's** Big Tate | 190 |
| w sour cream and chives / **Betty Crocker** Sour Cream 'n Chive | 140 |
| Potatoes, sweet, frozen | |
| Candied: 4 oz / **Mrs. Paul's** | 180 |
| Candied w apples: 4 oz / **Mrs. Paul's** | 160 |
| Candied, orange: 4 oz / **Mrs. Paul's** | 180 |
| Glazed: 1 cup / **Green Giant** Boil-in-Bag Southern Recipe | 340 |
| Pumpkin, canned: 1 cup / **Del Monte** | 80 |
| Pumpkin. canned: 1 cup / **Libby's** Solid Pack | 80 |
| Pumpkin, canned: 1 cup / **Stokely-Van Camp** | 90 |
| Sauerkraut. canned: 1 cup | |
| **Del Monte** | 50 |
| **Libby's** | 40 |
| Bavarian style / **Stokely-Van Camp** | 70 |
| Chopped / **Stokely-Van Camp** | 50 |
| Shredded / **Stokely-Van Camp** | 50 |
| Soup greens, in jar: 1 jar / **Durkee** | 216 |
| Spinach, canned: 1 cup / **Del Monte** | 45 |
| Spinach, canned: 1 cup / **Libby's** | 45 |
| Spinach, frozen | |
| In butter sauce: 1 cup / **Green Giant** | 90 |
| Chopped: 3.3 oz (about ½ cup) / **Birds Eye** | 20 |

|  | CALORIES |
|---|---|
| Chopped: ½ cup / Seabrook Farms | 25 |
| Creamed: 3 oz (about ½ cup) / Birds Eye Combinations | 60 |
| Creamed: 1 cup / Green Giant | 190 |
| Creamed: ½ cup / Seabrook Farms | 104 |
| Leaf: 3.3 oz (about ½ cup) / Birds Eye | 20 |
| Leaf: ½ cup / Seabrook Farms | 24 |
| Souffle: 1 cup / Green Giant Bake n' Serve | 300 |
| Souffle: ⅓ pkg / Stouffer's | 135 |
| Squash, cooked, frozen: 4 oz / Birds Eye | 50 |
| Squash, cooked, frozen: ½ cup / Seabrook Farms | 46 |
| Squash, summer, in cheese sauce, frozen: 1 cup / Green Giant Boil-in-Bag | 120 |
| Squash, summer, sliced, frozen: 3.3 oz (about ½ cup) / Birds Eye | 18 |
| Stew, vegetable, canned: 7½ oz / Dinty Moore | 160 |
| Stew, vegetable, frozen: 3 oz / Ore-Ida | 60 |
| Succotash | |
| Canned: 1 cup / Stokely-Van Camp | 170 |
| Frozen: 3.3 oz (about ½ cup) / Birds Eye | 80 |
| Frozen: ½ cup / Seabrook Farms | 87 |
| w cream style corn, canned: 1 cup / Libby's | 190 |
| w whole kernel corn, canned: 1 cup / Libby's | 150 |
| Tomato paste, canned | |
| Contadina / 6 oz | 150 |
| Del Monte / 6 oz | 150 |
| Hunt's / 3 oz | 70 |
| Town House / ⅔ cup | 150 |
| Tomato puree, canned: 1 cup / Contadina | 120 |
| Tomatoes, canned: 1 cup unless noted | |
| Stewed / Contadina | 70 |
| Stewed / Del Monte | 70 |
| Stewed: 4 oz / Hunt's | 30 |
| Stewed / Libby's | 60 |
| Stewed / Stokely-Van Camp | 70 |
| Stewed / Town House | 70 |

CALORIES

| | |
|---|---|
| Wedges / Del Monte | 60 |
| Whole / Del Monte | 50 |
| Whole: 4 oz / Hunt's | 25 |
| Whole / Libby's | 45 |
| Whole: ½ cup / S and W Nutradiet | 21 |
| Whole / Stokely-Van Camp | 50 |
| Whole / Town House | 50 |
| Turnip greens | |
|    Chopped, canned: 1 cup / Stokely-Van Camp | 45 |
|    Chopped, frozen: 3.3 oz (about ½ cup) / Birds Eye | 20 |
|    Chopped, frozen: ½ cup / Seabrook Farms | 22 |
|    Chopped w diced turnips, frozen: 3.3 oz (about ½ cup) / Birds Eye | 20 |
|    Leaf, frozen: ½ cup / Seabrook Farms | 22 |
| Zucchini, frozen: 3.3 oz (about ½ cup) / Birds Eye | 16 |
| Zucchini sticks, in light batter: 3 oz / Mrs. Paul's | 180 |
| Zucchini, in tomato sauce, canned: 1 cup / Del Monte | 60 |

# Vegetable Juices

CALORIES

**6 oz glass unless noted**

| | |
|---|---|
| Sauerkraut, canned / Libby's | 20 |
| Tomato | |
|    Bottled / Welch's | 38 |
|    Canned / Campbell | 35 |
|    Canned / Del Monte | 35 |

CALORIES

| | |
|---|---|
| Canned / **Libby's** | 35 |
| Canned / **S and W Nutradiet** | 22 |
| Canned / **Sacramento Plus** | 35 |
| Canned: 4 fl oz / **Seneca** | 27 |
| Canned: 1 cup / **Stokely-Van Camp** | 45 |
| Canned / **Town House** | 35 |
| Tomato cocktail, canned / **Ortega Snap-E-Tom** | 38 |
| Tomato-flavored cocktail, bottled or canned / **Mott's "Beefamato"** | 70 |
| Tomato-flavored cocktail, bottled or canned / **Mott's "Clamato"** | 80 |
| Tomato-flavored cocktail, bottled or canned / **Mott's "Nutrimato"** | 70 |
| Vegetable cocktail, canned | |
| **S and W Nutradiet** | 21 |
| **Town House** | 35 |
| **"V-8"** | 35 |
| **"V-8" Spicy Hot** | 35 |
| Low sodium / **"V-8"** | 35 |

# Wines and Distilled Spirits

The caloric content of all distilled spirits—gin, rum, vodka, whiskey, tequila—is determined solely by the amount of alcohol present. Thus the calorie count is higher or lower depending upon the proof (a measure of the alcohol content). The following figures apply to all plain distilled spirits, all brands: 1½ fl oz (one jigger)

| | |
|---|---:|
| 80 proof | 100 |
| 86 proof | 105 |
| 90 proof | 110 |
| 94 proof | 115 |
| 100 proof | 125 |

| | CALORIES |
|---|---:|
| **4 fl oz** | |
| Altar, red / Gold Seal | 132 |
| Altar, red / Henri Marchant | 132 |
| Blackberry / Manischewitz | 180 |
| Bordeaux | |
|     Red / B & G Margaux | 83 |
|     Red / B & G Prince Noir | 81 |
|     Red / B & G St. Emilion | 84 |
|     White / B & G Graves | 87 |
|     White / B & G Haut Sauternes | 132 |
|     White / B & G Prince Blanc | 83 |
|     White / B & G Sauternes | 127 |

## Burgundy

| | |
|---|---|
| Red / **B & G** Beaujolais St. Louis | 80 |
| Red / **Gold Seal** | 85 |
| Red / **Gold Seal** Natural | 82 |
| Red / **Henri Marchant** | 85 |
| Red / **Henri Marchant** Natural | 82 |
| Red / **Manischewitz** | 85 |
| Red / **B & G** Nuits St. George | 93 |
| Red / **B & G** Pommard | 89 |
| Red / **Taylor** | 100 |
| Sparkling / **Gold Seal** | 97 |
| Sparkling / **Henri Marchant** | 97 |
| Sparkling / **Taylor** | 104 |
| White / **B & G** Chablis | 80 |
| White / **B & G** Pouilly Fuisse | 85 |
| White / **B & G** Puligny Montrachet | 81 |
| White / **Gold Seal** | 85 |
| White / **Henri Marchant** | 85 |

## Catawba

| | |
|---|---|
| Pink / **Gold Seal** | 132 |
| Pink / **Henri Marchant** | 132 |
| Pink / **Manischewitz** | 130 |
| Pink / **Taylor** | 128 |
| Red / **Gold Seal** | 130 |
| Red / **Henri Marchant** | 130 |
| White / **Gold Seal** | 132 |
| White / **Henri Marchant** | 132 |

## Chablis

| | |
|---|---|
| **Gold Seal** | 90 |
| **Gold Seal** Nature | 88 |
| **Henri Marchant** | 90 |
| **Henri Marchant** Nature | 88 |
| **Taylor** | 96 |
| Rose / **Gold Seal** | 99 |
| Rose / **Henri Marchant** | 99 |

## Champagne

| | |
|---|---|
| **Gold Seal** Blanc de Blancs | 86 |
| **Gold Seal** Brut | 87 |

CALORIES

| | |
|---|---:|
| Gold Seal Extra Dry | 96 |
| Henri Marchant Blanc de Blancs | 86 |
| Henri Marchant Brut | 87 |
| Henri Marchant Extra Dry | 96 |
| Manischewitz | 85 |
| Mumm's Cordon Rouge Brut | 87 |
| Mumm's Extra Dry | 109 |
| Taylor Brut | 100 |
| Taylor Dry | 104 |
| Pink / Gold Seal | 97 |
| Pink / Henri Marchant | 97 |
| Pink / Taylor | 108 |
| Claret / Taylor | 96 |
| Cold Duck / Gold Seal | 97 |
| Cold Duck / Henri Marchant | 97 |
| Cold Duck / Taylor | 120 |
| Concord | |
|    Cream red / Manischewitz | 160 |
|    Cream white / Manischewitz | 130 |
|    Dry / Manischewitz | 85 |
|    Medium Dry / Manischewitz | 120 |
|    Red / Gold Seal | 132 |
|    Red / Henri Marchant | 132 |
| Labrusca | |
|    Gold Seal | 132 |
|    Henri Marchant | 132 |
|    Red / Henri Marchant | 116 |
| Lake Country | |
|    Taylor Gold | 104 |
|    Pink / Taylor | 108 |
|    Red / Taylor | 108 |
|    White / Taylor | 104 |
| Madeira / Gold Seal | 144 |
| Madeira / Henri Marchant | 144 |
| Malaga / Manischewitz American Extra Dry | 180 |
| Moselle / Julius Kayser's Graacher Himmelreich | 80 |
| Moselle / Julius Kayser's Piesporter Reisling | 76 |
| Moselle / Julius Kayser's Zeller Schwarze Katz | 76 |

CALORIES

| | |
|---|---:|
| Niagara, cream white / **Manischewitz** | 130 |
| Pinot / **Gold Seal** Chardonnay | 85 |
| Pinot / **Henri Marchant** Chardonnay | 85 |
| Port | |
|     **Gold Seal** | 166 |
|     **Henri Marchant** | 166 |
|     **Taylor** | 192 |
|     Ruby / **Gold Seal** | 166 |
|     Ruby / **Henri Marchant** | 166 |
|     Tawny / **Gold Seal** | 166 |
|     Tawny / **Henri Marchant** | 166 |
|     Tawny / **Taylor** | 184 |
| Pouilly Fume / **B & G** | 80 |
| Rhine | |
|     **Gold Seal** | 91 |
|     **Henri Marchant** | 91 |
|     **Julius Kayser's** Liebfraumilch Glockenspiel | 76 |
|     **Julius Kayser's** Niersteiner | 72 |
|     **Taylor** | 100 |
| Rhone / **B & G** Chateauneuf du Pape | 93 |
| Riesling / **Gold Seal** Johannisberg | 92 |
| Riesling / **Henri Marchant** Johannisberg | 92 |
| Rose / **Gold Seal** Vin | 99 |
| Rose / **Henri Marchant** Vin | 99 |
| Rose / **Taylor** | 96 |
| Sancerre / **B & G** | 81 |
| Sangria / **Taylor** | 132 |
| Sauterne | |
|     **Gold Seal** Dry | 97 |
|     **Gold Seal** Haut Altar | 109 |
|     **Henri Marchant** Dry | 97 |
|     **Henri Marchant** Haut Altar | 109 |
|     **Taylor** | 108 |
| Sherry | |
|     **Gold Seal** | 147 |
|     **Henri Marchant** | 147 |
|     **Taylor** | 164 |
|     Cocktail / **Gold Seal** | 127 |

|  | CALORIES |
|---|---|
| Cocktail / Henri Marchant | 127 |
| Cocktail / Taylor | 130 |
| Cream / Gold Seal | 172 |
| Cream / Henri Marchant | 172 |
| Cream / Taylor | 184 |
| Vermouth, dry / Taylor | 132 |
| Vermouth, sweet / Noilly Prat | 171 |
| Vermouth, sweet / Taylor | 176 |

# Yeast

CALORIES

| | |
|---|---|
| Bakers: 1 oz | 24 |
| Brewer's, debittered: 1 tbsp | 23 |
| Brewer's, debittered: 1 oz | 80 |
| Dry, active: ¼ oz pkg / **Fleischmann's** | 20 |
| Dry, active, in jar: ¼ oz / **Fleischmann's** | 20 |
| Fresh, active: .6 oz pkg / **Fleischmann's** | 15 |
| Household: .5 oz / **Fleischmann's** | 15 |
| Torula: 1 oz | 79 |

# Yogurt

CALORIES

**1 cup unless noted (8 oz = ⅞ to 9/10 cup)**

| | |
|---|---|
| All flavors: 8 oz container / **Dannon** | 200 |
| All flavors w fruit: 8 oz container / **Dannon** | 260 |
| All fruit flavors / **Lucerne** Lowfat | 260 |
| Apple, spiced / **Borden** Swiss Style | 270 |
| Apricot / **Borden** Swiss Style | 270 |
| Apricot / **Sealtest Light n' Lively** Lowfat | 240 |
| Apricot / **Viva** Swiss Style Lowfat | 250 |
| Black cherry / **Sealtest Light n' Lively** Lowfat | 240 |
| Black cherry / **Viva** Swiss Style Lowfat | 250 |

| | |
|---|---:|
| Blackberry / **Viva** Swiss Style Lowfat | 250 |
| Blueberry | |
|     **Borden** Swiss Style | 270 |
|     **Europa** / 6 oz container | 210 |
|     **Meadow Gold** Western Sundae Style Lowfat | 270 |
|     **Sealtest Light n' Lively** Lowfat | 240 |
|     **Viva** Swiss Style Lowfat | 250 |
| Blueberry-vanilla / **Sealtest Light n' Lively** Lowfat | 240 |
| Boysenberry / **Borden** Swiss Style | 270 |
| Boysenberry / **Meadow Gold** Western Sundae Style Lowfat | 270 |
| Boysenberry / **Viva** Swiss Style Lowfat | 250 |
| Cherry / **Borden** Swiss Style | 270 |
| Cherry: 6 oz container / **Europa** | 210 |
| Cherry-vanilla / **Borden** Swiss Style | 270 |
| Coffee / **Borden** Swiss Style | 270 |
| Cranberry-orange / **Borden** Swiss Style | 270 |
| Fruit salad / **Viva** Swiss Style Lowfat | 250 |
| Lemon / **Sealtest Light n' Lively** Lowfat | 240 |
| Lemon / **Viva** Swiss Style Lowfat | 250 |
| Lemon-lime / **Viva** Swiss Style Lowfat | 250 |
| Lemon-lime-flavored / **Sealtest Light n' Lively** Lowfat | 230 |
| Lime / **Borden** Swiss Style | 270 |
| Orange, mandarin / **Borden** Swiss Style | 270 |
| Orange, mandarin / **Meadow Gold** Western Sundae Style Lowfat | 260 |
| Orange, mandarin / **Sealtest Light n' Lively** Lowfat | 240 |
| Orange, mandarin / **Viva** Swiss Style Lowfat | 240 |
| Peach | |
|     **Borden** | 261 |
|     **Europa** / 6 oz container | 210 |
|     **Meadow Gold** Western Sundae Style Lowfat | 260 |
|     **Sealtest Light n' Lively** Lowfat | 240 |
|     **Viva** Swiss Style Lowfat | 240 |
| Peach Melba / **Sealtest Light n' Lively** Lowfat | 240 |
| Pear / **Borden** Swiss Style | 270 |

Pineapple / **Meadow Gold** Western Sundae
  Style Lowfat                                        270
Pineapple / **Sealtest Light n' Lively**
  Lowfat                                              250
Pineapple-coconut / **Viva** Swiss Style Lowfat     250
Pineapple-orange / **Viva** Swiss Style Lowfat      250
Plain
    **Borden** Lite-Line Lowfat             140
    **Borden** Swiss Style                  167
    **Dannon** / 8 oz container             150
    **Europa** / 6 oz container             130
    **Lucerne** Lowfat                      160
    **Sealtest Light n' Lively** Lowfat     140
Prune / **Borden** Swiss Style                      270
Prune: 8 oz / **Light n' Lively**                   257
Raspberry
    **Borden**                              278
    **Europa** / 6 oz container             210
    **Meadow Gold** Western Sundae Style Lowfat   270
    **Sealtest Light n' Lively** Lowfat     230
    **Viva** Swiss Style Lowfat             250
Red cherry / **Viva** Swiss Style Lowfat            250
Strawberry
    **Borden**                              266
    **Europa** / 6 oz container             210
    **Meadow Gold** Western Sundae Style Lowfat   270
    **Sealtest Light n' Lively** Lowfat     240
    **Viva** Swiss Style Lowfat             250
Strawberry-banana / **Sealtest Light n' Lively**
  Lowfat                                              270
Strawberry fruit cup / **Sealtest Light n' Lively**
  Lowfat                                              250
Vanilla / **Borden**                                276
Vanilla: 8 oz / **Light n' Lively**                 195

## FROZEN

**Danny** Flip / 5 fl oz                            175
**Danny** In-A-Cup / 8 fl oz                        180

|                                                        | CALORIES |
|--------------------------------------------------------|----------|
| **Danny** Parfait / 4 fl oz                            | 160      |
| **Danny** Sampler / 3 fl oz                            | 70       |
| **Danny-Yo** / 3½ fl oz                                | 110      |
| Fruit: 8 fl oz / **Danny** In-A-Cup                    | 210      |
| Peach: ½ cup / **Sealtest**                            | 110      |
| Red raspberry: ½ cup / **Sealtest**                    | 110      |
| Vanilla: ½ cup / **Sealtest**                          | 120      |
| Bars                                                   |          |
| Carob-coated: 1 bar / **Danny** On-A-Stick             | 125      |
| Chocolate-coated: 1 bar / **Danny** On-A-Stick         | 125      |
| Uncoated: 1 bar / **Danny** On-A-Stick                 | 65       |
| **Yosicle** / 2½ fl oz                                 | 90       |

# FAST FOODS

# Fast Foods

## ARBY'S

## ARTHUR TREACHER'S

## BURGER CHEF

| | |
|---|---|
| Mariner Platter | 680 |
| Rancher Platter | 640 |

## BURGER KING

| | |
|---|---|
| Whopper | 650 |
| Double Beef Whopper | 850 |
| Whopper w Cheese | 760 |
| Double Beef Whopper w Cheese | 970 |
| Whopper Junior | 360 |
| Whopper Junior w Cheese | 420 |
| Whopper Jr. w Double Meat | 490 |
| Whopper Jr. Double Meat Pattie w Cheese | 550 |
| Hamburger | 310 |
| Hamburger w Cheese | 360 |
| Double Meat Hamburger | 440 |
| Double Meat Hamburger w Cheese | 540 |
| Steak Sandwich | 600 |
| Whaler | 660 |
| Whaler w Cheese | 770 |
| Onion Rings—Large | 330 |
| Onion Rings—Regular | 230 |
| French Fries—Large Bag | 360 |
| French Fries—Regular Bag | 240 |
| Chocolate Milkshake | 380 |
| Vanilla Milkshake | 360 |
| Apple Pie | 240 |

## CARL'S JR.

| | |
|---|---|
| Famous Star Hamburger | 480 |
| Super Star Hamburger | 660 |
| Old Time Star Hamburger | 440 |
| Happy Star Hamburger | 290 |
| Steak Sandwich | 630 |
| California Roast Beef Sandwich | 380 |
| Fish Fillet Sandwich | 550 |

CALORIES

| | |
|---|---|
| Original Hot Dog | 340 |
| Chili Dog | 360 |
| Chili Cheese Dog | 400 |
| American Cheese | 40 |
| 11 oz Regular Salad w Condiments | 170 |
| 2 oz Blue Cheese Dressing | 200 |
| 2 oz Thousand Island Dressing | 190 |
| 2 oz Lo-Cal Italian Dressing | 48 |
| French Fries | 220 |
| Onion Rings | 320 |
| Apple Turnover | 330 |
| Carrot Cake | 380 |
| 20 oz Shake | 310 |
| 20 oz Soft Drink | 200 |

## CHURCH'S FRIED CHICKEN

| | |
|---|---|
| 1 average piece, boned, dark | 305 |
| 1 average piece, boned, white | 327 |

## DAIRY QUEEN / BRAZIER

### Snacks and Desserts

| | |
|---|---|
| Cone—Small | 110 |
| Cone—Regular | 230 |
| Cone—Large | 340 |
| Chocolate Dipped Cone—Small | 150 |
| Chocolate Dipped Cone—Regular | 300 |
| Chocolate Dipped Cone—Large | 450 |
| Chocolate Sundae—Small | 170 |
| Chocolate Sundae—Regular | 290 |
| Chocolate Sundae—Large | 400 |
| Chocolate Malt—Small | 340 |
| Chocolate Malt—Regular | 600 |
| Chocolate Malt—Large | 840 |
| Float | 330 |

CALORIES

| | |
|---|---|
| Banana Split | 540 |
| Parfait | 460 |
| "Fiesta" Sundae | 570 |
| Freeze | 520 |
| "Mr. Misty" Freeze | 500 |
| "Mr. Misty" Float | 440 |
| "Dilly" Bar | 240 |
| "DQ" Sandwich | 140 |
| "Mr. Misty" Kiss | 70 |

**Fast Foods**

| | |
|---|---|
| Hamburger | 260 |
| Cheeseburger | 320 |
| Big "Brazier" | 460 |
| Big "Brazier" w Cheese | 550 |
| Big "Brazier" w Lettuce and Tomato | 470 |
| Super "Brazier" / The "Half-Pounder" | 780 |
| Hot Dog | 270 |
| Hot Dog w Chili | 330 |
| Hot Dog w Cheese | 330 |
| Fish Sandwich | 400 |
| Fish Sandwich w Cheese | 440 |
| French Fries | 200 |
| French Fries—Large | 320 |
| Onion Rings | 300 |

## DUNKIN' DONUTS

| | |
|---|---|
| Cake and Chocolate Cake Donuts (includes rings, sticks, crullers) | 240 |
| Yeast Raised Donuts | 160 |
| Glazed Yeast Raised Donuts | 168 |
| Fancies (includes coffee rolls, danish, etc). | 215 |
| with filling and topping | add 45 |
| Munchkins—Yeast Raised | 26 |
| Munchkins—Cake and Chocolate Cake | 66 |
| with filling and topping | add 13 |

## HARDEE'S

|                               | CALORIES |
|-------------------------------|----------|
| Hamburger                     | 276      |
| Cheeseburger                  | 321      |
| Huskie                        | 648      |
| Big Twin                      | 447      |
| French Fries—Small            | 239      |
| French Fries—Large            | 381      |
| Apple Turnover                | 282      |
| Milkshake                     | 391      |
| Roast Beef Sandwich           | 390      |
| Fish Sandwich                 | 468      |
| Hot Dog                       | 346      |

## KENTUCKY FRIED CHICKEN

Chicken Dinner:
3 pieces chicken w mashed potatoes
  and gravy, cole slaw, and roll

|                               |      |
|-------------------------------|------|
| Original Recipe Dinner        | 830  |
| Extra Crispy Dinner           | 950  |

Individual pieces, Original Recipe:

|           |      |
|-----------|------|
| Wing      | 151  |
| Drumstick | 136  |
| Keel      | 253  |
| Rib       | 241  |
| Thigh     | 276  |

## LONG JOHN SILVER'S SEAFOOD SHOPPES

|                                                  |      |
|--------------------------------------------------|------|
| Fish w Batter (2 piece order)                    | 409  |
| Fish w Batter (3 piece order)                    | 613  |
| Treasure Chest (1 piece fish & 3 peg legs)       | 467  |
| Chicken Planks (4 piece order)                   | 458  |
| Peg Legs w Batter (5 piece order)                | 514  |
| Ocean Scallops (6 piece order)                   | 257  |
| Shrimp w Batter (6 piece avg order)              | 269  |

CALORIES

| | |
|---|---|
| Breaded Oysters | 460 |
| Breaded Clams | 465 |
| S.O.S. Super Ocean Sandwich | 554 |
| Fryes | 275 |
| Cole Slaw | 138 |
| Corn on the Cob | 174 |
| Hush Puppies | 153 |

## MCDONALD'S

| | |
|---|---|
| Hamburger | 260 |
| Cheeseburger | 300 |
| Quarter Pounder | 420 |
| Quarter Pounder w Cheese | 520 |
| Big Mac | 540 |
| Filet-O-Fish | 400 |
| Egg McMuffin | 350 |
| Hot Cakes w Butter and Syrup | 470 |
| Scrambled Eggs | 160 |
| Pork Sausage | 180 |
| English Muffin (Buttered) | 190 |
| French Fries | 210 |
| Apple Pie | 300 |
| Cherry Pie | 300 |
| McDonaldland Cookies | 290 |
| Chocolate Shake | 360 |
| Vanilla Shake | 320 |
| Strawberry Shake | 340 |

## PIZZA HUT

**Serving size: one half of a 10-inch pizza (3 slices)**

Thin 'N Crispy Pizza
| | |
|---|---|
| Beef | 490 |
| Pork | 520 |
| Cheese | 450 |
| Pepperoni | 430 |
| Supreme | 510 |

CALORIES

Thick 'N Chewy Pizza
   Beef                                    620
   Pork                                    640
   Cheese                                560
   Pepperoni                          560
   Supreme                           640

## STEAK N SHAKE

| | |
|---|---:|
| Steakburger | 276 |
| Steakburger w Cheese | 352 |
| Super Steakburger | 375 |
| Super Steakburger w Cheese | 451 |
| Triple Steakburger | 474 |
| Triple Steakburger w Cheese | 625 |
| Low Calorie Platter | 293 |
| Baked Ham Sandwich | 451 |
| Toasted Cheese Sandwich | 250 |
| Ham & Egg Sandwich | 434 |
| Egg Sandwich | 275 |
| Lettuce & Tomato | 4 |
| French Fries | 211 |
| Chili & Oyster Crackers (⅔ oz.) | 337 |
| Chili Mac and 4 Saltines | 310 |
| Chili—3 Ways & 4 Saltines | 402 |
| Baked Beans | 173 |
| Lettuce & Tomato Salad (1 oz, 1000 Island dressing) | 168 |
| Chef Salad | 313 |
| Cottage Cheese (½ cup) | 93 |
| Apple Danish | 391 |
| Strawberry Sundae | 329 |
| Hot Fudge Nut Sundae | 530 |
| Brownie Fudge Sundae | 645 |
| Apple Pie | 407 |
| Cherry Pie | 334 |
| Apple Pie a la Mode | 549 |

CALORIES

| | |
|---|---|
| Cherry Pie a la Mode | 476 |
| Cheese Cake | 368 |
| Cheese Cake w Strawberries | 386 |
| Brownie | 258 |
| Vanilla Ice Cream (1½ Scoops) | 213 |
| Vanilla Shake | 619 |
| Strawberry Shake | 648 |
| Chocolate Shake | 608 |
| Orange Freeze | 516 |
| Lemon Freeze | 548 |
| Coca-Cola Float | 514 |
| Orange Float | 502 |
| Lemon Float | 555 |
| Root Beer Float | 529 |
| Orange Drink | 83 |
| Lemon Drink | 86 |
| Orange Juice | 104 |
| Coffee | 2 |
| Hot Tea | 4 |
| Iced Tea | 6 |
| Milk | 146 |
| Root Beer | 115 |
| Dr. Pepper | 137 |
| Hot Chocolate | 686 |

## TACO BELL

| | |
|---|---|
| Bean Burrito | 343 |
| Beef Burrito | 466 |
| Beefy Tostada | 291 |
| Bellbeefer | 221 |
| Bellbeefer w Cheese | 278 |
| Burrito Supreme | 457 |
| Combination Burrito | 404 |
| Enchirito | 454 |
| Pintos 'N Cheese | 168 |
| Taco | 186 |
| Tostada | 179 |

## WHITE CASTLE

|                        | CALORIES |
|------------------------|----------|
| French Fries           | 225      |
| Cheeseburger           | 185      |
| Hamburger              | 160      |
| Fish (wo tartar sauce) | 192      |

# Index

## ABOUT THE AUTHOR

JEAN CARPER is a freelance writer, specializing in consumer and health subjects. She has written numerous articles for national magazines (*Reader's Digest, Consumer Reports, Saturday Review, Today's Health*) in the medical field, including articles on food. She is the author of seven other books: *Stay Alive!, Bitter Greetings: The Scandal of the Military Draft, The Dark Side of the Marketplace* (co-written with Senator Warren G. Magnuson), *Not With a Gun, The All-in-One Carbohydrate Gram Counter, The All-in-One Low Fat Gram Counter,* and *Eating May be Hazardous to Your Health.* Ms. Carper writes a syndicated column for Princeton Features and is the national consumer reporter for Westinghouse Broadcasting. She is a graduate of Ohio Wesleyan University and lives in Washington, D.C.

# BE A WINNER
# IN THE RACE FOR
# FITNESS

These physical fitness titles give every member of the family the guidance they need for getting in shape and keeping fit. Choose the program most suited to you whether it be yoga, jogging, or an exercise routine. You'll feel better for it.

| | | | |
|---|---|---|---|
| ☐ | 23801 | **THE OVER-30, 6 WEEK, ALL NATURAL HEALTH AND BEAUTY PLAN**  Elizabeth Martin | $3.50 |
| ☐ | 23309 | **KARATE: BEGINNER TO BLACK BELT**  B. Tegner | $3.95 |
| ☐ | 23211 | **THE ATHLETE'S KITCHEN**  N. Clark | $3.95 |
| ☐ | 23195 | **THE BEVERLY HILLS EXERCISE BOOK**  R. Krech w/ B. Libby | $3.50 |
| ☐ | 13812 | **RICHARD HITTLEMAN'S YOGA FOR TOTAL FITNESS** | $2.95 |
| ☐ | 23901 | **DR. SHEEHAN ON RUNNING**  George A. Sheehan | $3.50 |
| ☐ | 22972 | **RUNNING FOR HEALTH AND BEAUTY**  Kathryn Lance | $2.95 |
| ☐ | 23089 | **JAZZERCISE**  Missett & Meilach | $3.50 |
| ☐ | 23546 | **AEROBICS**  Kenneth H. Cooper | $3.95 |
| ☐ | 23899 | **AEROBICS FOR WOMEN**  Cooper & Cooper | $3.50 |
| ☐ | 23348 | **THE AEROBICS WAY**  Kenneth H. Cooper | $3.95 |
| ☐ | 23415 | **THE NEW AEROBICS**  Kenneth H. Cooper | $3.95 |
| ☐ | 22776 | **THE ALEXANDER TECHNIQUE**  Sara Barker | $2.95 |
| ☐ | 23544 | **INTRODUCTION TO YOGA**  Richard Hittleman | $3.50 |
| ☐ | 20999 | **YOGA 28 DAY EXERCISE PLAN**  Richard Hittleman | $3.50 |
| ☐ | 22881 | **90 DAYS TO SELF-HEALTH**  Shealy, M.D. | $2.95 |
| ☐ | 01443 | **THIN THIGHS IN 30 DAYS**  Wendy Stehling | $2.95 |
| ☐ | 01472 | **30 DAYS TO A BEAUTIFUL BOTTOM**  Julie Davis & Deborah Cox | $2.95 |

Buy them at your local bookstore or use this handy coupon for ordering:

# How's Your Health?

Bantam publishes a line of informative books, written by top experts to help you toward a healthier and happier life.

# SPECIAL
# MONEY SAVING
# OFFER

*Now you can have an up-to-date listing of Bantam's hundreds of titles plus take advantage of our unique and exciting bonus book offer. A special offer which gives you the opportunity to purchase a Bantam book for only 50¢. Here's how!*

*By ordering any five books at the regular price per order, you can also choose any other single book in the catalog (up to a $4.95 value) for just 50¢. Some restrictions do apply, but for further details why not send for Bantam's illustrated Shop-At-Home Catalog today!*

*Just send us your name and address plus 50¢ to defray the postage and handling costs.*